Advance Praise for *Home Now*

"The arrival of thousands of African refugees in a fading Maine city is a situation ripe for a writer as gifted as Cynthia Anderson. *Home Now* is immediately relevant and universally resonant, as it illuminates the explosive politics of immigration and explores complex issues around our relationships to places and each other. The richly told stories of Fatuma, Jamilo, Nasafari, Abdikadir, Carrys, and the other remarkable people in these pages will deepen and expand the ways that readers see the world."

—Mitchell Zuckoff, *New York Times*–bestselling author of *Fall and Rise: The Story of 9/11*

"In this journalist's beautifully written, balanced, personal account, we learn how a former mill town losing business 'like a mouth losing teeth' begins in 2001 to absorb 6,000 Somali, Congolese, and Sudanese refugees. . . . In discouraging times, such an honest and heartening read."

—Arlie Hochschild, bestselling author of *Strangers In Their Own Land: Anger and Mourning on the American Right*

"*Home Now* is a thrilling narration of the lives of the new Mainers settled in one of America's whitest towns—Lewiston, Maine. Cynthia Anderson humanizes the stories of the recent immigrants, many of them Somalis, who helped reawaken a sleepy town. As a recent Somali immigrant myself, I saw in this book a true, intimate, and timely account of what I live every day. This book should be read by everyone to learn about the stories, geography, tradition, strength, and resilience of their new neighbors."

—Abdi Nor Iftin, author of *Call Me American*

"A compassionate and insightful account of the human stories behind one of the most divisive issues in American politics."

—FARAH STOCKMAN, *New York Times* reporter and Pulitzer Prize winner

"*Home Now* is a breathtaking work of journalism and heart. Following several 'new Mainers' who arrive from war-ravaged African countries, Anderson brings her own deep Maine roots to bear as she illuminates [the new immigrants'] culture, assimilation, trauma, and homecoming. Her writing is graceful and clear-eyed and brimming with compassion both for the intrepid newcomers and the often ambivalent citizens who receive them. I found it instructive, poignant, and riveting. We need this book right now."

—MONICA WOOD, author of *The One-in-a-Million Boy* and *When We Were the Kennedys*

"An essential book to remind us that racism and prejudice will never be more powerful than what binds us together in the great American mosaic—community, family, faith, and ultimately, hope. Cynthia Anderson provides an honest portrayal of being a Muslim immigrant in Trump's America."

—ALI S. KHAN, dean of the School of Public Health, University of Nebraska

"*Home Now* folds us into a nonpolemical but clear refutation of the villainization of immigrants. Families we come to know and respect have survived appalling hardship in Africa and settled in a Maine mill town that's been demoralized after factories closed or moved on. Nasafari Nahumure, Jamilo Maalim, and the many others on these pages—they stand in for about 6,000 new immigrants in all—help revitalize Lewiston's spirit and commerce. Cynthia Anderson's expert reporting welcomes us, in highly readable style, to the complex and constructive fate of the real America. Her careful rendering, and her insights, deepen our understanding of what's happening here and now."

—MARK KRAMER, founding director of the Nieman Program on Narrative Journalism at Harvard University

"With great clarity and honesty, Cynthia Anderson blends intensely personal narratives with first-rate reporting to produce an indisputably necessary book for our times. Both an homage to those fearless immigrants who, through their industry and dedication, remake our country, and a wake-up call, *Home Now* gives us an America as it is now, today, not some bogus vision of what it never was. There's hope in this book, and struggle and endurance—all beautifully and intimately captured. And you want to know what it is like at the Walmart at 9 PM in late August in Lewiston? Anderson can tell you; she's been there."

—PETER ORNER, author of *Maggie Brown & Others* and *Am I Alone Here?*

"With the depth and detail of a skilled reporter and the narrative grace of a master storyteller, Cynthia Anderson brings to life one of America's unlikeliest immigrant communities: the six thousand people from Sub-Saharan Africa who have made a home for themselves in one of the coldest states in the nation. In *Home Now* she carefully strips away the politics surrounding Muslim refugees in the United States to reveal human beings whose relationships with each other are anything but foreign. These individuals are recognizable as mothers, daughters, fathers, and sons and recognizably American in their dreams of a better future."

—PAUL DOIRON, author of *The Poacher's Son*

HOME NOW

How 6000 Refugees Transformed an American Town

Cynthia Anderson

PUBLICAFFAIRS
NEW YORK

PublicAffairs
Hachette Book Group
1290 Avenue of the Americas, New York, NY 10104
www.publicaffairsbooks.com
@Public_Affairs

Printed in the United States of America
First Edition: November 2019

Published by PublicAffairs, an imprint of Perseus Books, LLC, a subsidiary of Hachette Book Group, Inc. The PublicAffairs name and logo is a trademark of the Hachette Book Group.

Print book interior design by Linda Mark.

Library of Congress Cataloging-in-Publication Data has been applied for.

ISBNs: 978-1-5417-6791-1 (hardcover), 978-1-5417-6788-1 (ebook)

LSC-C

10 9 8 7 6 5 4 3 2 1

for my mother

Contents

People Who Appear in This Book

PRIMARY THREADS:

Abdikadir Negeye—Somali Bantu refugee and cofounder of Maine Immigrant and Refugee Services (MIRS). Husband of Ikran; they have two daughters and two sons.

Carrys Ngoy—asylum seeker and high school student from Congo, recently arrived in the United States.

Fatuma Hussein—community leader and mother of eight. Founder of United Somali Women, now the Immigrant Resource Center of Maine.

Jamilo Maalim—young single mom who recently found her birth parents in a Kenyan refugee camp. Mother of Aaliyah and Hamzah.

Nasafari Nahumure—high school student navigating the college process and beyond. Lives downtown with her family.

OTHERS:

Aba Abu—single mom, caseworker, and bus driver who arrived in Lewiston in 2003.

Farah Adan—owner of Juba Halal Market on Lisbon Street.

Frank—friend of Jared's who also leads an ACT for America chapter.

Heidi Sawyer—close friend of Jamilo, Ikran, Abdikadir, and other Somalis.

Jared J. Bristol—head of an inland Maine chapter of ACT for America.

Jihan Omar—cofounder of Minds for Health. Also works at MIRS.

Mohamed Heban—owner of Baraka Store on Lisbon Street.

Nabega Nankema—older sister of Nasafari and mother of Azaleah.

Norbert Rwambaza—father of Nasafari. Married to Kamakazi; they have five children.

Phil Nadeau—former deputy city administrator of Lewiston.

Sadio Aden—Lewiston High School student and cross-country runner. Friend of Nasafari.

Shukri Abasheikh—owner of Mogadishu Store and a wedding hall. Mother of eight.

Zamzam Mohamud—Somali leader and single mom who arrived in Lewiston in 2001.

Glossary of Somali, Arabic, and Other Terms

Abaya—loose overgarment worn by Muslim women.

ALAC—American Laws for American Courts (legislative bill).

Alhamdullilah—Praise be to Allah.

Aroos—Somali wedding reception.

Asylum seeker (asylee)—someone in the United States or a port of entry claiming inability or unwillingness to return to his/her country because of persecution or fear thereof.

Baati—casual Somali dress.

Biil—Somali custom of resource sharing. In the United States, often takes the form of sending money to family members in Africa.

CMCC—Central Maine Community College.

Dadaab—Somali refugee camp in eastern Kenya.

Dagahaley—subcamp in Dabaab where Jamilo's birth family lives.

Dirac—full-length diaphanous dress worn for special occasions.

Dugsi—Muslim religious classes for children.

Eid al-Adha—Muslim commemoration of Abraham's willingness to sacrifice his son.

Eid al-Fitr—the celebration at the end of Ramadan. Commonly called Eid.

Eid Mubarak—Happy Eid.

FGM—female genital mutilation.

Guriga waah Lewiston—Lewiston is home.

Halal—meat prepared according to Muslim guidelines. More generally: permissible.

Haram—forbidden.

Hijrah—the prophet Muhammad's journey from Mecca to Medina. Islamic term for migration, taken by anti-Islamists to mean territorial incursion.

Hooyo—Somali word for "mother." More broadly connotes the mother-child relationship and nurturance.

Iftar—meal after sundown that breaks the daylong fast during the month of Ramadan.

Inshallah—God willing.

JAG—judge advocate general (military lawyer).

Jumuah—Friday afternoon prayer observed in congregation by Muslims.

Kafir—infidel (sometimes used derogatorily for ill-intended nonbeliever).

Kameez—white garment men wear to the mosque for prayers.

L-A—the Lewiston-Auburn area.

LHS—Lewiston High School.

Macawis—sarong-like garment worn by Somali men.

Mashallah—praise or thanks to God; more informally, "Well done."

Masjid—mosque.

Nikah—Somali wedding contract and ceremony.

ORR—Office of Refugee Resettlement (federal).

Salah—Muslim prayer. There are five requisite prayer times in Islam.

Sambusa—pastry stuffed with minced meat and vegetables.

Shaash—scarf.

Shaax—spiced tea similar to chai.

Sharia—Islamic law primarily derived from the Quran and the Hadith (sayings and practices of Muhammad).

Somaalinimo—pride in being Somali.

TANF—Temporary Assistance for Needy Families (federal program).

Taqiyya—deception to protect oneself or the Muslim community.

Tarawiy—nightly Ramadan prayers during which the Quran is read.

Wallahi—used for emphasis: "I swear to God . . ."

Introduction

WHEN I WAS GROWING UP, LISBON STREET IN LEWISTON, Maine, was the center of the world. A few times a year, my family drove there from our village forty-five miles up the Androscoggin River to shop and to see my great-aunt. Aunt Nell had moved to Lewiston decades earlier; her husband worked in a mill there. Now in her seventies, widowed, she lived on the left side of a tidy duplex with an upright bass in the living room. During our visits, she served rolls hot from the oven and lemonade. The bass grumbled whenever my sister or I plucked it.

In the early 1970s, Lisbon Street formed the spine of the small city. The sidewalks were filled with families and couples and old men wheeling handcarts. After shopping for school supplies at Kresge's, we'd head to Ward Brothers department store, where the saleswomen spoke English to us and French to each other. The smell inside Ward's was a heady mix of everything the cosmetics counter had to offer, the carpet plush underfoot.

As I got older, a friend and I sometimes walked along the busy streets in the evenings. Laughter and smoke wafted from the doors of restaurants, and the nearby river was a vast, unseen presence. We got sundaes or stopped at Ward's to sample makeup and try on clothes our mothers wouldn't have approved. We didn't know it, but even then Lisbon Street was in decline. The city's glory years manufacturing textiles and shoes—decades that brought trains filled with French Canadians in search of jobs—were fading as one by one the mills closed and commerce slowed. Maine's once-richest city, its Bates Mill the state's largest employer for over two decades, would struggle for years to come.

It wasn't until the '80s, passing through on the way to and from college and later from my home in Massachusetts, that I realized how much Lewiston was changing. The couples and young families had vanished, and Lisbon Street was losing businesses like a mouth losing teeth, until only scattered stores remained.

The city was headed the way of other once-prosperous American industrial centers—jobs gone, the young moving out for good. Welfare set in: subsidized housing and unemployment benefits, food stamps—a sadder kind of commerce that swelled City Hall and social agencies. Kresge's closed, Ward's left, and the studio where I'd taken ballet attracted fewer and fewer students.

The secondhand store stayed open. It had seemed unremarkable before, but the rest of downtown was so bleak that its bright front was a beacon. I went there often. Sometimes I walked the neighborhood off Sabattus Street, past the house with the bay window where my Aunt Nell had lived until she died at eighty. Eventually, I'd wind up by the Androscoggin. The river was cleaner than when I was growing up; the mist rising from the falls no longer stank of processed pulp from upstream paper mills.

The city was in tough shape overall. Yet whenever I came back to the fine old buildings and the river and the hills beyond, I thought, Here is a *place*. Even at its nadir the city retained grandeur and suspense, like a stage between acts. By the mid-'90s a tenuous renaissance was taking form—though some would have called it barebones accommodation—with health care, banking, and other services beginning to fill the postindustrial void. Former mill spaces were converted into restaurants and galleries. Unemployment fell, though the population continued to dwindle and downtown remained stagnant. Of the families who stayed, half of those with children under five lived below the poverty level.

Such was the situation in February 2001 when the first Somali refugees came north from Portland, forty miles away, where housing was short. Maine was cold, and homogeneous (the second-whitest state in the nation, also the oldest), but it offered safety and access to services, and a lower cost of living than large cities where the federal government had first resettled the refugees. Moving to the extreme Northeast was their choice—a gutsy one considering that photos shared through social media showed snow banked four feet high.

By the beginning of 2003, more than 1,400 newcomers had come to Lewiston. They settled into triple- and quadruple-deckers on Spruce and Birch and Pine—the tree streets neighborhood off Kennedy Park. When I came north that spring to visit friends, women in hijabs were shepherding kids down streets that for years had been all but empty. It was an incongruous, astonishing sight. On Lisbon, a few closed stores had reopened under Somali ownership. I went into one, bought cardamom, wondered at signs offering translation and money-wiring services and—back out on the sidewalk—at the palpable energy. In a place where businesses rarely stayed open after five p.m., these were still lit at eight thirty.

Refugees kept coming. People I knew in Lewiston responded to the changes in accordance with their nature: curious or suspicious, or holding off on judgment. In 2005, the *New Yorker* called what was happening in Lewiston a "large-scale social experiment"—a blunt but not inaccurate assessment. There were, after all, now several thousand African Muslims in an overwhelmingly white town not known as a liberal outpost. Pickups flying American flags regularly drove down Lisbon Street, and stories in the local *Sun Journal* about the newcomers triggered online rants.

Yet I was seeing a slow, quiet shift—Somalis stocking shelves at the supermarket; white and black kids sitting together at the library; white people buying goat meat on Lisbon. A high school acquaintance who had a daughter in kindergarten with Somali children was happy about the new diversity. "I only knew white kids when I was growing up," he said. After one of the kindergartner's family came home to find "Get Out" scrawled on their apartment building, longtime residents helped paint over it. They worked late into the night, he said, so the message would be gone when kids left for school in the morning.

If there was a hostile undercurrent, and if some complained Somalis consumed the city's resources, other Lewistonians were reaching out and seeking accord. In 2006, a man rolled a pig's head through the doorway of a mosque. Residents rallied around the city's Muslims. The deed was denounced, the offender criminally charged. But the act spoke to a bitterness that remains.

I've been reporting on Lewiston's transformation for more than a decade. Early on, the narrative I embraced was of passive refugee-victims. The trauma of wars they left Africa to escape—the loss of loved ones, sexual assault, splintered families and years of privation—means that most newcomers do bear heartache. But over time I came to see that they were not passive. Their resilience moved and inspired me. One early acquaintance, Fatuma Hussein, founded United Somali Women of Maine to promote gender equality. She'd come to the United States at thirteen, from a Somali refugee camp. The first line in my Lewiston notebook was hers: "We are making new lives here."

The new lives were complex, often delineated by loss. Jamilo Maalim had been separated from her parents as a toddler. When the Somali civil war intensified and militants attacked their village, relatives took her to a refugee camp in Kenya. She lived there eight years. I met

Jamilo when she was twenty-two, or maybe twenty-three. (Record keeping, especially during escalations in the war, was haphazard and many refugees don't know their birthdate.) Her downtown apartment was spare but comfortable, decorated with swags of plastic flowers and photos of her daughter and son. The living room held a leatherette sofa and TV, and a soft rug where the family sat to eat their meals.

Jamilo's physical traits—the slight set to her chin, upright posture, a warm but searching gaze—suggest both sensitivity and grit. When she arrived in Lewiston as a nine-year-old, she entered third grade. She was quick—learned English easily, made friends, loved gym class. Yet she struggled at home, shuttled among relatives and sometimes harshly punished.

At seventeen she left school and moved out of state to live with a Somali boy she'd met online. She named the baby born that fall Aaliyah—Arabic for "ascending." A year later, the relationship dissolved. Jamilo and Aaliyah wound up in a shelter for several months. After they returned to Lewiston, her family maneuvered her into an arranged marriage. That ended after two years, just after her second child, Hamzah, turned one.

In spite of the instability, Jamilo has kept moving forward. She returned to high school while pregnant with Aaliyah, got promoted to team leader within weeks of a new job, played on a women's soccer team. Almost daily, her extended family pressured her to return to the marriage, in which she felt unloved. She wants to raise her kids, work, find a man with whom she can have a marriage that feels mutual. She wants to sort through her past and choose her future.

"Inshallah, someday I will have a happy life," she says.

LEWISTON NOW HAS the fifth-highest per capita Muslim population of any US city, most of it Somali, along with rising numbers of immigrants from other African nations. Its challenges—strained resources, a still-struggling older generation, teen anomie, de facto segregation—mirror those in other places with large refugee communities. For some, the long-term effects of trauma hinder acculturation. Yet Lewiston is more vital than it was two decades ago. The stakes are high, progress real but precarious.

Into this mix came the 2016 elections and a rise in anti-immigrant sentiment around the country. From spring 2016 through winter 2019, a time when national realities were colliding with those in Lewiston, the lives of five new immigrants play out on these pages. Jamilo and Fatuma each carry a thread. Three others belong to Nasafari Nahumure, Abdikadir Negeye, and Carrys Ngoy. All granted me sustained access to their lives—for which I'm abidingly grateful. A sixth thread examines my family's leave-taking of the village where we'd lived for generations and the factors that led us to go.

A note about the writing: This is a work of journalism. But it's not without bias. I talk with my students about the lens of subjectivity—the attributes and accumulation of experiences through which each of us views the world. My lens: I'm female, middle-aged, and married with children. White. I'm registered as Unaffiliated, socially progressive, and attended college in New York before moving to Boston. I now live part-time in Maine.

Getting to know Lewiston's new-immigrant community changed my lens. The beliefs of strong Somali women made me reevaluate my views on Muslim gender bias, which made me wonder about what I'd absorbed—was still absorbing—about Islam overall. During the thousand-plus hours I spent reporting, a parallel track emerged—this one personal. Trying to understand Islam from the Quran and other primary sources led me to comparisons with the Bible and then from my meditation practice back to the Christianity I've grappled with for years. This search had unintended consequences. I sifted through my family's past, grew closer with my mother.

Some Mainers I interviewed described a reexamination of values that stemmed from what they saw as cultural richness in the new immigrants. One Lewiston man put it like this: "My Somali friends changed [my perspective]. What matters are relationships. Material things do not equate with happiness." His observations resonated with me. For close to two centuries, my family's life had revolved around community, family, and faith. The values we abided by were like the ones many of Lewiston's newcomers hold close today. How had these values sustained them through hardship in Africa and equipped them for new challenges in the US? What had my family given up?

A sizable minority of Mainers remains unhappy about the presence of the city's newest residents. Lewiston sits in the state's second congressional district, where the political right has hold. Trump's win here was his sole district victory in New England. The expansion of the city's services to include translators and English as a second language (ESL) instructors is anathema to many, as is coexistence with Islam. In recent years the region's anti-Islam faction has gained momentum and new followers. In my reporting, I set out to get to know them, too.

So much overlays the social landscape through which Jamilo and her friends move. On a sunny autumn day she hosted Aaliyah's fourth birthday party at an orchard outside Lewiston. Most of the guests were Somali. Among the tree-lined rows, women hoisted kids onto their shoulders and handed them bags for apples. One woman's fiancé—the only male guest—helped. "So many Eves, only one Adam," another woman joked.

At the cash register, one of Jamilo's friends commented that, picking the apples, she'd thought they were free. The cashier's face hardened. "You shouldn't take produce you can't pay for," she said.

The friend protested—she was paying; that's why she'd brought her bag of apples to the register. If she didn't have enough money, she'd take some out.

The cashier narrowed her eyes. "It's wrong."

"I didn't come here to steal your apples," the friend said.

The cashier glared. The friend swore. The cashier threatened to call the police. Party guests backed away from the register. Jamilo and a friend hurriedly cleaned up the remains of the lasagna they'd brought. The cashier chastised me for letting "them" bring their own food, as if that was my call. "This is a family place," she said.

The party wasn't ruined. The kids didn't overhear the confrontation, and Jamilo shrugged it off. Her friend had a temper; the cashier was rude. Jamilo had dealt with worse.

So they packed up the gifts. Aaliyah would open them and they'd eat the cake inscribed with her name when they got home.

A month later, Trump won the election. Jamilo texted me the next day. She'd voted for the first time—for Hillary. She was shocked at the outcome, she said, and worried for herself and other Muslims. Then she added, "God bless America! I still love this country!" That was Wednesday. Thursday at noon she left work to go home and make chicken for lunch. It was chilly outside, and overcast. As she stepped into a crosswalk, a motorist sped past and shouted at her to take off her hijab. Soon afterward Jamilo texted, "I'm terrified."

A few days after the incident, though still shaky, she reiterated her love for the US. "This is my home," she said.

In the eighteen months to come, Jamilo would question her goals and priorities at work and at home. The strain of being Muslim in America under the new president would magnify her struggles.

But Jamilo never thinks about leaving the US. After Trump was elected, Somali social media lit up with rumors. Muslims would be required to wear identification bracelets. They'd have to sign a national registry. Muslim men would be monitored.

Since then, fear in Lewiston has flowed and ebbed based on the president's latest pronouncement on refugees, or on public reaction to it, or on actions taken by local anti-Islamists. But the city's Muslims aren't easily deterred. These are people who trekked miles across the desert, often under attack, to reach refugee camps where conditions too were perilous. Those who made it to the United States—even more, those who left primary resettlement sites to move to an isolated city in western Maine—did so with intention. The same is true of the city's more recent wave of African asylum seekers who, though less overtly targeted than Muslim refugees, also have sometimes faced unwelcome.

So here we are. The first Somali American kids born in Lewiston are teens now. They're Mainers, kids who grew up with snow and the piercing blue of a winter sky. They wear wool hats over their hijabs and go to sleep at night with the nearby Androscoggin flowing beneath the ice.

1

Early Spring 2016

Nasafari, Fatuma, Carrys

FRIDAY, TEACHERS' WORKSHOP. SEVENTEEN-YEAR-OLD NASAFARI Nahumure streams *The Bold and the Beautiful*, fixated on her iPod when she knows she should be studying for her SAT. But these few hours are her haven. She got up this morning glad for a break from the intensity of school and homework and the youth center where she volunteers.

The condo smells of citrus and last night's jasmine rice. It's atypically quiet—her little brother and sister upstairs in their rooms, father at work, mother helping out at a friend's store. Her mom asked Nasafari to tidy the house, so she swept and quickly wiped surfaces with Lysol. This bit of time belongs to her. She sits in her place at the kitchen table, close to a heat vent that keeps away the chill, flicking back a braid or two when they fall forward. She's lanky, with a fine-boned oval face.

Wind pushes at the windows. Behind the complex a dog barks and barks. Onscreen, the Forrester family schemes to stay on top of the Los Angeles fashion world.

The SAT is April 12, and Nasafari needs to do well. Her dream—she calls it that: "my dream school, it means everything to me"—is to attend St. John's University in New York for the paralegal studies that will set her up for law school. She hopes to apply early decision next fall. But her parents, conservative Christians and watchful, aren't sure they want Nasafari that far away, especially given what's happened with her two older sisters. The oldest moved to Arizona with her youth pastor's family. The middle sister left high school and lives with her boyfriend, who's neither born-again nor African.

Nasafari's father, Norbert, keeps a close eye on his third daughter. She has no phone and little in the way of a social life, does not have a curfew because mostly she doesn't go out. In navigating Lewiston High School, where she's a junior, it helps that Nasafari is outgoing. Other students know the slim girl in boots and jeans even though they rarely see her at night or on the weekends. Nasafari isn't alone; a lot of teens with new-immigrant parents are kept close to home.

It's possible her mother and father won't let Nasafari go away for college at all. She knows this. She doesn't want to know this. She forges ahead.

In school, her strengths are history and English. "I like words, adding to my vocabularies." She's been learning languages all her life: Kinyamulenge in the refugee camp where her mother, in her third trimester, fled after rebels jailed her husband and pillaged the Congolese village where the family farmed. Nasafari (whose name means "journey") was born on the way to the camp. While her father remained imprisoned, the rest of the family resettled in Rwanda. Nasafari learned Kinyarwanda there.

After the rebels released her father, he applied for asylum in the United States. Eventually the family reunited in Maine. Nasafari has lived eleven years in Lewiston, longer than anywhere else. Her English bears traces of Down East: occasional dropped consonants at the ends of words, a two-syllable "there." She loves Portland ("booming and friendly") and Freeport for good deals at the outlet stores. Her father's wages at Pioneer Plastics pay the mortgage on their two-story condo.

Around town, kids who arrived as refugees or asylum seekers are applying to college or gearing up for the SAT. Other immigrants are finishing the semester at universities across the state and elsewhere. Will they come back to Lewiston when they graduate? Will there be jobs if they do? Nasafari sees herself going away for college and then returning; maybe she'll open a law practice on the lower end of Lisbon, alongside the other offices with their plate-glass windows.

School superintendent Bill Webster hopes so. "The city needs these kids," he says. "We need their energy and their talents. If they settle here, if they have their own families, [Lewiston] will be a place that can keep pace with the rest of the country." Webster likes what he's already seeing: As Maine's leaders lament its aging, Lewiston is younger than it has been in decades. A new elementary school will soon be built, as schools around the state have had to close their doors.

Five years ago Nasafari walked into the office of Tree Street Youth, the after-school program where she now volunteers, and announced she wanted to be a JAG (judge advocate general) military lawyer. Director Julia Sleeper remembers: "She was twelve, a sixth grader. I didn't even know what a JAG was." Nasafari can't recall where she got the idea. "I just knew I wanted to serve my country and also to be a lawyer and advocate for kids."

To launch her on her way—St. John's. Nasafari sees herself as equal parts homebody and adventurer. She likes the idea of college in New York—the pace, the crowds, the rush. Why not? She's seventeen, impatient—"If I want something done, I want it done *now*." And nice but not naive. This is a self-description. Nice but not naive, caring, assertive. And impatient. Two weeks from now she'll attend her first high school dance. Her parents have allowed it, at last.

Sun patterns the room in blocks of light and dark. *The Bold and the Beautiful* is over. Nasafari switches off her iPod, takes out her math homework. College. If she gets in. If her parents agree to it.

A few blocks away, Kennedy Park teems with kids and the energy of a no-school day. Children play tag beneath bare-limbed trees, criss-cross the paths on bikes. Flags fly straight in the March wind. A few kids, impervious or optimistic, have shed their jackets, and a couple of boys wear shorts, but otherwise hoods are up and coats are zipped. The forecast calls for snow. Periodically a car pulls up, someone honks, and children come running—a girl in a long skirt and hijab with a ball under her arm, a pair of middle schoolers who were part of tag.

Before refugees began moving here, Kennedy Park would have been all but empty on a cold spring day. Now, close to 6,000 of Lewiston's 36,000 inhabitants are African immigrants, about three-quarters of whom are Muslim. The last time this many people under age eighteen lived in Lewiston was the 1950s, when families were settling into tract homes in the city's outskirts. What's happening here is *isbeddal*, the Somali word for "transformation."

A van pulls up. A woman gets out, wind billowing her abaya as she walks to the basketball court. A boy in a T-shirt disentangles himself from a group, pulls his coat from a pile. The woman speaks pointedly in Somali, chastisement clear. As the boy thrusts his arms backward into the jacket—"Like this?" he asks, in English—she puts back her head and laughs.

~

DOWNTOWN ON LISBON Street, Fatuma Hussein is running late. She is thirty-seven, and her days are packed, this one no exception. She needs to get to court in Portland, a forty-minute drive if she pushes the speed limit.

The hearing is on behalf of a woman whose husband violated a restraining order. Fatuma will be there as an advocate. She has fifty-eight minutes, and she hasn't eaten lunch—which she must because she just learned she's pregnant with her eighth child. This wasn't something she was hoping for, exactly, but weeks of denial ended four days ago when the midwife swept a probe across Fatuma's belly and a baby materialized onscreen.

So there's lunch to be gotten through and a long drive, and Portland traffic, and Fatuma's caught in the doorway while her assistant, Rosaline, issues updates on who's called and why. Finally Fatuma puts a hand on Rosaline's arm. "I really have to go."

As Rosaline disappears, a man emerges from an adjacent office. "Did you get my messages?"

"Yes." Fatuma beams at him. The worry on his face dissolves. "I'm sorry," she says. "I've been so busy."

He waves both hands. "It's okay, okay. I just wanted to check on a few things. About the wedding."

"Of course," Fatuma says. "I'll get back to you, I promise." The wedding is the man's daughter's, and Fatuma's hoping, planning, to go even though it's on a Saturday a few weeks from now that's already full.

Whenever the topic of Somali leadership comes up, so does Fatuma's name. The reason for this is partly her charm but also her resolve and the circumstances that gave rise to it. She was eleven, visiting relatives, when the Somali civil war erupted in 1991 after the collapse of Siad Barre's government. Her memories of what happened are fragments: being pressed into the back of a crowded flatbed truck, the truck tipping over, people on the ground, gunshots and smoke, bodies motionless. Fear in Utanga, the refugee camp where she wound up. Heart-aching separation from her parents and siblings.

Fatuma arrived in the US in 1993 and was resettled with distant relatives in Atlanta. She married at sixteen and moved to Maine soon after, determined to make a life. The organization she founded in 2001, United Somali Women of Maine, has grown into a large non-profit now known as the Immigrant Resource Center (IRC). But there are stresses, too: family responsibilities, this pregnancy—which she's not told her children about—and a perpetually jammed schedule plus funding pressures as other Somali nonprofits crop up. Then there's Fatuma's de facto role as spokesperson. She's become the voice of Somali women in Maine, quoted by the media and asked to testify whenever the legislature considers refugee-related bills.

There's also the presidential candidacy of Donald Trump. A couple of weeks ago on national television he said, "I think Islam hates us." Later, on another network, he called for surveillance of mosques. "We're having problems with Muslims coming into the country." And still later: "There's no assimilation.... They want sharia law. They don't want the laws that we have." At rallies Trump has taken to reading the lyrics from Al Wilson's song "The Snake." In it, a woman nurses a sickly snake back to health only to receive a fatal bite when it revives. The lyrics, Trump tells supporters, provide an allegory for domestic terrorism.

Fatuma's reaction to Trump's pronouncements is an exasperated exhale. "He's putting fear in so many people. Muslims, of course, but really all Americans." More and more she feels like a mandated emissary of the Lewiston Somali community, demonstrating through action that Muslims are not to be feared.

The strain of it all sometimes shows on Fatuma's face. It's showing now. Even so, at the restaurant across the street she and the proprietor greet each other warmly. *"As-salaam alaikum." "Wa-Alaikum-as-Salaam."* ("Peace be upon you." "Peace with you also.")

Within minutes a steaming platter of chicken and rice appears at her table, where Fatuma perches watching the clock. Save for the table, TV, and a prayer rug in the corner, the persimmon-hued room is empty. It typifies the Somali aesthetic for indoor spaces: bright and uncluttered, pared of possessions.

Dutifully, Fatuma finishes her chicken and takes a long drink of orange Fanta. Her phone rings—Rosaline. The client is en route to court.

Outside, the sky spits sleet. Fatuma steps cautiously around curds of snow, favoring the knee she shattered last winter in a fall, held together now by a plate and pins. She gets to Portland just in time to sit beside the woman and listen to the long proceedings. Then she's back in the car, driving northwest into a reddening sky. At home, she puts together a quick dinner of pasta with meat sauce. Later she supervises bath time for the three younger kids while sitting on the toilet with her laptop open. They play and she triages her work email, blotting the occasional splash on her screen with a towel. Long day—what she really wants to do is get into bed.

It's easier when Fatuma's husband, Muktar, is home, but he's a long-distance trucker and often on the road. When he's here, Fatuma sleeps longer than her usual six hours and leaves some meal prep to him. If that means McDonald's or cereal, so be it. Muktar's longest breaks come at the end of the year. This is the reason, Fatuma jokes, that five of their children have autumn birthdays.

The next morning—22 degrees with a bitter wind, colder than March has a right to be, even in Maine. It's Saturday, but Fatuma's working while her teenaged kids babysit the younger. She heads north to Augusta then south to Portland for an observance of International Women's Day. This time, Rosaline goes with her. "We both have drive," Fatuma says in explanation of why she hired her. Recently arrived from South Africa with her husband and two kids, Rosaline offers wry commentary on settling into Lewiston: "Someone asked, 'Did you wear clothes in Africa?' I told them, 'Oooh no, just a little bitty thing that covered me down there. And an elephant came and stopped in front of my house every morning to carry me to school.' They believed me!"

In Portland, the celebration is under way—a six-hour mash-up of simultaneously translated speeches, skit, African buffet, and a dance. There's a fashion show, too, and many of the women are dressed accordingly. Fatuma—small, no makeup, dark clothing—is a wren to their cardinals and orioles. Eventually she takes the microphone. For a few long seconds, she stands quietly. A hush grows; people lean forward. Such is Fatuma's ability to command a space.

"We fight very hard," she says of the IRC's work. "If I have to go to [governor] LePage, if I have to play politics, I will." Her rounded voice lingers over vowels as she talks about the need for women's rights advocacy—"A safe woman, educated and empowered, will build a good foundation for generations to come"—and, more generally, about the state's immigrant presence. "We are not a burden. We come, and we succeed," she tells the crowd to echoes of "That's right." Applause builds as she continues. "The state of Maine is lucky to have us."

The early years were rocky. Tensions rose as more and more Somalis settled their large extended families into downtown tenements and city officials scrambled to provide language and social services. "The large number of new arrivals cannot continue without negative results for all," Mayor Laurier Raymond wrote in a now-infamous letter in October 2002. "We need breathing room."

If Raymond had thought the letter would unify residents behind efforts to dissuade more refugees from coming, his plan backfired. Hate groups rushed to align themselves with the cause; most other people distanced themselves, fast. It became clear that most Lewistonians didn't want to be associated with racism or religious intolerance, which the letter came to symbolize over Raymond's protests. Volunteerism rose, as did efforts to integrate the newcomers into the community. The Chamber of Commerce urged members not to look past the newcomers when hiring.

TV and newspaper accounts about Lewiston's new immigrants focused almost entirely on dramatic incidents: the mayor's letter, the hate groups, the pig's head. Mostly what was happening was quiet forward motion, a lot of work by longtime residents and newcomers alike. But incremental, imperfect progress is not the stuff of headlines. For years, whenever Muslims or refugees appeared in the national news, reporters called deputy city administrator Phil Nadeau looking for edgy follow-up.

"What's happening in Lewiston?" they'd ask.

"Nothing's happening in Lewiston," Nadeau would tell them.

In his City Hall office, surrounded by photos of Lewistonians and a huge street map, Nadeau grins as he recounts the exchange. "I love saying that." Then, uncharacteristically, he's silent. After a while he says, "Let's hope it stays that way."

I'll think of his words when Jamilo is harangued over her hijab, and on the afternoon an anti-Islamist tells me the best thing for our country would be if all Muslims were deported. A year from now, after Nadeau has reluctantly retired, he'll describe the presidential election as among the most upsetting events in his life—and, in particular, the uptick in anti-immigrant activism. "There's this sense that everything we've worked toward in Lewiston could come undone," he'll say. In retirement, Nadeau will create a website celebrating Lewistonian accord. "I love this place," he says of the city where he was born. "I want to make sure we go down on the right side of history."

It won't be easy. National politics will be one thing, the city's own complexities another. In June 2018, a man will die after being assaulted during a dispute in Kennedy Park. New-immigrant teens are involved. Many will see things in an Us vs. Them reduction: The death of Donny Giusti is more evidence the newcomers are a net loss for Lewiston. Or conversely, that view is nothing more than deep-rooted prejudice.

But some of those who live in or know the city well—including family members of Donny Giusti—take a more nuanced stance. For sixteen years they've lived the city's progress and its setbacks. They've felt the discomfort of navigating religious and racial difference. Of worrying there's not enough of everything to go around. Of change. They've also sensed that Lewiston is somehow a bigger place for all of that.

These are the people who, black and white, put on a yellow T-shirt and head out in pairs to patrol the park after Donny's death. To let Lewistonians know that, in spite of the tragedy, the park is theirs and the city is theirs and there's distance yet to go.

~

TREE STREET YOUTH sits in the flats below the spires of the Basilica of Saints Peter and Paul. In the afternoons, girls race down the hallway, hijabs flying, to get first dibs on supplies in the art room. Teens sandwiched into a music studio play Beyoncé and Stevie Wonder and their own compositions on a keyboard, while outdoors bystanders cheer as goals accrue in a pickup soccer game. Soccer is huge in Lewiston. Last fall, the high school boys' team won the city its first-ever state soccer championship, capping a 17–0 season. More than four thousand people packed the stands that day. The team included seven Somali players who'd lived together in a refugee camp.

On an April afternoon at Tree Street, Carrys Ngoy practices keyboard for an upcoming performance, though not wholeheartedly. Whenever he stops, hip-hop filters in from down the hall where kids work on a dance routine. The floor reverberates with bass and pounding feet. In two weeks Carrys will perform his piece with his best friend and housemate, Isaac Kabuika, who right now is at Bowdoin for a three-day visit for accepted students. It's hard to play without him.

Carrys and Isaac have much in common: born three days apart, both high school seniors, both in the US without parents, both from the Democratic Republic of Congo (DRC). Carrys grew up in the mining city of Lubumbashi, a transportation hub for copper and the coltan used in cell phone production. His dad works in a shipping office. The area around Lubumbashi is also the site of fierce, ongoing clashes between the DRC government and rebel groups. Isaac comes from the capital, Kinshasa, where his father is a Christian minister.

Both boys are seeking asylum because of peril in Congo—and their families' fears for them. Thousands of young men in the mineral-rich but beleaguered nation have been killed or threatened into joining militias in recent years. Over two decades of fighting, more than six million people have died. Carrys arrived in the US last spring; Isaac, in 2014. Their friendship was cemented in AP Calculus II at Lewiston High School.

At home in the railroad-style apartment they share, Carrys and Isaac split chores and hang out when they're not at their desks. They enjoy sitting outside on their porch overlooking Kennedy Park, but mostly they stay inside because their neighbors smoke a lot of weed. Isaac and Carrys dislike that, but don't want to make it into a big deal. "You just get along," Carrys says. At night the two talk philosophy and politics, wash down any disagreements with Welch's sparkling grape juice.

For all they have in common, they have different styles: Isaac forthright; Carrys deliberative and wry. Recently Isaac announced that he didn't like to cook and hoped to marry a woman who does. Carrys eyed him sidelong. "She might not like to cook, either," he said. Isaac nodded. "We'll take turns and eat out on my nights." In the meantime, Isaac buys stuff to microwave, and Carrys experiments with cooking from scratch. His pasta is al dente, his rice sautéed with bits of vegetables.

With Isaac away, Carrys is spending much of his time at Tree Street. "Actually, it's lonely at home," he says in French-inflected English.

Carrys has no idea where he'll wind up next fall. The University of Maine at Orono accepted him into its engineering program, but unlike Isaac, who got a scholarship, Carrys doesn't know how he'll pay the tuition. As an asylum seeker, he can't apply for federal loans, and though he filed for an interview with US Citizenship and Immigration Services soon after he arrived, a large backlog of cases means it could be years before he learns whether he can stay. Meanwhile, even if he can get a job permit and work full-time while in school, it will be hard to cover the costs.

Phil Nadeau, for one, wishes the asylum process were easier and faster. He's seen asylees in limbo for years they could have committed to investing in new lives and becoming real contributors. Carrys and Isaac—strong, self-directed students who might well remain in Maine and forge lives after college: "Aren't these the kind of new Americans we want, young people who will give back?" And asylum seekers are well positioned, Nadeau says. Many arrive speaking English and acclimate quickly.

So Carrys waits—for his hearing date, for acceptances from other colleges, for private grants, or for job alternatives if he can't make full-time school happen. Maybe he'll take classes at the community college. Maybe he'll apply to stay on at Tree Street as staff—he does love Lewiston. For tonight, he'll eat leftover pork and beans he made. Isaac will be home on Sunday.

In a Tree study room, Nasafari is in her own state of uncertainty. The SAT was Tuesday. She's not sure how it went. The verbal portion seemed okay, the math was pretty hard. Plus, she felt off that morning. It was raining, she got to school late, ate too little breakfast. She sighs, flicks a braid. "Maybe I did fine."

A boy appears in the doorway. He smiles at Nasafari, leans there for a while waiting. Finally she smiles back. After he leaves, she's quiet. They are not dating, she tells me. He is a friend who is a boy. "I mean, I don't do relationships. School and my family come first."

As she speaks, she looks older than seventeen and also very young. Crosscurrents run through her Facebook posts: "Blessed to see another week go by . . . All thanks to the most high" followed by "I will never feel bad for doing what is best for me." And "Did you know? The love of darkness or night is called 'nyctophilia.'" After midnight, with everyone asleep upstairs, the downstairs is hers—TV, fridge with leftover chicken and beans. Sofa to herself. Nasafari sprawls on it and dreams.

Last week a woman came to Tree Street to talk to students about her path to becoming an attorney. Nasafari's face regains composure as she recounts how the woman raised her siblings and married young before attending law school. "It was really inspiring. I'd love to job-shadow her," she says. For a lot of kids, the college-prep program culminates their Tree experience. Application essays paper one wall, acceptance letters another.

More than one hundred kids come through the doors every day. Most are African immigrants, a few are white Mainers. Hand-painted lettering on the dance room wall sums up the ethos: "Respect yourself. Respect others. Respect the space. Participate." The place is not always a model of good behavior—there are back-talking kids and misbehaving ones, children in whom the effects of trauma are clearly evident—but it emanates structure and a steady warmth.

At thirty, Julia Sleeper has worked in Lewiston's immigrant community for more than a decade, since she was a student at nearby Bates College. She founded Tree Street in 2011 and recently raised more than a million dollars to renovate and expand its quarters in a former paint shop. Her investment in the kids is obvious two weeks later at the Tree performance. From the front row she mouths the words to all the songs and spoken pieces. The kids perform dances titled "Powerful" and "Cultural Mash-up." Julia sways and bounces in her seat, anticipating every move.

2

May–June 2016

Jamilo, Fatuma, Abdikadir

WHILE NASAFARI WORRIES ABOUT HER SAT SCORES AND Fatuma figures out the best time to tell her kids about the new baby, Jamilo Maalim feels stronger than she has in years.

She grew up thinking she'd never see her parents again, that probably they had died. In 1994 an aunt fled with baby Jamilo—then her parents' only living child—after militants invaded their village in southern Somalia, leaving it in chaos. Villagers were attacked, women raped, homes pillaged.

For the next eight years Jamilo lived in Dadaab, a Somali refugee camp in eastern Kenya. No one knew what had happened to her mother and father. Then, something Jamilo hadn't allowed herself to imagine: two years ago, after she'd been in Lewiston more than a decade, she learned her parents had made it to Dadaab.

Right away she began to set aside money for a trip. Three months ago, with a leave from work and with Aaliyah and Hamzah cared for by relatives, she flew to see her parents for six weeks. "When I got there, I was in such a rush. It was like, *There's this lady, I'm told she's my mother.*" That first hug from her sweet-faced mom—it felt as though Jamilo had been with her always, as though they hadn't been separated at all. Same with her dad, especially when he picked her up and whirled her around. Jamilo couldn't stop laughing, and then she cried. They'd been apart for more than twenty years.

As the first days turned into a week, it seemed her parents were vying for her attention. She and her mom would sit side by side telling stories, giggling, when suddenly her dad—a big guy with a henna-dyed goatee—would be in the doorway with a look on his face that made Jamilo think he felt left out. It made her giddy, so much attention after too many years of so little.

She missed Aaliyah and Hamzah, but she also felt at peace in Dadaab, happy to be back in her extended family's compound of huts on dusty ground. Not much had changed. There were two stick-framed huts for sleeping, one for cooking, another with a latrine shared with neighbors. In the main hut, everyone gathered to listen to her father's prized radio.

The heat—*that* took getting used to. It was the cusp of Gu, the rainy season, but the sun still shone oppressively. All winter in Lewiston, as sidewalks iced over and snow piled up and her fingers numbed, Jamilo had longed for warmth. Now, the heat and the brightness sometimes overwhelmed her.

Yet, family. She loved being with her parents and getting to know her four younger siblings. She braided her sisters' hair, played tag with them and the boys. In some ways, the extended family of thirty was as settled in Dagahaley, the northernmost subcamp of Dadaab, as they'd been in their village near the Jubba River.

"Camp" conjures a place far more temporary than Dadaab, the world's largest refugee settlement. It's been sheltering refugees for twenty-five years. A generation born there has grown to adulthood, and those who arrived as teens when the camp first opened are grandparents. Members of Jamilo's extended family who got there when she did—and haven't been lucky in the international resettlement lottery, which places only a fraction of those who register—still live there among 300,000 others in five spread-out subcamps. Taken as a whole, Dadaab is Kenya's third-largest city.

Jamilo's weeks in Dagahaley became regular. Everyone got up early, before the heat set in. In the kitchen hut Jamilo helped her mom and aunt fix breakfast—usually anjera, a sourdough flatbread, with bits of meat or vegetable. They brewed tea, spicy and sweet. Ingredients were sparse; food tasted good from the care it took to make it. When the meal was ready, everyone sat down on the rug to eat. This was Jamilo's favorite time of day, voices still low with the earliness of the morning, before the clamor from neighboring huts took over. Afterward her mother would go to milk her goat or head to the market. Wherever she went, so did Jamilo.

Dagahaley felt poor and crowded but full of life. Kids played soccer in any open space, with rags wrapped in plastic if they didn't have a ball. People bargained at an open market that sold produce and cookware, clothing and electronics, and other items the aid agencies didn't give out. Camp regulations forbade refugees from working, out of concern they'd take jobs from Kenyans, but entrepreneurism flourished on the gray market. One of Jamilo's relatives worked at a food stall and another ferried shoppers' purchases. Other residents had jobs as teachers or goat herders in the desert scrub that surrounds Dadaab for a hundred miles. Kids earned small amounts by taking the thorn-hedge-lined road out of camp to forage for firewood. Money also came from relatives abroad and from the sale of UN rations of maize and wheat.

In midafternoon, when the sun stared down and the temperature tipped into the 90s, people rested in whatever shade they could find. Jamilo listened to the radio with her dad, or he told stories about how he'd met her mother and the prized watermelons they'd grown back in their village. The women cooked again in late afternoon, often rice with goat and whatever vegetables they could find. Her mother's resourcefulness astounded Jamilo—she cooked so well with so little. At home Jamilo had all of Walmart or Hannaford to choose from, yet the meals she made for Aaliyah and Hamzah didn't taste half as good. "I told her, 'Mom, you have an amazing way with food.'"

She felt frightened at times, especially at night. Her cousins had warned her about thieves, and men who slip into compounds to assault women. Many people slept outside in courtyards. At night the ubiquitous Dadaab wind died to a breeze that cooled things without raising the red dust that found its way into everything. Jamilo was surrounded by family, but even so she lay awake. She'd been told the men greased themselves so they could get away, that they touched people's heads so they could tell women from the men. Those images—and what it would feel like—lodged in her.

But then—Mashallah—morning would come. The muezzin called, Jamilo prayed. Women gathered in the cooking hut. Another day, begun.

Now, back home as the grass in Lewiston begins to green, Jamilo carries with her those memories of Dagahaley mornings and the long afternoons. The trip marked a turning point: "I came back with a clearer sense of who I am and where I want to go." She feels more centered than she has in years. She can't say why, exactly, but it has something to do with the way her mom's eyes softened whenever she looked at Jamilo, and the feeling she'd had when her father spun her around "like I would Aaliyah or Hamzah!" Something to do with love.

Jamilo needed fortification. Ever since she and Hamzah's father split up, members of her extended family in Lewiston have been trying to push her back into the marriage. Again and again she's refused. "I'm like, this time it's not gonna be how you want it," she says. "First, when I was young, you didn't do what a child needs. Second, you didn't support my first relationship, with someone I really cared about. Then you pressured me into this marriage." She pauses, chews on her lower lip. "It goes all quiet when I talk like that, but I don't care. Now I'm going to do what I think is right."

What Jamilo thinks is right, for now, is making the best home she can for Aaliyah and Hamzah. She liked her time in Africa but wouldn't leave Lewiston permanently; she's a single, working mom who values health care, education, the conveniences of Wi-Fi and big-box stores. She arrived here with the malleability of youth, and in many ways the city has formed her. In Lewiston she's worked as a customer service rep and now at a resource center as a youth specialist. She gets some assistance—a partial housing voucher and fuel credits—but pays the bulk of the cost of babysitters, utilities, groceries, and rent.

Since Dagahaley, she's also begun sending a few dollars to her parents—a Somali custom of sharing known as *biil*. "Food is very, very expensive there. I feel I should do what I can to help." Her relationships in Africa are sustained by social media; whenever something happens in Dagahaley, Jamilo hears about it within minutes on her cell.

Like many young immigrants in Lewiston, she seems less interested in conventional assimilation than an additive acculturation in which her American identity exists alongside her Somali one. Her computer fluency, close ties to Kenya, love of hip-hop, her hijab and full-length baati, her trilingualism and abstinence from alcohol—all of it is who she is. Or as she puts it, "Somali and Mainer and American are parts of me." On Friday nights she gets pizza from Papa John's and lets the kids watch cartoons on YouTube while she and a friend dig into their caches of makeup to try out different looks on each other. She's devoutly Muslim—follows *salah* and when stressed turns first to Allah.

The way Jamilo sees it, she's picked what feels right from both cultures. One evening when toddler Hamzah spikes a fever of 103, she takes him to the ER—"Grateful for hospitals" she posts at two a.m., which garners a slew of Likes from other new immigrants.

In Lewiston, Jamilo lives an American life infused with Somaalinimo—a sense of her Somaliness. Not that she spends much time worrying about how Somali she is or how American. Post-Dagahaley, she wants to concentrate on being a person of character. That's how she puts it, and to become "someone I'm proud of, aside from what others think."

There's a story she tells: When her little sister needed eye surgery, her mother walked three days from Dagahaley to Hagadera camp, to take the child to the hospital. On their way home, Gu rains flash-flooded the road. Both nearly drowned—her mom had to rush for help. Telling me this, Jamilo's eyes shine. Her mother is the kind of person she wants to be. Devoted, strong, resourceful.

The next two years will test her.

~

IN MAY, CARRYS learns the University of Southern Maine (USM) has accepted him—he applied last minute, when other prospects weren't looking good financially—with a $2,500 scholarship. None of the other grants came through. During the school year he'll live off-campus in Portland, to save money, and he'll start out studying math since USM doesn't have engineering. He doesn't know how he'll pay the rest of the tuition (and his asylum situation will become more complicated before it gets less), but at least he's in. For days, he goes around smiling.

Nasafari's news isn't so good. She didn't do well on the SAT—badly enough that she won't reveal her scores. She points out, though, that while she used the word *impatient* to describe herself, her last name (Nahumure) actually translates as "patient." She'll redouble her prep efforts, especially in math, for the fall retest. She reminds herself she has other things going for her besides academics: class board and prom committee as well as Street Leader at Tree. The prom—she hopes her parents let her go.

At the IRC Fatuma finds out her assistant, Rosaline, is moving to Dallas, where her husband got a new job. Fatuma's happy for Rosaline and her family, yet the timing isn't great. Fatuma, five months pregnant, is fatigued and a little overwhelmed realizing how much she has to do to prepare for upcoming conferences.

But a few weeks later, as head of a celebration of World Refugee Day at Lewiston's Simard-Payne Park, she's her usual self—greeting people, accepting an award, dancing with others on the outdoor stage. She hesitates to dance at first, but Muktar joins her on the platform and the Somali music takes hold. It's not formal dance, more like the onstage group sway at the end of televised fund-raisers. People clap, cheer. Steam rises from tables of African food. Fish stew and pork, muamba (an Angolan stew), cassava, and sambusas—all free, and popular. Women refill serving dishes.

The site, fittingly, is a former rail yard for trains that carried nineteenth-century immigrants to new lives in Lewiston. The recent influx of immigrants is significant, but the city has seen much more rapid growth before. After a slow, primarily agricultural start by English settlers, the city's population doubled between 1840 and 1850, then again by 1860. By 1885, more than twenty thousand people lived here. The Yankee girls who worked the textile mills in Lewiston and shoe shops in Auburn were joined by thousands of French Canadians who often disembarked at Grand Trunk Station one day and started jobs the next.

The newcomers and their families settled in this neighborhood near the river, in Old World–style blocks of tenements. The area came to be known as Little Canada. New immigrants moved, too, a quarter mile north to the tree streets neighborhood. Today that same grid work of streets is called Little Mogadishu by some Lewistonians and the Village by those who live there.

The rail yard is now part of the Androscoggin Riverwalk and a recreation space. Hot air balloons ascend from the field during an annual festival. Aloft, you get a bird's-eye view of the city and a hint of the way things used to be: the brick mill buildings churning out goods; Lisbon Street bustling with shoppers; hydropower canals shooting off from the big, serpentine river; the spires of the basilica looming over it all.

Today's event was months in the planning. Wearing business attire—full-length plaid skirt, beige headscarf, black jacket—Fatuma had ticked off items during a City Hall meeting. Corporate sponsors: Walmart, Central Maine Power, and Poland Springs—check; a larger site because last year's World Refugee Day was crowded, check; partnership with the Chamber of Commerce, check. Fatuma hoped for a thousand participants, she told the group. Fund-raising goal of $10,000. "Nothing too aggressive, but we want to do a little magic."

She cochaired the meeting with Joel Furrow, who heads a Christian organization that serves new immigrants. Later Fatuma would say that around Joel she's "mindful of his male privilege"—but she seemed the one in charge, even though Joel opened the meeting and did much of the talking. As the group broke into subcommittees, Fatuma stood. "I'm going to step out now, okay?"

Joel chuckled. "If we said no, would it matter?"

Fatuma smiled. "Of course it would." She was humoring him. She hoisted the file-stuffed tote she carries everywhere. "See you next time, everyone."

This morning Fatuma woke worried the leaden sky would keep people home on the big day. But a crowd that's half black, half white mills around the park, kids darting among adults who step aside as they balance plates. Teens jockey for position around Mike McGraw, who coached the LHS soccer team to its state championship last year. Later Fatuma will say that while dancing, she looked out into the crowd and felt relief and gladness. "Everyone did their part," she says, by which she means organizers and sponsors, new immigrants, and all the Lewistonians who showed up.

On nearby Oxford Street a truck slows, honks, then revs its engine and speeds by. A couple of the food servers glance up apprehensively; the national rise in anti-immigrant sentiment has people on alert.

Acts of aggression toward or by the newcomers are uncommon—police say crime dropped in the city from 2006 to 2016—but tensions linger. So does a conviction that the newcomers disproportionately and unfairly consume welfare dollars, a view less and less borne out by the numbers. According to Phil Nadeau, Somali refugees received General Assistance at a lower rate than the nonimmigrant community in 2015, for instance, and housing vouchers commensurate with their population.

Primary-resettlement refugees do get eight months of medical care and cash assistance from the Office of Refugee Resettlement (ORR). In Lewiston, they're eligible to apply for General Assistance for two years after that and state-run Temporary Assistance for Needy Families (TANF) under the same rules as other permanent residents.

One challenge to cohesion is that, other than schools and commerce, the orbits of longtime residents and newcomers often barely overlap. Abdikadir Negeye, the thirty-one-year-old human resources director of Maine Immigrant and Refugee Services (MIRS), says connecting the two communities is a pressing need. "We need to integrate more. We should know each other better. . . . It will make the city stronger."

The closeness of the Somali community itself is a source of resentment for some. A storeowner complains mildly about low-interest business loans available to refugees, then more heatedly says the newcomers "don't do things like the Dempsey Challenge (a fund-raiser for cancer) or the balloon festival. They keep to themselves. . . . You can see it as exclusive."

Robust support structures among Somalis, in particular, may foster this perception. Women shop collectively and watch one another's children; inside the mosque, preschoolers often flow from mom to mom as a single unit during prayers. Rotating, interest-free credit makes possible the purchase of big-ticket items like cars. And hospitality is reflexive, a cultural mandate. Somalis wouldn't think of letting someone show up at the bus station to begin anew without an acquaintance or a friend of a friend there to welcome them.

Obligatory hospitality doesn't mean everyone always gets along. Sometimes it seems the opposite, like a big bickering family with feuds and rifts—but ultimately allegiance. When someone's in need, the community is there; Jamilo will learn this firsthand a year from now.

Some believe the African emphasis on mutuality will translate well in Lewiston. At World Refugee Day, a woman puts it like this: "Mainers are warm and so are the Somalis. We have our children and our city in common, and this beautiful state. There's a lot to care about."

In a city that loves its sports, soccer is another unifier. The 2015 championship team included players from Somalia, Kenya, Congo, Turkey, and the US. From the start, McGraw told me, he insisted they were "one team, together on and off the field." *Pamoja ndugu!*—Swahili for "Together, brothers!"—became the team's rallying call. As the season went on and LHS kept winning, the fan base grew to include many longtime Lewistonians. Several thousand people traveled to the state championship. At the end of that game, Lewiston players raced across the field and leaped into the arms of their fans.

Abdikadir coached many of the championship players as kids, including the captain and the player who did crowd-pleasing flip throw-ins. "To see that team win, what it meant to our city, it still makes me emotional," he says.

Fatuma attended the celebration held later at the Ramada Inn. "It was so diverse. I looked at the crowd and I thought, 'This is who we are.'"

Bridging differences matters to Fatuma, but for Abdikadir it's keenly personal. He's Somali Bantu, a marginalized ethnic minority from the southern part of the country. More than two thousand Bantus live in Lewiston. Most descend from various African tribes whose people were captured and sold during the Indian Ocean slave trade. Even after slavery was abolished at the turn of the twentieth century in Somalia, a vast class divide remained.

Direct yet tender, Abdikadir has a habit of following a factual statement with its emotional correlate. For instance, "Somali Bantus could not easily access opportunity in Somalia. We suffered because of that." Now he's married to Ikran, an ethnic Somali woman. He refers to it as a "mixed marriage," suggesting the long-standing gulf between the two groups.

But Abdi and Ikran: a single entity. There's the tidy townhouse in Tall Pines, three kids with a fourth on the way, Ikran a let-it-loose extrovert to Abdikadir's introvert. On their seventh anniversary she posts on Facebook, "Thank you for being my husband, my partner, my lover and my best friend... Thanks for making [my life] better and happier... Happy Anniversary, hubby!" Usually he responds to her posts with a Like. This one gets a Love.

It's opposites attract, Ikran says. She operates on instinct; Abdikadir is methodical, "step by step by step," she says. He's the kind of guy who double-checks his cheeseburger to make sure it has no bacon.

Abdikadir's family was okay with the marriage; hers pushed back and then relented. Abdikadir says he worried at first, when they were still engaged. But—he loved Ikran. Their marriage would work.

His sense of self-determination has its origins in Dadaab, the same refugee camp where Jamilo lived. His family, too, had fled Jubba Valley after militants invaded their village. The family walked for more than two weeks—two hundred miles through desert scrub—taking turns carrying five-year-old Abdikadir when he tired. The hunger was terrible; the thirst, worse. At night they hid from animals and bandits while an adult went sleepless to keep watch. Night or day, roving militias made the journey even more dangerous. Conditions in the part of Dadaab where the family wound up were makeshift, with hunger and disease still constants. But the peril had abated. Refugees could attempt a daily life.

In Dadaab, Bantu kids who went to school did so alongside ethnic Somalis. Abdikadir was the second oldest of what would eventually be ten children, and the first in his family to attend school. He'd leave their one-room hut early to walk two miles along the dusty road—a compact boy with a round face, making his way in flip-flops past hundreds of other huts with just-woken inhabitants. If he'd gotten to eat something that morning, good; if he hadn't, he went anyway. His parents insisted, his grandparents too. They had not carried him all those miles to Dadaab on their backs for nothing.

But Abdikadir likely would have gone without being urged. Even at seven years old, he sensed the rows of shared desks linked him to something big. The teacher kept chalk in one hand and a stick in the other. No worries. Abdikadir went to learn, not to act out. If his mind wandered to what could happen to his family while he was away—his uncle had been threatened at gunpoint one afternoon and robbed of a sack of grain—he pulled his focus back to two-digit subtraction or the English alphabet.

When classes ended in the afternoon, he'd begin the walk back. It took longer now with the sun high and his belly emptier. The ground was bare and dusty except during Gu, when mud clung to his ankles and he walked hoping the plastic tarp that roofed his family's hut hadn't torn or come loose. If all was well when he got there, his mother would be putting together an evening meal. Sometimes she had money to boost the UN rations the family stood in long lines for, sometimes not.

By the time the family left Kenya for the US, after ten years in Dadaab and four more in another Kenyan camp, Abdikadir had the equivalent of a tenth-grade education. He was nineteen when the family moved to Lewiston in 2006. He got his high school diploma from a specialized school for older students in Limestone, near the Canadian border. Certain things stood out there, Abdikadir says—stars in the clear sky, the open land.

And snow. "It was everywhere. Sometimes so high you couldn't see out the windows." He laughs. "It was fun before I realized how much you have to shovel it." New immigrants all share anecdotes about Maine winters, cracking up about the kid who during his first snowfall ran inside to tell his mom, "I was eating sugar from the sky!"

After high school, Abdikadir moved back to Lewiston and started community college. Nights he worked on the shipping floor at L.L.Bean. With his associate's degree, he transferred to the University of Southern Maine to study social and behavioral science. He was a solid student—and devoted. Doing well in school gave him confidence. He imagined a happy future: well-paying job, loving wife, children.

Later, while working at Geiger Elementary School as a translator, Abdikadir passed his citizenship test—one hundred questions, such as "How many amendments does the US Constitution have?" "What is the number of members in Congress?" "Why did the colonists fight the British?" That Monday when he showed up at Geiger in a white dress shirt and an American flag tie, dozens of kids greeted him, waving little flags and cheering. "I will never forget that celebration," Abdikadir says.

In 2007 he met Ikran at a friend's wedding. "Full of life," he thought. Ikran remembers liking his smile. In Africa, marriage between a Somali Bantu and an ethnic Somali likely wouldn't have happened, but things were different in Lewiston. An affinity had emerged between the two groups, born of mutual dislocation and hardship, and shared cultural and religious values.

What had seemed big differences in Somalia seemed less so in America. Longing supplanted so much else. People missed different things—a white stucco house, a camel herd, the rain-swollen Jubba—but everyone missed something. There was also the fact that as a group Somalis had suffered deeply—many were physically or sexually assaulted, or endured famine, or saw loved ones die. "Some people lose everything, everyone," artist Jawab Aden told me in in 2006. "Only his or her life is left." Because of the depth of loss, many Somalis fixed firmly on the present. "We don't have a back. Only a front," another man said.

Among survivors in the US, kinship mattered. "We lost many, many things," says Abdikadir. Without the support system of shared housing and cars, collective shopping, loans, and group childcare, "we would have been more shocked than we already were."

The communality represented another form of biil. Abdikadir's experience was typical. The day after he and his family arrived, an acquaintance drove them around and showed them things—grocery stores, city hall, schools, Lisbon Street shops. Initially the family moved into his sister's apartment, but Abdikadir lived with many other people, too. "Eventually I was in the position to start helping others. To return the help," he says. Paying it forward, reflected in the Somali maxim *Iskaashato ma kufto*: If people support each other, they do not fall.

The togetherness wasn't absolute. Lineage-based bias remained, especially among the older generation and kids whose families emphasized it at home. And some complain about what they call the Old Guard, a small group of Somalis who came to the US in the 1990s and who, they claim, set themselves apart. The Old Guard typically had money enough to leave Somalia early; some never lived in refugee camps or, if they did, not for long.

Abdikadir views the world through a lens of commonality. "How are we more alike than different? This is what we should focus on." He's studied the teachings of Nelson Mandela, the Dalai Lama, Martin Luther King Jr. And the US Declaration of Independence—it, too, emphasizes parity, along with opportunity: "We hold these truths to be self-evident, that all men are created equal, that they are endowed by their Creator with certain unalienable Rights." Heady stuff—of course he and Ikran could make their marriage work.

In mid-May, the Lewiston Auburn Metropolitan Chamber of Commerce names Abdikadir to its "40 Under 40" list. Profiled in the *Lewiston Sun Journal* with other winners, Abdikadir again cites integration as a priority. "More learning from each other," he says of what the city most needs. He's lauded for his roles as youth soccer coach and as cofounder of MIRS, which employs forty people.

What goes unsaid: As Mainer, Somali Bantu Muslim, and transnational citizen still linked to loved ones in Kenya, Abdikadir is quietly transforming what it means to be American.

~

THE SOMALI STORES on Lisbon Street stay open late. Often I wind up downtown in the evening for a cup of tea. It's habit-forming, this shaax, creamy and spice-warmed. One night I stop in at Baraka, formerly Twins Variety, sandwiched between a Somali clothing store and Doucette Insurance. Like many of Lewiston's African stores, Baraka sells a little of everything—produce and goat meat, luxury soap, yogurt drinks.

From behind the counter the owner inquires, as he often does, after my mother. "How is your mom?" he asks, the letter *M* emphasized so the word pops. *Mom!* The two hit it off when they met, bonding over a shared love of warm weather, which my mother gets plenty of in Florida and Mohamed finds lacking in Maine. He described the Somali beaches of his youth: Soft sand. Sunshine. The aqua water of the Indian Ocean. She closed her eyes and nodded. "That sounds beautiful."

This evening, no shaax. "I'm sorry," Mohamed says. "I cleaned the thermoses already." As I'm turning to leave, he speaks in Somali to another customer. She nods. "Go with her," Mohamed tells me. "She will make it." I recognize the woman, tall and somber, as the owner of a café down the block.

At Banadir, a block from Mohamed's place, the woman unlocks the door and flips on lights. "Few minutes, please," she says, gesturing to a booth.

I sit, moved that she would reopen her store to make a cup of tea, that Mohamed would think of asking her. It reminds me of something the manager of a Lisbon Street smoke shop told me. One day a woman who runs programs at the mosque next door came into his store, which is loaded with pot paraphernalia. She was carrying one plate of sambusas for him, another for the elderly tenant upstairs. *Give these to Uncle*, she said. "Now we talk all the time," he said. Perhaps this is how community forms, one gesture at a time.

I smell a familiar spicy scent. The woman reappears with two cups of shaax. "For you. For me," she says. She smiles, but shakes her head when she sees me reaching for my wallet. "No," she says. I thank her, ask her name—"Muna." I tell her mine and she repeats it.

Muna hands me a cup. I inhale the aroma and sip. Delicious.

IN JUNE, A few weeks after Jamilo gets back from Africa, the Kenyan government announces it will shut down Dadaab within the year, citing security and economic concerns. The secretary of the Interior Ministry issues a vague call for the international community to take responsibility for the humanitarian needs that will arise as a result of the closure. Doctors Without Borders and other aid agencies urge Kenya to reconsider, warning the shutdown will jeopardize lives.

In Lewiston, people who haven't talked much about Dadaab before begin sharing stories. I hear about a two-week journey a mother of five made from Mogadishu to the camp by bus, truck, and finally on foot. Two of the children died on the way. A man describes overcrowding, sexual assault, and an outbreak of cholera in the camp. The stories are harrowing, yet people agree Dadaab should stay open. Almost everyone in Lewiston has a relative, friend, or acquaintance there.

The news dismays Jamilo deeply—members of the extended family whom she just visited have lived in Dadaab for two decades. It's frightening to imagine their humble compound emptied or razed. An idea begins to form in her mind: Could she bring her relatives to America? Is there an alternative to the conventional resettlement process? She begins to research possibilities online.

Jamilo and others question Kenya's claim that the camp provides a haven for the terrorist group al-Shabaab and is a conduit for weapons. They believe money is the primary driver. When Kenya threatened previously to shut down the camp, aid agencies upped their funding and Dadaab stayed open.

What's clear is that every time politicians announce that the camp will close, things get harder for those who live there. The place goes into bare-maintenance mode, and agencies depart. Remaining programs shift their focus to repatriation. But few refugees have actually wound up leaving. When past shutdowns were threatened, some went to the coastal city of Kismayo in southern Somalia. But with al-Shabaab there, Kismayo is too dangerous now.

The question of whether camps like Dadaab should be lifelong homes for refugees warrants consideration. But it's academic in the absence of alternatives. Somalia remains too unstable and too poor to safely repatriate people. Other African nations already hold large refugee populations. And existing resettlement programs in Africa and abroad can't realistically relocate an additional third of a million people in the span of a year—especially with the worsening crisis in Syria.

In Lewiston, Jamilo's thinking in practical terms. She wishes her parents spoke English, wishes they had technical skills that would merge them with the US workforce. The likelihood she'll succeed in getting them here within a year is small. She knows that. But the seed is there.

3

Beginnings

FATUMA WAS IN THE SHOWER ON A COLD MORNING IN 2002 when the FBI showed up. It was early. She heard banging on the bathroom door and distress in Muktar's voice. "Fatuma, please come!"

She shut off the water, hurriedly dried and dressed. In the living room of their apartment, her husband stood with a man in a suit. The agent introduced himself, said he wanted to ask her a few questions. Would that be all right? Fatuma's heart thudded. She nodded. The family recently had moved from Atlanta to a town forty miles southeast of Lewiston. Now it was just months after 9/11. Fatuma still felt shocked and grieved about what had happened. She hoped that wasn't what he wanted to talk about.

It was. The agency had received thousands of tips, the agent said, and one involved her. She'd been spotted in her hijab and abaya, walking in the town center alongside a man with "black, black skin," the agent said. According to the witness, the man resembled one of the suspects in the Twin Towers' collapse.

Fatuma knew the man the agent was talking about—he was the imam of the Lewiston-Auburn mosque. She'd met him through mutual Somali friends and bumped into him often. That day he'd come south for a meeting. She took a deep breath, explained this, worried the whole time that her still-sleeping children would awaken upset. The baby she was carrying inside—a son—shifted and resettled. Fatuma folded her hands over her belly.

The agent looked at her. "Okay," he said. He asked for the imam's name and address. Fatuma told him. He left. She sat on the sofa and cried. Muktar locked the door, went to check the kids.

The imam was cleared in a few days, but the act of having to reveal his identity would haunt Fatuma for years to come: "He was an innocent man."

As warm weather came, the welcome she'd felt during the family's early months in Maine continued to erode. Another morning, as she was going to her car, a leaflet fluttered to the ground. One side showed a white family with an estimate of the amount it earned in wages; the other side pictured a dark-skinned woman in hijab surrounded by kids, with a figure of how much she "took" from government sources.

The implication offended Fatuma. She did not consider herself a taker. Her family had been forced to leave Somalia by the civil war. Before their losses—including their home and daily life and, most searing, one of Fatuma's sisters, who died under circumstances she doesn't talk about—her family was middle class in Mogadishu. After the hard months in Utanga and more upheaval in Atlanta ("We moved from place to place to place"), she found stability with Muktar. They'd met through friends and settled comfortably into marriage.

Fatuma had been a spirited child. At twenty-two in Maine, ambition still burned inside her. In that way, she differed from laid-back Muktar. What might have seemed a mismatch was instead a good fit.

She missed her parents though. "It was so hard not to have [them] here," she says. "But I decided that I was going to do something with my life. If I made it, I made it for them, too." Maine was the place, she decided, where she would make it. Fatuma took the "Welcome to

Maine, The Way Life Should Be" border sign to heart. She set about making a new home and getting to know her neighbors and the handful of Somali families in the southern part of the state. And watching for her future.

People were drawn to her quiet confidence. Someone on the Lewiston city council asked her to give a presentation on Somali culture. Fatuma liked feeling needed, liked the role of leader. One morning a man approached her about a talk he was giving on Lewiston to the state advisory council on refugees. He wanted her help. "It's a woman's world," he said.

Telling the story years later, Fatuma raised her eyebrows. The man's name was Ali, and he was the only caseworker for the city's new immigrants. By "woman's world," she wasn't sure whether Ali meant Lewiston or the United States in general. She didn't share his view either way, but was glad for the offer. She saw what was happening—the refugees who kept arriving, the challenges—and wanted to help make things work. There were physical, immediate necessities—and deep emotional needs. "These are people who have really suffered a lot," Fatuma told me the first time we met.

She especially wanted to reach out to women, many who had survived sexual assault and the loss of children or their husbands. Then and now, single moms headed more than a third of new-immigrant households. With help from Coastal Enterprises, she submitted a proposal and received a $40,000 state grant. A hundred women showed up for the first meeting of United Somali Women of Maine.

By early 2002 more than one thousand refugees had moved to Lewiston, with more arriving every week. The Greyhound bus would pull into the station, and family members or friends would whisk the newcomers away—to feed them, to offer clothing and provide a place to sleep. Word traveled that new people were coming. Even those who knew no one in Lewiston could expect someone to be waiting when they got there.

That the newcomers were African and the women wore hijabs made them stand out in overwhelmingly white Lewiston. Fatuma's take on how her fellow Somalis came across: "Very proud, wearing very bright colors, very large families." Of those early years she says, "It was clear we were from someplace far away."

The new immigrants did look as though they were from someplace far away, yet the city seemed somehow more itself than it had in decades. There were moms and kids on Lisbon Street, people picnicking in the park. The city felt alive to me again, as it had in the '70s when my family spent so much time here. Was this part of its destiny all along?

Among longtime residents, the rumor mill was churning—most of it negative. The city gave cars to the refugees. They got food stamps and free childcare while people who'd lived in Lewiston for years were denied benefits. Refugees went to the top of subsidized apartment waitlists and got the best units. In handing all this out, the city was going under and would soon have to stop providing basic services. Much of it was untrue or exaggerated—nearly half of Somali adults under fifty found jobs within a year, often doing minimum-wage work, and perks like cars were never part of the equation.

Fear and misgiving distorted the facts. In my first Lewiston interview, a woman said, "They're everywhere I go," even though Somalis then numbered around one thousand. "I consider myself an open-minded person," the woman said as we sat in Kennedy Park. "But it's too much, too fast."

The city did struggle. It would be difficult to overstate how unprepared it was. When Portland officials reached out, Lewiston had agreed to help find apartments for a few families. It seemed win-win: the city would fill units, and refugees would have homes. No one anticipated how quickly the refugees would take to Lewiston's quiet, to the low cost of living, the safety. Or how quickly other Somalis would move from large cities around the country to join them. Cold, yes, western

Maine winters were frigid. But as struggles go—*Walwal lahayn* (no worries). These were people who had endured far worse. They went to Goodwill, bought boots and big coats. Shared them if they had to. Wrapped scarves around their kids' necks and sent them to school.

In 2001, Lewiston had one English language learner (ELL) teacher in the whole K–12 system. And city coffers were far from full. Relatively low property values meant less tax revenue. The year before, the General Assistance budget had been halved. As a significant complication, federal money allocated for new refugees did not follow them to Lewiston because they'd chosen to leave the cities where they'd been resettled. General Assistance records show 443 Somalis applied for help that first year.

Phil Nadeau was the acting city administrator then. Intense and kinetic, Nadeau gives the impression of being caffeinated even when he's not. In addition to the photos and the big street map, his office is filled with devices that impart information: two phones, three computer monitors, a laptop, and two televisions on simultaneously, and loudly, on different channels whenever there's breaking news.

"At first it was, 'We can handle this,'" Nadeau says. "So we tried the business-as-usual approach, but that didn't work." The summer of 2001, he says, was the summer of *Who authorized this?* The city needed many things, and needed them in a hurry: translators in the schools and hospitals, case managers, a greatly expanded ESL program and other social services. "We never felt hopelessness or panic," Nadeau says of City Hall, which could make you think panic was a possibility. (Fatuma would later tell a radio host the number of Somalis showing up early on was "alarming.")

Who would pay for what—and how? General Assistance funds were drying up, with almost half the already halved amount then going to new immigrants. And who were the newcomers, exactly? Nadeau, for one, didn't really know. "In the beginning I wasn't even sure where Somalia was on the map," he says with an almost laugh.

Like many Lewistonians, Nadeau had seen the movie *Black Hawk Down*—hardly an endorsement of Somalia or its people. The fact that Sgt. Tommy Fields, one of the Army Rangers who'd been killed by a mob in Mogadishu, grew up one town away in Lisbon heightened the emotional stakes. "Having [Somalis] here dishonors his memory," one man told me. Part of State Route 196, which goes through both Lisbon and Lewiston, is designated the Thomas Field Memorial Highway.

Phil recalls a general sense of confusion. "I had an urgent sense of needing accurate information," he says in understatement. And he remembers a lot of pushback. Almost from the beginning, he and the city's social services director received daily complaints about Somalis and their too-big families getting benefits that "rightly" belonged to longtime residents.

Phil's own history is largely the history of Lewiston: French Canadian blue-collar upbringing, strong work ethic. He served four years in the US Air Force and worked in the Pentagon before moving back to Lewiston and entering Bates College. After three semesters, he ran out of tuition money and had to drop out. In the 1980s he helped run Friends Deli, his family's restaurant and catering business. A fire destroyed Friends in 1989. Nadeau went back to school, this time the University of Maine at Augusta. Employed by the city for eighteen years, he tends to work through problems methodically, although—or maybe because—he's deeply emotional. "I'm not paid to have opinions," he tells me more than once, but his passions are clear: his wife, the state of Maine, the people of Lewiston—including its new immigrants.

The first financial score for the city came at the end of 2001, when Lewiston and Portland got a joint four-year $1.2 million "Unanticipated Arrivals" grant from ORR. It was the first time cities, rather than nonprofits like Catholic Charities or Lutheran Services, had been awarded money. The grant would do a lot to support more programs, but it didn't quell unease. New rumors cropped up: Somalis kept live chickens in their cupboards and fish in their bathtubs. They got free medical care at local hospitals. They received tens of thousands of dollars in interest-free loans.

There was also a sense that previous generations of immigrants had behaved differently—found work right away, assimilated rapidly, spoke English, set aside their ethnicity. I heard this a lot, that whether you were French Canadian or Irish or Italian back when earlier immigrants had arrived, within a year or two you became American. The fact that manufacturing had been in its heyday then, that technology and globalization hadn't yet eroded other jobs, that unlike earlier immigrants Somalis were neither white nor Christian and many had endured profound war trauma—none of these factored into the views some Lewistonians held. Nor did the fact that expenditures on refugees averaged about 3 percent of the city's budget.

At an open forum in May 2002, citizens lined up behind the microphone—mostly to complain about or berate the newcomers. Here, Nadeau does admit to frustration: "It was like, you realize the things you're saying about the Somalis and their religion were the same things being spread when the French Canadians first came."

The pot boiled over on Wednesday, October 1, 2002. Mayor Laurier Raymond, acting, he said, at the behest of citizens, sent an open letter to the Somali community. Nadeau, whose office sat across the hall from the mayor's, had helped him revise an earlier version to tone it down. But the letter still had an edge. "The press is going to be rough," Nadeau told him.

He was right. Hours after the letter's release, someone posted it on the Internet. Within days, news outlets across the world were running stories about Lewiston, the little city in Maine with the xenophobic mayor. The TVs in Nadeau's office ran for days. That Raymond received hundreds of supportive emails and letters from residents only implicated the city more broadly.

The letter itself was a curious combination of addressing the newcomers directly and speaking about them in third person:

> I assumed that it would become obvious to the new arrivals the effect the large numbers of new residents has had upon the existing Staff and City finances and that this would bring about a voluntary reduction of the number of new arrivals—it being evident that the burden has been, for the most part, cheerfully accepted, and every effort has been made to accommodate it.... [T]he Somali community must exercise some discipline...We have been overwhelmed and have responded valiantly. Now we need breathing room. Our city is maxed-out financially, physically and emotionally.

Many Somalis didn't then speak fluent English, but certain words etched themselves into the collective psyche: "burden," "maxed-out," "exercise some discipline." It's likely no coincidence Fatuma often includes *We are not a burden* even now when she gives a speech.

That weekend, Somali elders hunkered down and drafted a response. They handed it out on Monday at a press conference. It read, in part:

> We react to your letter in mixed feelings ranging from dismay, astonishment and anger. This is because of the fact that you have never given us a chance to meet with you and discuss our future plans with you during your term in office...[Your] letter is an attempt to agitate and incite the local people and a license to violence against our people physically, verbally and emotionally.

On Friday, Raymond finally sat down with Somali leaders. He issued a statement that said, in part, "Those who have interpreted my letter as a 'call to draw lines in the sand' totally misunderstood my message." Soon after, he acknowledged he should have met with the leaders before releasing the letter.

By then it was too late—the lines were there. On Sunday about three hundred people marched with a local church in support of the newcomers. A few weeks later the Illinois-based World Church of the Creator (WCC), which brands itself "white racial loyalists," announced plans to hold a January rally in Lewiston. Shortly thereafter, Maine civic and religious leaders formed the Many and One Coalition. On the same day WCC came to Lewiston, coalition leaders said they would hold a counterrally at Bates College. Another pro-immigration group planned a more confrontational rally for the National Guard Armory, where WCC was holding its gathering.

As the date approached, the city and state amassed one of the largest law enforcement teams in Maine's history. There was reason for concern. WCC, now known as the Creativity Movement, holds among its core beliefs that "the white race is nature's finest." A web homepage disclaimer that the movement is "non-violent, progressive . . . [and embraces only] 100% legal activism" is inconsistent with its sixteen "Commandments." Among them: "Show preferential treatment in business dealings with members of your own race. Phase out all dealings with Jews as soon as possible. Do not employ n—ers or other coloreds" and "It is our immediate objective to relentlessly expand the White Race, and keep shrinking our enemies."

On the January day of the rally, more than four thousand people showed up at Bates. To enter the auditorium, they walked through metal detectors and past bomb-sniffing dogs and a line of police. Those who couldn't fit inside chanted and sang outdoors for hours. The turnout included both of Maine's US senators and its US representatives. The state Speaker of the House read from a resolution unanimously passed by the legislature that said in part, "Hate and bigotry have no place in the great state of Maine."

Meanwhile, across town, hundreds of pro-immigrant protestors marched outside the armory. Police snipers lay on rooftops, and armed officers amassed on the frozen ground. In the end, only about forty WCC members and supporters showed up. Their message was a watered-down version of the group's online content but chilling nonetheless. Speakers vilified Somalis along with Jews, US political leaders, and organized religion. "There is no stopping us," one speaker said of the WCC movement. Even so, the riot-ready ranks turned out to be unnecessary; at the end of the WCC gathering in an outbuilding, police hustled the white supremacists away.

Most surprised by what happened that day were refugees themselves. Many expected animosity and opposition—not a wellspring of support. Years later, shop owner Hussein Ahmed would tell a *Sun Journal* reporter that the Many and One Rally opened his eyes to how many Mainers cared. "It made me realize there was big support that we were not aware of. It motivated a lot of Somalis, gave them hope that they can stay here."

The refugees' most illustrious supporter that day was Muhammad Ali, who sent a letter referencing the 1965 World Heavyweight Championship in which he'd knocked out Sonny Liston—in Lewiston. Ali said he was now "concerned about an even greater contest going on in Lewiston, one between those ingrained in bigotry and those who have embraced freedom." He went on, "I was especially troubled by [Raymond's] suggestion that the 'Somali community must exercise some discipline' in their preference of Lewiston as a place to live. This insinuation was, at best, irresponsible. At worst, it was evidence of a deeper prejudice."

In a bizarre coincidence, Larry Raymond had been the one who, as a thirty-four-year-old district attorney, gave consent to the 1965 fight, which had been hastily relocated from Boston Garden. Thousands poured into Lewiston that May weekend, including Joe Lewis, Frank Sinatra, and Elizabeth Taylor. Ali stayed at the Holiday Inn for three days, his big red bus parked in the hotel lot. People I knew while growing up talked about it for years; many older Lewistonians still do.

Another coincidence: It was in Lewiston that the twenty-three-year-old champion was introduced for the first time as Muhammad Ali. The year before, he'd joined the Nation of Islam and then, to honor slain civil rights leader Malcolm X, changed his name from Cassius Clay to Cassius X and later to Ali. Most media there that night didn't call the champion by his new name, even though fight tickets clearly stated it. The next morning both Lewiston newspapers referred to him as Clay.

Thirty-six years later, Raymond released his letter. Almost everything that followed was a stinging rebuke. Raymond did not respond to the onslaught of calls from national media, did not attend the Bates rally. Then-governor Angus King Jr. came to his defense—"I know Larry Raymond and he is not a racist. . . . Lewiston has really dealt with a situation that would be difficult for any community"—but most Maine leaders remained critical.

Fatuma's take, in retrospect: The situation *was* overwhelming. One morning in 2002 she showed up at City Hall and counted forty-seven Somali newcomers. "Unsustainable," she says of that first influx, with so much pressure on General Assistance and on city services overall.

"Looking back now, the mayor was addressing an issue—absolutely," Fatuma told students in a talk she gave at Bowdoin College. She didn't agree with Raymond's approach, but it was clear Lewiston was changing and everyone—the city's residents, new immigrants, state and city officials—had a lot to figure out.

When the first Somalis were arriving in Lewiston, my father lived briefly in Auburn. Even after he moved, he kept a close eye on what was happening. He believed Raymond's shortcoming was one of leadership. In those early years, the city needed a strong hand to guide it, he said. A lifelong Democrat, progressive to his core, my dad admitted the sudden appearance in the city of so many African Muslim immigrants had surprised and startled him. "People didn't know what to make of it," he said. But Raymond misstepped in issuing an open letter, my father said—and by saying he'd done so on behalf of residents. From my dad's perspective, Raymond should have publicly supported the refugees while working with Somali leaders to sort through issues. Instead of being shaped by public opinion, the mayor should have been the one shaping it.

Those few months tainted Raymond's legacy in Lewiston, mayoral and otherwise. In the aftermath, he seemed resigned to being painted broad-brush as a bigot. "Somebody had to say something. I guess it was me," he later told a filmmaker who directed a documentary about the city.

Somalis themselves, it turned out, acknowledged parts of Raymond's message. In a second statement, released after they met with him but barely covered by the press, they said: "We understand the social and economic pressure that new entrants bring to the community." They hoped, they wrote, that Lewiston in turn would see "the potential richness and opportunity newcomers bring."

Even now the mayor's letter remains a tender topic in Lewiston—it's referred to as "the letter," and remembered well. One afternoon I ask Phil Nadeau whether it was heavy-handed. Maybe, he says. Racist? "No." Nadeau contends that in the end the letter did the city good, that it was a catalyst. "We realized then that if this experience was going to work, it had to be an all-hands-on-deck effort. The whole community—civic, nonprofit, newcomer, religious, corporate—needed to be a part of what was going on."

Fatuma agrees. "People from every sector worked really hard to come together." It was a time of confusion and anxiety, she says, but also one of hope. The broad bases that formed in the aftermath of the letter widened support for civic and school programs that might otherwise have failed. And Somali emphasis on communitarianism introduced new conventions—for instance, that a public meeting should not adjourn until all who wished to speak had done so.

In the end, Fatuma and Phil Nadeau may have been right that the letter unified the city. The racist label horrified many residents, who worked to distance themselves from it. Volunteerism spiked at language centers and food pantries. Employers hired more refugees. My friend whose daughter was in kindergarten described white parents reaching out to newcomers for playdates. Some Somalis reciprocated. And refugees kept coming. There was a brief lull, but by mid-2003 the numbers were up again. Somalis still liked Lewiston enough to encourage those who wanted out of big cities to give it a try.

To many, Lewiston felt a lot safer than the urban neighborhoods where agencies had first settled them. Aba Abu, a single mom of two who moved here in 2003, remembers being frightened in Atlanta, so much so that she kept her kids inside. Her fears were not unfounded: a US Senate Committee on Foreign Relations report would later describe the part of the city where Aba and other Somali refugees were being sent as "shattered" by crime and police brutality.

Jamilo remembers feeling more welcome than she had in Dallas, where her extended family was first sent: "People were just friendlier in Lewiston."

Fatuma saw steady improvement in relations between Somalis and native Lewistonians. "We are starting to know each other," she told me a few years after her family moved to Auburn. She noted similarities between Somalis and Mainers—both were reserved on the surface and caring underneath. She'd also developed a liking for the civility she'd observed. "In Georgia, the attitude was in the air," she said. "If [Mainers] have an opinion, they tell you in a respectful way or they keep it to themselves."

~

WHILE FATUMA AND Jamilo were settling into Lewiston, my family had dispersed. For four generations we'd lived in a rambling colonial on the Androscoggin. My mother left first, separating from my father and moving to Farmington to teach at the university there. My sister and I stayed with our dad.

In towns across late-twentieth-century America, millions of other families were dissolving or taking leave around the time ours did. My parents' divorce led to my family's breakup; different forces disrupted other families—job loss or substance abuse or, on a larger scale, the closure of a factory. The need to move away or move on brought more change. Families lost their origins, grew less securely underpinned. And with each family that left, the town grew that much smaller.

I'd grown up believing my family was deeply rooted—my great-grandfather had helped build the village church; my grandfather had owned the general store; my dad was the tenth-generation male to bear his name. Successive generations had left evidence of their commitment to the house: gardens, inlaid floors, stained-glass windows.

After my sister and I graduated from college and our father moved out, the house stood empty. It fell into disrepair. My mom had remarried; she and her husband spent part of the year in Florida and part in southern Maine. My sister and I avoided going back to the village. We drifted from former neighbors and cousins. We rarely visited our family plot in the cemetery behind the church.

Finally, facing health challenges, Dad agreed to sell the house and settle closer to my sister. Within a few months of the closing, the place looked better than it had in years. Fresh paint coated the clapboards, the hedges were trimmed.

By then I was living in Boston. But Boston didn't really feel like home. Maine did. Especially the western part of the state, where the land opened up, where moose grazed matter-of-factly beside wheelless cars on blocks. I went inland often, on magazine and newspaper assignments or to see friends. When I drove up along the river, it was no longer with uneasiness about what I'd see when I entered the village.

But there was an emptiness. My mother's Portland condo was spanking new and painted white throughout. Occasionally small groupings of the family reconfigured there. My father came at Christmas, fiddling the whole time with his Red Sox cap, visor-up-visor-down-visor-up. In spite of the presents my mom heaped beneath the tree, those were diminished occasions. We watched old movies on TV in place of caroling. We sat around her new glass table, not the dinged-up mahogany one that had seated twelve.

~

IN 2006, WHEN Farah Adan moved to Lewiston from Missouri, he followed the same trajectory as the more than two thousand Somali secondary migrants before him. He and his wife found an apartment, settled the kids in school, applied for assistance. Within months Farah was doing seasonal work at L.L.Bean.

In his longing to open a business—a halal butchery—Farah was like other Somalis, too. By now, certain things about the newcomers had become clear. As Muslims, they didn't drink alcohol or use drugs; that included most teens. Apart from occasional domestic issues, the new immigrants mostly stayed clear of the law. They threw big weddings and Eid celebrations. And many were strivers—eager for education and start-up opportunities, often self-assertive.

It was taking white residents time to get used to the self-assertion. The word *refugee* conjured victimhood, but the newcomers didn't seem particularly helpless. Many came across as active seekers, intent on creating new lives. Refugees, yes, but also survivors who'd navigated an arduous process to qualify for UN refugee status. Who had reestablished close communities once they got to the US.

On the whole, the newcomers were not ungrateful. But they weren't *just* grateful.

One day I watched two Somali women sort through a prepacked box at a food pantry, setting aside chips and sweetened cereal, keeping potatoes and canned tuna. One of the volunteers seemed displeased—she shook her head, frowned—but it was clear the women intended no offense. They would take what they would use; some items didn't figure into the mix.

Longtime residents had many opinions. What they hadn't necessarily counted on was that the newcomers did, too.

Moe Landry owns a barbershop in the heart of the tree streets neighborhood. His daughter cuts hair alongside him. It's a busy part of Lewiston. Jamilo's former mother-in-law lives across the street. Nasafari's family's condo is nearby. "I've never once had any trouble," Moe says of relations with new immigrants. His biggest problem is trash thrown in back of his shop. He parks his SUV there, doesn't appreciate stepping out onto soda bottles and frozen-dinner trays. He got fed up and installed a camera. It's not his African neighbors, he says. White people occupy the apartments adjacent to the lot.

But Moe doesn't cut the newcomers' hair—"They're particular," he says. A pause. "I can't blame them. Cutting African hair is a skill." One day, he said, four Somali men came in saying they'd pay for haircuts but one of them would do the work with Moe's instruments. Moe said no way. He tells the story with a degree of delight: "I didn't see a license hanging on the wall with that guy's name on it, but it was a good try."

Some in Lewiston criticized the refugees for receiving assistance *and* for taking initiative. Downtown, people complained Somalis would displace longtime residents who were struggling or marginalized. Besides the envy of Somali support structures—loan pools, childcare, shared vehicles—I sensed resentment of their community. White residents living downtown often seemed more isolated. It's likely some felt bitter, period, and the newcomers served as a locus for that bitterness.

Somalis for the most part ignored what they could and coped with what they couldn't. They averted their eyes from the "Go Back to Africa" sign a man posted in his yard. Carpooled when they realized some taxis drivers wouldn't pick them up. And when kids told Fatuma's children that welfare bought their clothes and they shouldn't get to wear brand names, Fatuma went out and bought more.

In 2013, Farah opened his store, midway down on Lisbon Street. His older son helped out at the register. After a while, Farah moved up the street to a better location. He named the new place Juba, after a river in Somalia. Juba stayed open from ten a.m. to eight p.m., long hours that didn't bother Farah—they meant more business.

After a couple of years, as more stores began to sell halal goat, competition stiffened. Farah's profits dipped. One of his kids went off to college, then a second. Farah turned fifty-two. He was working a seventy-hour week.

On a spring Saturday, people trickled in and out of the store. A customer wanted a leg of lamb, cubed, and ground beef. The beef was ready, but Farah had to cut the lamb. In the rear of his store he prepared: washed his hands, tied an apron over his gingham shirt, inserted earplugs. An extrovert with a penchant for conservative politics, around the meat saw he exudes focus. No one but he crosses the line painted on the floor between the butchery and shelves of spices and dried goods.

The customer settled into a chair, ran her fingers over a stack of prayer rugs. Her outfit was a season-straddler—plaid wool coat, long skirt, silver sandals. She watched the proceedings closely. The saw droned, the blade cutting through frozen meat as if it were butter.

Finally Farah switched off the saw. The chunks he swept into a plastic tote had the look and sound of a child's blocks.

The woman stood. "And the beef!" she commanded. Farah pulled a bag from a freezer. They moved to the register.

"That's fifty-five," he told her.

"I have fifty."

"I can't do fifty."

"I don't have the five!"

Farah reached for the bag of lamb. "Then I'll take it out."

The woman paused, then rummaged for a few singles and handed them over.

Farah pushed the bags toward her. She smiled for the first time since entering the store. "Thank you."

Later Farah would say he hates bargaining, that his profit margin is already slim, but he returned her smile. "Thank you."

The morning wore on, customers here and there—mostly Somali, a few Congolese or Burundian. Outside on the sidewalk, two elderly women passed arm in arm. A family stopped to reallocate bundles. A tattooed man ambled by with a dog on his shoulder. Farah sighed, said he needed shaax.

Lisbon Street was a tough place not long ago and still can be. When Farah opened Juba, dealers made deliveries on a nearby corner. Since then the city's drug problem hasn't lessened—opiates are a crisis—but police have heightened their presence. In 2015, they made a big bust in the building next door. After I left Juba that day, I stopped at the pawnshop a few doors away. A woman came in shoeless. She was clearly tweaking, belligerent when the manager wouldn't give her what she wanted for a scratched TV.

Farah's door banged open. Two women entered, with them the scent of baking bread from the Country Kitchen plant across the street. Customers kept coming, even if Farah's prices weren't the cheapest. His goat was imported from New Zealand, organic and tender, good enough that people drove up from Portland.

Farah turned to the women, nodded. "How can I help?"

4

Summer 2016

Jamilo, Nasafari, Carrys

ON THE MORNING OF EID AL-FITR, THE CELEBRATION AT THE end of Ramadan, shoes are piled everywhere at the entrance to the Lewiston Armory. Inside, hundreds of people sit on prayer rugs or on the floor of the huge space, men on one side, women on the other. People murmur greetings, embrace; girls take one another's hands and admire henna tattoos applied for the occasion. Almost everyone is dressed up: women in their best diracs, some of the men with suit jackets over white kameezes. Jamilo woke Aaliyah and Hamzah before dawn to get them ready. They were out of the apartment by six a.m., bumping into other families and posing for photos in front of City Hall.

The celebration ends the month of prayer and daylong fasting. Muslims believe fasting increases their closeness to Allah and helps them relate to the suffering of others. Giving money or food to the poor is customary. Ramadan also marks the first revelation of the Quran to the prophet Muhammad.

The month brought a sense of unity to Muslims—they did something hard, together—but also challenges. Jamilo kept reminding herself to be patient with the kids, who won't fast until after puberty and whose energy rose as hers flagged. On the hardest days, she gave in and ate. Abdikadir often ran out of steam midafternoon at MIRS after ten hours without water or food; he'd check and recheck his phone to see how close day's end was. National politics added to his stress. It's becoming more and more evident that Donald Trump will be the Republican nominee for president. Trump's divisiveness upsets and mystifies Abdikadir. "This is not how a leader should be," he says.

The service at the Armory begins: *"Allahu Akbar, Allahu Akbar."* As everyone kneels in unison and touches forehead to floor, fabric shushes like wind. The Armory is used for Eid al-Fitr and two months from now for Eid al-Adha because the city's two small mosques don't have enough room.

There's crossover, but most ethnic Somalis attend Masjid A-Nur on Lisbon Street, while Bantus go to the Bartlett Street mosque. Both mosques follow less austere forms of Islam than the Salafism or Wahhabism practiced in parts of the Middle East and Africa. Bantu culture also includes animist traditions. But today on Eid, after the long weeks of Ramadan, the city's Muslims are one, regardless of where they worship.

After the half-hour salah, people stream into the July day. Kids shout and run beneath the trees. Moms pull cell phones from their dirac. Photos, and more photos: *Pose here by the flowers with your cousins. Now gather around Granddad; again, and this time keep your eyes open.*

Eid Mubarak, everyone calls. Happy Eid! From the Armory, families spread out in different directions—for meals that have been days in preparation, for trips to parks and lakes and relatives in other cities.

Abdikadir goes with Ikran and the kids to his mother's, where she's made food enough for thirty-five. The apartment smells of grilled meat, shaax, and oud, a perfume Somalis like. People keep coming.

Shoes stacked by the door topple. Jamilo takes Aaliyah and Hamzah to her aunt's apartment and then with friends to the play space at the Auburn Mall. Fatuma and her extended family head for Six Flags so the kids can ride the Buzzsaw and the Wicked Cyclone. Stomachs flip-flopping, the adults watch.

Other families drive to Boston, Old Orchard, Rhode Island, upstate New York, toddlers buckled into their boosters and, later, parents drinking coffee or shaax to stay awake on the long trip home. Many Somalis love to travel—some attribute it to their nomadic roots—and there's no better excuse for a road trip than Eid.

That evening in Kennedy Park, benches are still occupied as dusk gives way to dark. A couple of families wind up picnics of goat or beef, rice, and salad—and the ubiquitous bananas that accompany every meal, to be sliced into the rice. By the basketball courts, two women watch a man and a girl trace figure eights with sparklers left over from the Fourth of July. Little kids rest in parents' laps. Couples sit on benches near a latticed gazebo—the same gazebo in one of my family's photos from Great-Aunt Nell's time, girls astride Victorian-era bicycles in front of it.

Inside Speaker's Variety, the cashier is a little testy. "No more dollar bills!" she tells the kids gathered on the other side of the counter. "I've gotten three hundred of them today and I'm out of change." But she's not stern as she says it, and the kids crack up. It's true they've brought in a lot of singles: Say "Eid Mubarak" to an adult, and it sometimes elicits a dollar—a magical transaction that's occurred countless times today.

On the sidewalk a group of boys peel wrappers from candy and open chips they bought after coaxing the cashier to take their singles anyway. When I ask a fifth grader what Islam means to him, he recounts its pillars: care for the poor, the Hajj (pilgrimage to Mecca) once in your lifetime, pray five times a day, fast during Ramadan. He pauses. The Quran, another boy says. Right, says the first. Say you believe in Allah, and that Muhammad is his messenger. The other kids nod; he's got it.

~

IN MID-JUNE, THE day after twenty-nine-year-old Omar Mateen kills forty-nine people in an attack on an Orlando nightclub, Donald Trump lashes out at Hillary Clinton: "[Her] catastrophic immigration plan will bring vastly more radical Islamic immigration into this country, threatening not only our society but our entire way of life." Two days later, at a rally in North Carolina, Trump points out that Mateen's parents are Muslims from Afghanistan. He claims the children of Muslim immigrants are "responsible for a growing number . . . of terrorist attacks." On Fox News the next night, he says of Muslims: "They come, they don't, for some reason, there's no real assimilation."

In July, in his acceptance speech for the Republican nomination, Trump mentions "brutal Islamic terrorism" several times. Three days later he vows to go forward with his proposal to restrict Muslim entry into the US and, on NBC News, suggests that maintaining the status quo is akin to suicide. "Why are we committing suicide?" he asks. "Why are we doing that?" Two weeks later, in Orlando, Trump says that Syrian Muslims find it far easier to come to the US than do Syrian Christians. He later vows to "screen out anyone who doesn't share our values and love our people."

~

IN JAMILO'S KNOX Street apartment, the curtains are drawn against the sun. Outside, when she and the kids climbed to the third floor, the heat was a wall. Neighbors in the four-story complex fanned themselves on stair decks that double as porches. The doors to units with AC were closed, the ones without open to the hope of a breeze.

Here it's cool, or cooler, and quiet. Three-year-old Aaliyah sits on the sofa beside Jamilo and licks a Popsicle. Fifteen-month-old Hamzah sleeps upstairs. "Careful you don't drip," Jamilo says. Aaliyah nods, cranes her neck to see photos her mother swipes through on her phone: Eid, pictures of the kids wading in Sabattus Lake, some shots from May, then back to March when Jamilo arrived in Dagahaley camp.

She looks often at the photos from her trip—if they were prints, they'd be dog-eared. She stops at one of herself with five others in a dusty courtyard. "There they are," she says—her birth family. This photo gives her a lump in her throat. She still can't believe she was back there, can't believe she got to be with her parents and meet her younger siblings. "So many people remembered me," she says, wistful.

Here's her dad with his radio; here's the Dagahaley market; here's the shady spot where people gather in the afternoon. There's the hut where Jamilo got her hair braided when she was small. Then, "There's the hut where I got circumcised." Matter-of-factly she adds that family members sleep in that same space now. I sit there, stunned. She swipes to the next photo.

It will be nine months before Jamilo tells me her circumcision was the most extreme form, that they took her clitoris and labia. In a text, she'll add: "They lined up all my cousins, girls first and then boys. [Hearing] my cousins cry in pain pained my heart! When I realized I'd be next, I ran away far from everyone. I ran for what felt like two days. Some guy [who] knew my people and the village I'm from found me and brought me back. They called the scary man on me! They held me down, about four people. I'm only 5-6 years old. The man who is about to ruin my privates says Look there's an airplane—I went out, woke up. Why am I in pain? . . . I couldn't stop crying, it hurts so much, where's my hooyo (mother). I need someone to hold me."

That hot day in her apartment when she first tells me, Jamilo's face takes on the look it sometimes gets. A stillness, almost as if she's holding her breath. We sit quietly for a while. Nine months from now, when Jamilo sends that text, the state legislature will be battling over a bill to ban female genital mutilation.

Aaliyah taps the screen. "Let's look at some more, Mama."

Instead Jamilo hands Aaliyah the tablet they share. "Here, you can play." She sits her daughter on the rug at her feet, briefly holding her shoulders, reassuring. It's the same gesture she used one day at Kennedy Park. Aaliyah had gone down on her own to the swings but rushed back after a man passed with a snake wrapped around his torso. "That was really scary!" Jamilo reached for her. "You're safe here," she told her.

Traveling to Dadaab and back to America has given her new perspective, made her question things. When she first arrived in the US and lived in Dallas, a boy touched her inappropriately. She told adults. Why was nothing done, she now asks. And why was she treated differently from the family's biological children, who she says were well cared for and punished less harshly for misbehavior. Jamilo doesn't have answers, yet her new, stronger self knows this: Her extended family may have done the best they knew in the midst of their own struggles, but she grew up with care that sometimes bordered on indifference.

The questions she's asking now have lurked, unarticulated, for years. In Kenya, she used to get up before the sun rose, find wood and start the fire. That way, when the grown-ups woke, they could put on water for shaax and whatever they were cooking for breakfast. Sometimes the adults smiled at Jamilo or said *Shaaqo wanaagsan* (Good job). Often they shooed her away. Why?

At Tree Street Youth, Julia Sleeper recalls a teen-aged Jamilo as a charismatic pleaser. Also vulnerable: "A lot of the time it seemed like she was taking care of herself. Like she was on her own." Many of the city's refugee families have emerged from hardship strong, Julia says, but there are other kids growing up as Jamilo did—separated from their birth parents or in families compromised by PTSD and other effects of trauma.

Maybe it was inevitable that with longing as deep and wide as the oceans separating her from the parents she thought she'd lost, Jamilo would find and follow a man who said he loved her. She was seventeen, he nineteen. "He encouraged me, he listened to me," she says. "For the first time, I was happy." Jamilo loved him, too, and when Aaliyah was born knew she'd care for her daughter in a way she never remembered being cared for herself. That her relationship with Aaliyah's dad broke down—she was too young, unready, unsupported—saddens her still.

Often I'm struck by the initiative I see in Lewiston's new immigrants. Isaac sets his sights on Bowdoin, gets in; Fatuma founds a nonprofit and manages her big family; Nasafari plans her career as an attorney. Initiative for Jamilo means something different, a less direct trajectory. There's the past to reckon with, a lot to come to terms with before the future can be mapped. In that way, she's like many of the city's refugees—dealing with aftereffects of sexual assault and other attacks, of uprooting and deep loss. Some manage to move forward, others do not.

"People respond differently to pain and trauma. They have different thresholds, based on how their brains are wired," says Jihan Omar, cofounder of Minds for Health in Lewiston. "Some are able to process things and apply coping skills. Others are unable to move from that time, those experiences... It can take a long, long time to work through, and that's if you have the mental health resources to help."

Many new immigrants, particularly older ones, feel reluctant to get help, Omar says. Within the community, people are sometimes ostracized for going to a counselor; clients often won't acknowledge her if they see her on the street. "When we go into homes we can't use the word *mental* with *health*," she says. "Mental illness means something severe, like schizophrenia. Not PTSD or depression. Sometimes family members are told that if they followed Islam more closely, they wouldn't be struggling. They're told they need to learn how to forgive. Learn how to manage their emotions."

In Jamilo, I see something I've seen in other refugee women in their twenties. Hardship has annealed her, given her a definition others her age don't have. She's small, five foot four and 125 pounds, but there's heft to her. What keeps her moving forward? For her, it's faith in Allah first. She's done therapy and tried antidepressants, finds it more helpful to pray and sort things through with friends. She has Aspen and Binto in Lewiston and another close friend, Fatima, in Massachusetts.

Inside the apartment, Aaliyah is climbing the carpeted stairs and riding down on her bottom. "Look!"

"Try to be quiet," Jamilo says, but it's too late—Hamzah appears. Aaliyah helps him down the steps. Jamilo hands him a Popsicle. He takes a few licks, widens his eyes. "No," he says, his current pronouncement to almost everything. Aaliyah tickles him. He giggles, keeps licking. "No."

Mostly Jamilo figures things out as she goes—wounded yet determined. In this and other ways, her independence works for and against her. Some things already are clear. She wants to be a good mom, even if she's not always sure what that looks like. Wants to try to bring her parents to the US, if she can raise the money and make her way through the bureaucracy. If Trump doesn't win the presidency and keep them out. She wants the love of a good man and a successful marriage, though that seems far off. More immediately, she'd like to figure out how to play in the city's women's soccer league a couple of nights a week.

For now—her job, healthy kids, nice apartment—she's in a good place. Among other young moms in Lewiston, her enterprise and spirit make her a leader. Yet, too often, the past presses in on Jamilo, makes her restless, pensive. The trip to Kenya did fortify her, and

Ramadan deepened her closeness with Allah. She turns to him to keep the restlessness away.

Mostly it works. Everywhere Jamilo goes, people tell her she has a beautiful smile. I mention this; she nods. "I always smile, no matter what." A pause. "I hope someday my eyes will match with the smile on my face."

~

DURING HER SUMMER stays in Maine, my mother sometimes comes with me to Lewiston. I work, and she reads the *Sun Journal* or does crosswords in a café. One afternoon we walk around Aunt Nell's old neighborhood. Mom says it feels busier than she remembered. Students from Bates College room in what used to be single-family homes, and new immigrants live in several of the duplexes. Aunt Nell's house looks worn, but flowers bloom along the driveway.

Another day we cover Park Street and the length of Lisbon, buying kefir along the way. In front of a three-story brick building, I have a sudden sense of having been here with her and Aunt Nell. Now the ground level holds a Somali store.

That night searching the address online, I find a photo captioned "1890 Pottle Building; 230-234 Lisbon St., Lewiston, Maine; Built by Cyrus Greeley for George Pottle, Lewiston mayor." George Pottle was Great-Aunt Nell's father-in-law; her son was named for him. She must have pointed out the building. (I hadn't known George Sr. was mayor—later I'll learn he served from 1899 to 1900, and that he was one of fourteen children.) My mom and I find another Pottle building farther down Lisbon. That one has the name etched into its facade.

"This will always be my home," Mom says one day as we cross the Androscoggin. I'm surprised—she's lived thirty years in Florida, grew up in Massachusetts. She always seemed impatient with Maine's slower pace. For that matter, she was impatient with my nonlinear father, and often with my sister and me.

After my parents married, they lived down east in Machias, where my dad owned a mobile motel on Route 1. They had a cat that rode on my father's shoulder, and a beagle. The idea was that each fall they'd flatbed the motel's units to Florida and reconstruct it for the season there, then truck it back north for the summer. My dad's biggest miscalculation was that my mom wouldn't mind cleaning the rooms. She minded. They sold the place and moved inland to the house where he'd grown up. Mom didn't like it much. I have early memories of her getting ready to go someplace else: work, school, the hairdresser, away.

But at eighty-five she's changing—content to sit on the porch with morning coffee when earlier she'd have penned a to-do list at the counter. She may even cede the day's plans to whomever she's with.

Is she also growing emotionally more attuned? The Lewiston café she likes is one where I go, too. One day, early to conduct an interview at the mosque, I head there first. I'm wearing a headscarf for the interview—inexpertly but painstakingly tied, so I don't want to take it off. At the café, the waitperson is cool, not unpleasant but not so friendly. She clearly doesn't recognize me when I greet her. My take: she sees a woman in hijab, someone who is "other."

When I tell my mom, she questions my interpretation that the waitperson was put off by the headscarf. Maybe I just looked like someone she didn't know? "Like a stranger," Mom says. "She would have gotten to know you with time."

~

NASAFARI IS MAKING progress toward St. John's. She hung in there prepping for the SAT retake, and her math skills especially feel stronger. *Alexis is half her sister's age. She will be three-fourths of her sister's age in 20 years. How old is Alexis?* Ten—Nasafari's got it. She's happy, too, that she earned a final grade of B+ in Algebra II, not bad for her weakest subject. Next month she'll take a weeklong college-prep course at the high school. She'll work on an application essay and the Free Application for Federal Student Aid (FAFSA), and research safeties in case she doesn't get into St. John's.

But she will. Surely St. John's will work out and she'll take the first steps toward becoming a JAG. She's possessed the dream for so long she no longer remembers not having it. It seems closer now, though, like she's ready, like when you're in eighth grade and that sophomore boy is nice but you're too shy to talk, then two years later you're a sophomore and he's a senior and everything feels different.

Her summer job at Tree Street, working with first and second graders, is going okay. The days get long, especially the hot ones because Tree has no AC. But Nasafari likes kids, and they gravitate to her. Together they draw and read, dance, hang out in the play yard. A couple of weeks ago they planted lettuce in Tree's garden; the first sprouts have popped. Nasafari looks forward to seeing everyone each morning—the littlest kids, and the uninhibited, climb into her lap and tell her she's pretty. She tells them they're pretty, too.

So it's not the most exciting summer but peaceful. Nights still belong to Nasafari. She keeps up with the Forresters on *The Bold and the Beautiful*, sometimes watches travel shows. Her parents finally let her get a phone; after they and her younger siblings Moses and Christina go upstairs to bed, she texts with friends and posts on Facebook from her spot in the crook of the sofa. She even texts with a boy, possibly the same one from the spring—but she guesses she won't name him yet.

She's doing some personal work too, she says, trying to be less self-absorbed, more attentive to other peoples' feelings. More mature, a better Christian. And she wants to be a better friend: "I mean, I don't really have that many. At LHS a lot of people know me, but I just go to school and stay focused on schoolwork and activities."

Sometimes it seems Nasafari is hard on herself. The friend thing—others see it differently. "She's totally loving and kind," says a classmate named Farhiya. They met in elementary school, and Farhiya says when she moved to Massachusetts no one kept in touch except for Nasafari. Farhiya's family later returned to Lewiston. Her devotion to Nasafari is steadfast: "She turned out to be the only real friend I have."

Julia Sleeper says Nasafari holds herself a little apart from other kids. "She puts pressure on herself, and she's under a lot of scrutiny from her parents. Sometimes we wish they could loosen up a little."

It's true that African parents tend to be stricter than American in Lewiston, and Nasafari's occupy the traditional end of the African spectrum. There are reasons for that. The family is active in the First Assembly of God in Lewiston. Conservative, Bible-based faith forms the core of their lives. Then there's Nasafari's father Norbert's temperament, and his harrowing history, and the way both elements have intertwined and propelled him through the past two decades.

Norbert: mild-mannered with a warm smile, a wiry five foot seven. Ex-president of his condo association and a trainer at Pioneer Plastics who knows how to run six machines. He allows beverages but never food in the mint-condition Toyota Avalon he polishes by hand.

One morning in 1998, Norbert left his western Congo village to make the journey to Lubumbashi on foot with seven of the family's cows. He was twenty-eight. He planned on selling the cattle at the city's market. His wife Kamakazi, pregnant with Nasafari, stayed home with their two daughters. It took Norbert a month to get there. The night after he sold the cattle, Congolese soldiers burst into the house where he was staying. They were targeting Banyamulenge, sometimes called Tutsi Congolese—the same Tutsis massacred in Rwanda earlier in the decade, more than 800,000 during a hundred-day genocide. Norbert and Kamakazi are Tutsi.

The soldiers robbed Norbert of the money he'd made selling his cows. They forced him from the house at gunpoint. That night he was stripped and chained to twenty-eight other men, tied by hands and feet and corralled by a cable. After a week, the men were transferred to a second jail so crowded the prisoners could only stand.

When he tells the story of his imprisonment, Norbert acts it out physically. He squats with arms wrapped around his knees to show how the men had to sleep because of the crowding. He steps over and around the remembered bodies of those who died of dehydration or disease.

"It doesn't leave you," he says. None of it—the abuse, the hunger, the stench. The fear.

Repeatedly the captors told their victims, *Tonight is the night you will die*. They threatened mass execution, once even loading the prisoners into vehicles and driving them to an isolated site in the woods. Night after night for a month, the terror went on. How did Norbert make it? He's not sure, he says—but he'd been a boy who preferred the serious world of grown-ups, hanging around them rather than playing with his cousins. "I learned to keep to myself," he says. While imprisoned, he mostly stayed silent, attentive but head down. He visualized Kamakazi's face, her high cheekbones and calm eyes, imagined holding his plump little girls in his arms. He prayed.

He got through it. Many did not. But by the time Norbert was released, after fourteen months, through an intervention by the Clinton administration that brought Banyamulenge prisoners directly to the US, his family had vanished.

While Norbert was jailed, Kamakazi had fled the village with their daughters after militants invaded it. Norbert had no idea where they were. He arrived in the US in 2000 with nothing. He had two goals: Find his family. Find a job. The job was relatively easy, the reuniting was not. It took months to locate Kamakazi and the kids—they'd gone from refugee camp to camp until finally reaching her parents in Rwanda. Two years after that, they made it to Portland, where Norbert was living. A year later, the family moved to Lewiston.

Telling his story, Norbert never tears up talking about the imprisonment. Here's where he does: "And now, look. We have our family together. God has blessed us with two more children. And this house, a car. A fine job. It is good."

That which haunts Norbert has driven him forward. Norbert's older daughters shied away from their father's intensity. Nasafari doesn't. She seems in some ways to have taken it into herself. Like him, she's affable yet watchful. Single-minded and unswerving. In their alikeness, sometimes she and her father clash—not in the same ways her sisters did, but still. And maybe Nasafari is hard on herself because, sometimes, her dad is hard on her.

I see it one day when they're driving in the Avalon so Norbert can drop her off at TJ Maxx for her second job, on weekends. Nasafari's something of a fashionista, a girl who can spot a Michael Kors bag from ten yards, always nicely dressed, even among the little kids at Tree Street. This day she remarks that she wants to go to St. John's for its curriculum, of course, but also because New York will be fun, with great shopping and a lot of culture.

Usually Norbert seems pleased by her style and sophistication (*She needs not one handbag, but six or seven!* said in mock dismay), yet now his face clouds over. "Nasafari. This is not what I want to hear." He grips the wheel, suddenly fierce. "I think your choice should not be for entertainment, not for what will be fun, Nasafari. You need to make sure why you're leaving your family. Why you're so far away. To better yourself, to get an education. I don't want to hear about fun."

Nasafari says nothing as Norbert keeps talking. She stares out the freshly Windexed window into a midsummer scene of maples waving their leaves like little hands. Her face says, *I'm out there right now, not in this car with you*.

Later, back at home while Nasafari works her shift, Norbert softens. He says Nasafari is a good, smart girl. She listens. She will not disappoint. In that moment, the African custom of naming children for the circumstances under which they were born seems achingly fitting. Nasafari Nahumure—Patient Journey. Nasafari, pressed between the old ways and the new, navigating everything that's happened along the way. Not just to her but to Norbert and Kamakazi and her older sisters. It's a lot for a kid to carry.

Crosscurrents of the family's struggles, American teen culture, her African identity in a very white state, the college process: all of this may be why she welcomes the littlest kids onto her lap at Tree and holds them for a while.

On a July day she tends to a series of small dramas at Tree Street. Outside on the basketball court, kids run around throwing water balloons *smack* on the pavement and, although they've been admonished not to, sometimes at one another. Nasafari hovers near the building, staying out of the sun. Other assistants hand out filled balloons. The younger kids are out here with the older ones. Nasafari's not keen on the activity, but the head teacher okayed it.

"This isn't going to end well," Nasafari says. Sure enough, the hilarity halts when a five-year-old falls and skins his elbow. He cries. Nasafari goes to him. "That must hurt. Come on, we'll fix it." Inside, she applies a Band-Aid, dries his tears. "Better now?"

The boy nods. He points to a nonexistent scrape on his other elbow. "Here, too." Nasafari bandages that one also.

Back outside, the kids have run out of balloons. They fill buckets with a hose and slosh each other. A girl rushes by with a full water bottle, "Getting you back, Hasan!"

A second girl chases the first: "That's my bottle, give it here!" Nasafari intervenes, hands the bottle over. She sighs. Ten more minutes until they go inside.

Then she's soaked—a full bucket dumped over her head by a teenaged boy. Nasafari gasps, sputters. Reaches reflexively for her phone. Dry, in a back pocket, thank God. But her velour Roxy jeans are wet, her shirt stuck to her back. She laughs as kids crowd around, but she's upset to the point of tears. Later she'll say she wanted to yell at the boy who poured the water on her, that for a second she even thought of walking away from Tree Street.

But, patience. She's working on that, too. She sucks it up, says, "That wasn't cool. That was not okay." The boy grins. Nasafari shakes her head, goes inside to do what she can to dry herself off. The kid with the Band-Aided elbows follows.

~

KIM WETTLAUFER WAKES early—there's no sleeping in with a two- and one-year-old. While his wife gets ready for work, Kim dresses the kids. Window fans do what they can to cool the three-bedroom ranch. By midmorning, it's pushing 90. Kim's a doer, but today he makes concessions—gives his son extra computer time, abandons chores to read to the baby. She leans in, sniffles. He puts a palm to her forehead. *Is she coming down with something?*

Before Kim became a stay-at-home dad, he ran a chain of Subway sandwich shops. He still owns several, but other people manage them. Before that, he reported sports for the *Sun Journal* and coached high school track; before that he was a Bates College student and All-American long-distance runner. Now he works part-time and takes care of the kids. He also coaches summer youth track. About eighty kids turn out for the team, many of them Somali. Kim knows each one well. He and his wife have close ties in the new-immigrant community; the kids' babysitter is Somali, as are many friends.

The next afternoon, still sultry. At the track, kids guzzle Powerade between sprints. Birds perch silent in the trees, but there's energy here—a shout of *Yes!* to a good time on the hurdles, a thunder of feet on the 100-meter dash.

Kim had to leave the kids with the babysitter to be here. He's cross that some team members arrived for practice late, that a few didn't show at all. "You need to pass the word to be here, and to be on time," he tells the kids gathered for roll call.

But minutes later, while everyone stretches through warm-ups, the mood lifts. It's "Kim, we're going to FunTown this weekend!" "Kim, look at my new sneakers!" Girls and boys crowd him like chicks around a hen. Kim laughs, relaxes into the high spirits. "Great sneakers, let's hope they're fast!" It's like this wherever Kim goes; his cell rings nonstop. A man needs help with his citizenship papers, a high school senior got accepted to USM, a mom asks him to drive her daughter home from practice.

On the track, boys push through the second lap of an 800-meter. High five from Kim as a heavyset kid crosses the finish.

The girls are practicing long jump. About half wear a headscarf, and several make the leap into the sandy pit in a long skirt with leggings underneath. Others wear just leggings with a T-shirt—they're the kids whose parents aren't as conservative about dress, which turns out to be a couple more each season. One girl consistently lands a foot beyond everyone else. Back in the lineup, she adjusts her hijab and offers advice: "Run hard as you can. Pump your arms, like this." The littler kids crack up, practice pumping. Kim smiles approval then turns to a girl who's fussing over a braid come undone from its weave. "Worry about that later."

The team is a winning one, a contender for this year's state championship title. Its girls' relay of ten-year-olds last year broke a long-standing state record.

In 2001, when Somalis began to arrive, Kim still worked full-time-plus at Subway. He volunteered a few hours a week at Trinity Jubilee, a downtown drop-in and resource center for low-income residents. Over time, new immigrants began showing up, too. Kim was struck by the newcomers' resilience. "I saw people who'd been through so much trying hard to make new lives.... It was very moving."

His own life, meanwhile, was in flux—divorce pending, Kim questioning his career and what came next. He sold some of the franchises, joined the Trinity board and then became director (a position he held nine years). His ties with refugees deepened; he found himself offering to drive people to medical appointments and the supermarket even when he wasn't at the center. New immigrants began to invite him into their homes. They became friends. After Kim married his second wife, a nurse who works in the immigrant community, the connections deepened.

In some ways, Somali values resemble the staunch Episcopal ones he grew up with, where faith and community came first, Kim says. Where conservatism was less about politics than lifestyle, and self-restraint and piety were encouraged. When one of his Somali Muslim friends wanted to send his son away to school, the friend zeroed in on Kent in Connecticut, where Kim had gone. Kim asked whether the school's Episcopal roots would bother him. The father said no. "He said, 'At least he'll be surrounded by people of faith.'"

Kim thinks about this, even though he's no longer a frequent churchgoer. "It's the secular world that's eating away at family and community. And materialism." One big difference between his former lifestyle and the new: de-emphasis on material possessions. "I never wanted for anything," he says. "But things aren't what make you happy. People are."

Through the summer, as the nation rushes toward the election and anti-Muslim sentiment rises, Kim's anxieties rise. "There's ugliness out there," he says. Recently he saw an oversized Confederate flag flying from a pickup. A Somali friend described being threatened at a gas pump while dressed for Friday prayers. Kim worries people may leave Lewiston. Go to Canada, or back abroad.

Look—he's not saying everything's perfect with the new-immigrant community. Are there some issues with employment and acculturation, especially for those over fifty? With language skills? With a few kids who've gone astray? Yes, yes, and yes—but Kim sees the community as a big net gain. "Even though we're not all the way there yet, we're closer every year. If [the newcomers] picked up and left, it would be devastating." He reconsiders: "I would be devastated."

Others feel the same. Heidi Sawyer, a lifelong Mainer and marketing director, has many ties among new immigrants. "These are people who have my back, and I have theirs," she says. Her first friend was Zamzam Mohamud, who served on the Lewiston School Committee. One night when Heidi showed up at a meeting—her son is in high school—Zamzam was "giving out hugs," so Heidi, a fellow extrovert, took one. They've been close since.

Heidi's overall take is like Abdikadir's. "We've come a long way, but there's still not enough community. People need to interact more, to mix—well, to integrate. Sometimes you might be nervous to say or do the wrong thing, but if your heart's in the right place, it usually works out."

Heidi says she sometimes sees another kind of division—between Lewistonians befriending newcomers and activists with a narrow definition of what's correct "waiting for people to screw up." She's been called out for a Facebook post in which she urged people to show up for a meeting not on "Somali time" and for referring to herself, Zamzam, and another woman as "rainbow sisters." People similarly criticized Zamzam for using "reverse Oreo" to describe a photo of herself between Heidi and another white woman.

In Lewiston, bridge builders do sometimes seem closely scrutinized. I heard a Somali woman complain that Abdikadir shouldn't worry about whether there are enough white kids on elementary school soccer teams. And at Tree Street, Julia Sleeper has been criticized for posting photos of Muslim girls in a pool. Years ago, when I first met her, Julia talked about the importance of sensitivity and, even with the best intentions, the inevitable missteps. She forges ahead, banking on hard work and her own evolving understanding.

Julia has watched the first wave of Tree Street kids graduate from college and move on to jobs or advanced degrees. Some have returned to Lewiston to settle down. And she's engaged to a Lewiston man who works with her at Tree. "We're here to stay," she says of herself and her fiancé. "Lewiston is going to be our lives."

~

CARRYS MANAGED TO get a work permit. He's lucky—some asylum seekers have waited over a year. And he found a summer job—telesales of medical equipment for Argo, a downtown marketing company and call center. If he adds most of what he makes to what he's saved, and if he's frugal, he can pay his in-state USM tuition by September. Big relief. He's worried about that ever since USM accepted him.

And he likes the work at Argo—especially the conversations with elderly callers who seem lonely to him. "Actually, I think I cheer them up." Occasionally someone gives him a hard time about his accented English. *Where are you from? India? South America?* Carrys tells them he grew up in Congo, in central Africa, and disarms them with attentiveness.

Argo's owner refurbished an old brick building slated for demolition. Now there's an aquarium and a rooftop deck. Carrys's workstation sits among dozens in a brightly lit space. During breaks he roams, chatting with co-workers. He's a people guy, curious about others, ready to talk about their families, their hobbies, the weather—whatever engages them. A few of his co-workers are other young immigrants. Most are white.

At home at night, he and Isaac follow their routine of shared meals (Carrys still experimenting) and long talks about things in Congo. They FaceTime and text with relatives. Carrys's father tells him he's relieved Carrys is in the US because of the peril. Joseph Kabila's second presidential term ends soon; he's promised to relinquish power. But will he allow an election? Will the fighting intensify?

No asylum hearing for Carrys or Isaac yet, no updates either. *"J'attends,"* Carrys says. *I wait.*

The governor of Maine, meanwhile, doesn't seem to want him in the state. In 2014, a year before Carrys arrived, Paul LePage vowed to stop reimbursing communities that give General Assistance to asylum seekers. Citing a federal law that restricts aid to undocumented immigrants, LePage ceased reimbursements in July 2014. The previous year, Lewiston had given those seeking asylum $152,000 in GA along with $21,000 to refugees. Total GA expenditures were $761,000. (The bulk of support for refugees comes from the federal and state governments.)

As asylum seekers continued to arrive, a legal battle escalated. Attorney General Janet Mills argued GA was meant to be based on need alone, independent of immigration status. Two cities sued to block implementation of the policy. LePage's administration countersued. In a radio address, the governor urged listeners to "tell your city councilors and selectmen to stop handing out your money to illegals."

Carrys doesn't consider himself illegal. He arrived on a student visa, which hadn't expired. Federal statute calls for asylees to be interviewed within 45 days of filing an application and to receive a decision within 180 days. But the wait for an interview in Maine is about two years, with indications it's getting longer. After that, it can take two more years to receive a decision. And seekers often don't receive asylum. A restaurant owner in Lewiston recently returned to Africa after his application failed.

The city didn't join the suit to block LePage. Mayor Bob Macdonald supported the governor. Macdonald, too, had referred to asylees as "illegal" for not following the conventional immigration process. The mayor did, on the other hand, advocate hastening the work-permit process—he favored letting asylees stay as long as they could pay their own way. By now, Macdonald had a reputation for hard-nosed views on welfare and on new immigrants. In a 2012 BBC interview he'd said Somalis coming to the US should "leave your culture at the door." A thousand people signed a petition demanding his resignation; a year later, Macdonald was reelected.

In June 2015, after the state Superior Court effectively upheld LePage's decision, the Maine House of Representatives voted to allow asylum seekers to receive GA for up to two years. The bill didn't receive enough Senate support to avoid gubernatorial veto, but LePage missed the deadline so the measure went forward. Meanwhile, the Lewiston City Council voted to continue assistance to asylees who were already receiving it on or before June 30, and to deny assistance to newcomers. So Carrys, a March 2015 arrival, cleared the bar—though barely.

Throughout the controversy he's kept his head down—studied, cleaned the apartment, waited for his work permit. His brothers and parents ask how it's going in the States. "*Ca va bien,*" he tells them. (Everything's fine.) And, actually, relative to things in Lubumbashi, it is. To Carrys, it's straightforward: "I want to contribute, to show my gratitude for being here," he says of his life in the US. "I want to finish my education and stay."

On August 4, while Nasafari is at Tree and Carrys at Argo, Donald Trump comes to Portland, campaigning for the presidency. It's his third time in Maine in recent months. The governor drives down from Augusta and introduces him. "We must elect Donald Trump the next president," LePage tells a packed audience Trump will later describe as "rambunctious and beautiful."

Trump doesn't say anything publicly about the state's asylum seekers but does go after its refugees. Jabbing his index finger in the air, he describes Islamic terrorism as a great danger. And then, "We've just seen many, many crimes getting worse all the time, and as Maine knows—a major destination for Somali refugees. Right? Am I right? Well, they're all talking about it. Maine, Somali refugees." The crowd is with him—even if the candidate's point is hard to pin down, he gives voice to angst that many feel.

Afterward, backlash against Trump's reference to Somalis is immediate. Senator Susan Collins condemns the comments, and a protest the next day in front of Portland City Hall draws hundreds. Mahmoud Hassan, president of the Somali Community Association of Maine, reads a statement: "It is damaging to the psyche of our youth to hear a major party presidential nominee insult our culture and religion, especially while standing next to the governor of our state."

Despite Trump's repeated trips to Maine, confidence he'll be defeated remains high among the City Hall protesters. Polls show Hillary Clinton with a big lead, from high single digits to 15 percentage points. "Never, never," says a woman named Gina Grisham, who drove from Augusta for the rally. "He'll never make it to the White House."

Three months from now, Trump becomes president. Voters in Androscoggin County, which includes Lewiston, choose a Republican for the first time in three decades. Grisham and a hundred thousand other Mainers awaken the morning after Election Day with a question: *How could this have happened?*

5

Opposition

IT BEGAN WITH 9/11. JARED J. BRISTOL WAS VISITING HIS daughter's family in a New York suburb. He'd driven down from Maine with his son-in-law's father—two grandpas on a road trip. Jared had taken early retirement a couple of years earlier. A former middle school teacher, he'd been named Maine State Conservation Teacher of the Year and now hoped to become a golf pro.

On that blue-skied Tuesday in New York, he and the other grandfather were getting ready to go into the city to sightsee and attend a Yankees game. Then the first plane struck the north tower of the World Trade Center. The two men stood in front of the television as the second plane hit the south tower, watched as both towers collapsed again and again onscreen. It was horrific—the World Trade Center, the Pentagon, the crash site in Pennsylvania.

Stunned, uncertain about what else might happen, the two decided to go home to Maine, to their wives. They drove north on jammed-up highways, listening to the radio as the death count rose, switching from station to station, not talking. Jared felt rigid with anxiety and sorrow. He kept thinking, *Things will never be the same again in this country.*

Jared was not the same. As the post-9/11 days turned into weeks and it became clear that what had happened was an act of terrorism, his sadness gave way to anger. *Our nation is vulnerable*, he thought. *Something has to change*. What, he didn't know. But he couldn't bear the feeling that radical Muslims wanted to destroy the country he loved.

Silver-haired and blue-eyed, Jared looks the part of the volunteer Santa he used to be at the local mall. Except he's not very plump—he walks miles on the golf course. For decades he played bass and guitar in bands and still carries himself with a rock musician's nonchalance. At home he dotes on his two granddaughters, who live nearby, attends as many of their gymnastics meets as he can. He's affable, puckish.

All of which is to say he comes across as an unlikely leader of a radical movement. But in 2008 Jared founded an inland Maine chapter of ACT for America, a 500,000-member group self-described as "the NRA of national security." ACT exists to oppose Islamic extremism, which Jared likens to a rabid dog. "It has to be eliminated." He and a handful of other men and women form ACT's inner circle in Maine.

Ask how he came to head the chapter, he'll offer up a story. One day as part of a workshop at his K–9 school, the teachers took a personality inventory based on animal traits. Most of the elementary teachers came up Saint Bernards—helpers, pleasers—while several of the middle school instructors were foxes. Jared was a lion. Okay. He liked this, relished it actually. Protective, sometimes gentle, ferocious when necessary. It was his lion that led him to ACT for America. If some people view him askance, if his own son, a physician, won't talk with a reporter about his father because, as Jared puts it, he doesn't think Jared should be putting himself out there as "a radical and a zealot," then so be it.

Jared wasn't always a lion. He grew up the middle of three kids, a tender boy with an affinity for the spiritual. He remembers being seven, "lying on my back in the yard and imagining falling up into the sky. What was there, and who was I?"

He was close with his mom: "loving, kind, generous, musical. Yep, [I'm] Oedipus all over the place." Not close with his army officer father, who drank and sometimes disciplined him harshly. His father had been an Olympic fencer and was also, Jared says, a genius with a photographic memory. He died when Jared was eleven. All of it left Jared aswirl in emotion. "My mother saved me," he says. "She was such a good person. But I don't have many warm memories of him."

Jared went two years to college, then did a stint in the navy. By the '80s he was back in school, by the '90s a psychology major turned teacher who led the student jazz band and sometimes played bass on weekends. He was also a husband and the father of three, forging a home life as different from his own father's as he could. Dinnertime, for instance. As a kid he'd been forced to eat everything on his plate. He remembers gagging on Brussels sprouts. At his own table, he and his wife asked their children to taste everything, and that was that. "There was no emotional distress," Jared says. He stayed away from booze. And family came before career. "I let them know I loved them."

Still, he felt a void. The longing for spirituality he'd felt as a child had remained, but skepticism held him back. His mom hadn't been a churchgoer; his father had been an atheist. Jared considered himself agnostic. In his thirties, his marriage rocky under the strain of young kids, he wasn't sure he and his wife would make it. It made him anxious, almost crazy, the idea of hurting her or the kids. He would not be his father. One evening he drove home too fast on winding roads, raging at God, "Show yourself if you exist." Suddenly he felt an all-encompassing force "like a hum, within me and without." And then a voice—but more a feeling than a voice: *Love nature*. Jared kept driving, unsure what had happened. Then the voice again: *Besides that, slow down!* Jared took all of it to mean love what he'd been given, including his family. He had no doubt a supreme being had spoken. He pulled over and cried.

But the voice didn't stay with him. It wasn't until he was fifty and depressed—he'd had depressions since his twenties, but this one was the longest—that the Holy Spirit came to him for good. Another teacher who knew Jared was struggling gave him a cassette of a Christian blues band one Friday. "I knew I was getting primed. I said something like, 'I don't know how you can believe. How can I be expected to accept all this from a book that's two thousand years old, just words on a page?'"

The other teacher looked at him. "Well, Jesus is there, knocking. If you open the door, he'll come into your heart."

"That would just be so wonderful," Jared said. He meant it. Then: "That was it. It felt like something being lit inside me. A small shock, like a candle lit in my chest." That night he still felt depressed, but less so, and better still by the end of the weekend. He's been a Christian ever since.

That sense of a discrete shift, of his life changing direction, happened again after 9/11. Jared had never been particularly political. Republican, yes, but also a freethinker with progressive views on some things. Not a reactionary. Now, a profound sense of patriotism took hold. A descendant of John Adams, Jared had roots that traced to the *Mayflower*. This mattered a lot to him even if three-plus centuries on millions could make the same claim. America had been good to him, to his loved ones. He wanted to protect her.

A close friend, Frank, felt the same way. At the golf course where they played, and where Jared worked part-time as a starter, people knew Frank as a big reader. Jared asked Frank to recommend a couple of books on Islamic terrorism. At home, he read what Frank suggested and burrowed online. The more Jared looked, the more troubled he became. Like nested wooden dolls, one website led to the next. Atlas Shrugs, Jihad Watch, Freedom Center. Center for Security Policy. World Net Daily. World Refugee Watch, Bare Naked Islam. There were so many. Jared's views slid more to the right with each: *Islam wasn't a religion of peace but a totalitarian political ideology that mandates submission. Islam could not coexist with Western culture and was, in fact, intent on destroying it.*

He learned about Dave Gaubatz, a former Air Force Office of Special Investigations agent who'd gathered counterterrorism intelligence abroad. Gaubatz founded the Mapping Sharia project and did undercover investigations of mosques across the US. Later he would coauthor *Muslim Mafia: Inside the Secret Underworld That's Conspiring to Islamize America*, an account of his son's infiltration of the Council on American-Islamic Relations.

Much of the material Jared took in was discredited in the mainstream. He read what detractors said, that the sites traded in misinformation and exaggeration. They put forth conspiracy theories about Islam. But people called Dave Gaubatz a conspiracy theorist, too, and a disseminator of distortion. The way Jared saw it, if Gaubatz, an Arabic-speaking counterterrorism specialist trained by the State Department and holder of the nation's highest security clearances, believed Islam was a threat, then likely it was. Heck, Gaubatz had committed his life to anti-terrorism work.

Plus, Jared prided himself on thinking deeply about things, and what he was reading and hearing online made sense to him. He felt the same way about one of the books Frank had recommended, *The Sword of the Prophet* by Serge Trifkovic, which posits radical Islam as the greatest danger to the West since the end of the Cold War.

"[I began to believe] that Islam and sharia [Islamic law] are not compatible with American democracy," Jared says. "I saw what was going on in other countries—women stoned, gay people killed. People murdered for leaving the faith, children used as soldiers." He was unbothered by the fact that he didn't know any Muslims personally, or that, actually, he did know one but he was a partier and a womanizer—clearly not an authentic Muslim.

Soon Jared was on the path of the ideologue. If something could be interpreted two ways, he chose the one that substantiated his new views. Take *taqiyya*, a Muslim term that derives from the Arabic root for "piety": Conventionally defined, taqiyya means the denial of one's beliefs in the face of persecution or, more broadly, in defense of Islam. Jared believes it means lying by Muslims to forward a covert Islamist agenda.

He and Frank befriended another golfer, Kevin Prescott, an FBI special agent who headed counterterrorism in the Northeast. Prescott had walked the crash site at the Pentagon. Found the wallet of one of the hijackers in the rubble. To Jared and Frank, he was the real deal. Both men felt aligned with Prescott's mission to prevent terrorists, and in particular Islamic jihadists, from striking out against America.

Each time there was a large-scale Islamist assault anywhere—car bombs outside Bali nightclubs, 202 dead; explosions on trains in Madrid, 192 dead; the seizure of hostages in a Russian school, 380 dead; bombs on Mumbai trains, 209 dead; car bombings in Iraq, 590 dead; an explosives-filled truck outside a Pakistani Marriott, 54 dead—Jared's resolve strengthened. It was only a matter of time, he felt, before the next big attack in the US. He wasn't worried about his family's immediate safety. He kept guns, and a 120-pound Rottweiler guarded his home. But there was no going back to pre-9/11 complacency—he needed to figure out what going forward looked like. How he could help. He wrote letters to newspapers, made frequent comments online. It wasn't enough.

In late 2008 he volunteered to start an inland-Maine ACT chapter. Around the same time, Frank founded one for the Portland area. Suddenly Jared had much to do—recruit members, establish an online presence for the chapter, spread ACT's message. He found himself busy, filled with intention, even driven. Finally he was doing something tangible.

First, fill the ranks. ACT's members tend to come from two sources: Tea Party Republicans and evangelical Christians. Both groups were growing in Maine. For a decade, the Tea Party had been drawing disgruntled Republicans and conservative Independents. And attendance at Bible-based churches was rising—nondenominational, Pentecostal, Baptist, Assembly of God—the faithful bound by belief in scriptural authority as well as by conservative politics. According to a 2008 survey by the Pew Forum of Religion and Public Life, a quarter of Maine's Protestant Christians identified as evangelical or nonmainline.

So Jared had a ready constituency, not just those who joined the chapter but also sympathizers. Still, early on the chapter wasn't part of mainstream discourse. Jared wanted to change that. He's succeeded. Maine ACT is the most dominant voice in the state in opposition to radical Islam (some would say Islam, period) and to the resettlement of Muslim refugees. It's behind proposed legislation to prevent the consideration of sharia law in court cases and to criminalize female genital mutilation. ACT also has paid for investigations of Maine mosques. Many call ACT's rhetoric Islamophobic. Jared disagrees. The header of every email he sends says, "Islamophobia is not a phobia because fear of Islam is rational."

In person, you get a guy who's softer than his online posts or email. Once, in the State House parking lot, he teared up when I grew emotional over the national divisiveness and left-right tensions in my family. "Oh, now," he said, rummaging his pockets for a tissue. "I didn't mean for you to cry." But he can be a hard man, too, prone to bitterness if you don't see things his way. Sometimes derisive.

Jared would say he's practical, a straight shooter. "Look, this isn't personal," he says. "I have no problem with any immigrant in Maine or anywhere else who comes here and assimilates to our laws and our values. I have a problem with those who refuse to assimilate."

He believes assimilation for Muslims means "you have to drop sharia totally"—and that it will never happen.

While Jared searched for concrete patriotic expression before landing on ACT, African Muslims were coming to Lewiston by the hundreds. By mid-2006 the city's population of African refugees had grown to nearly three thousand, approaching 10 percent of the population. According to Phil Nadeau, most were still secondary resettlers, relocating from dozens of US cities.

After living in the United States for a year, refugees can become lawful permanent residents. As such, they're fully protected by the Constitution. Newcomers in Lewiston exercised their First Amendment right to practice their religion. Masjid A-Nur held daily prayers and *dugsi* religious classes for children in a three-story row house at the foot of Lisbon Street. Known also as the L-A Islamic Center, the mosque was housed in a building owned by former mayor Laurier Raymond (more evidence, to some, that he wasn't simply the bigot people took him to be) that he later sold to the center.

Masjid A-Nur was a quiet, unmarked place you'd walk right by unless going there intentionally. On Fourth of July eve in 2006, several dozen men were observing *isha*, the nighttime salah, when the door swung open. It was a few minutes after ten. Shoulder to shoulder in prayer, foreheads to the carpet, none of the men saw who was entering; one later said they assumed it was a latecomer. Instead, the partially frozen pig's head rolled into their midst. The men recoiled. Muslims consider pigs unclean and do not eat or handle them. The worshippers and the imam rushed outside, but whoever had done it was gone.

By morning all the city's Muslims knew what had happened. That same day a thirty-three-year-old man named Brent Matthews showed up at the police station and turned himself in. He'd tossed the severed head as a joke, he said; he didn't know it was a mosque.

If people found it funny or believed Matthews didn't know what he was doing, few said so publicly. Even among those who didn't embrace the newcomers, there were limits to what was acceptable. The comments sections of local papers filled with condemnations, and people rallied around mosque members. Matthews was charged with desecration of a house of worship. The state filed suit, saying he'd violated the Maine Civil Rights Act. Matthews pleaded not guilty to the desecration charge. The story made national headlines for weeks—Lewiston, once again, *that city*.

Less than a year later, Matthews was dead. Early one April morning he called 911 from the parking lot of Mardens, a discount and salvage store two miles from Masjid A-Nur. When police got there, Matthews was holding a gun to his head. Minutes later, as a police officer urged him to put down the weapon, he shot and killed himself.

It's not clear how the mosque incident influenced Matthews's decision to take his life. He'd struggled with relationship and job issues before—and more so afterward. In a piece that ran in the *Sun Journal* after his death, friends and family said he was ashamed of what he'd done, and depressed. He didn't leave a note.

This much is clear: in tossing the pig's head, Brent Matthews created a divide between himself and other Lewistonians greater than the one between the newcomers and most Mainers had ever been.

~

DOWNTOWN LEWISTON—FEBRUARY 27, 2010, midmorning. A few stragglers made their way to school along icy sidewalks, and moms with bundled-up toddlers headed to the park. Just before ten o'clock, agents from US Immigrations and Custom Enforcement (ICE) pulled up to A&R Halal Market on Bartlett Street. The store was four blocks from Nasafari's family's condo and around the corner from where Jamilo lived.

ICE stayed inside A&R for hours. People who showed up to shop were turned away, as was a supplier with a meat delivery. Eventually the agents emerged with taped-up boxes and a computer hard drive. They packed everything into an unmarked car and drove off. Afterward, despite the cold that descended as the sun went down, people kept coming by, theorizing about what was happening.

Later, A&R owner Roda Abdi and her husband, Ali-Nassir Ahmed, were charged with felony theft by deception. Abdi was also charged with attempted theft for trying to redeem Supplemental Nutrition Assistance Program (SNAP) vouchers illegally. The couple was eventually convicted on the felony charge in connection with taking more than $40,000 in federal low-income housing subsidies while acquiring two properties and paying off $266,000 in mortgages.

The tip-off to ICE had come from Special Agent Prescott, who'd gotten word from a member of Jared's ACT chapter that A&R might have committed welfare fraud. The chapter was ramping up its tactics to include covert information gathering. By now, Jared had assumed the role of activist. He'd gotten a couple of useful traits from his hard-nosed father, he figured, one of which was that anything worth doing was worth doing 100 percent. Combine that with his lion—full bore ahead. He was more convinced than ever that taqiyya was insidious, that among the refugees were extremists, and that American Muslims eventually would try to impose sharia.

Increasingly, anti-Islamists around the nation zeroed in on Lewiston. Refugee Resettlement Watch founder Ann Corcoran cited the city as an example of what she called stealth jihad "changing a country from within to bring about Islamic dominance." And she and others claimed that Catholic Charities, the city's resettlement agency, was part of the problem.

In primary resettlement cities, volags (short for "voluntary agency") such as Catholic Charities, Lutheran Social Services, and Church World Service provide support to refugees through federal contracts. Refugees receive eight months of medical care and cash assistance at TANF levels, variable by state. Volags also contract with ORR to offer

English classes, job training, and other employment services for up to eight years. The way anti-Islamists saw it, volags relied on the government for their income. As such they were driven by self-interest, lobbying Congress for legislation that would benefit them financially.

Most anti-Islamists I met viewed volags in large measure as political entities doing the bidding of Big Government. To them, the resettlement program was an imposition on towns and cities that should have the right to self-determination. Stepping further back, they saw the refugee program as led by out-of-touch liberals who believed they knew best. Viewed through the anti-refugee lens, liberals were at best naïfs, at worst zealots trying to replace democracy with socialism and wanting refugees to boost their voting ranks.

The truth about how so many refugees wound up in Lewiston is complicated. Catholic Charities in Portland did initially send a few families to Lewiston. And Somali scouts gave Lewiston a thumbs-up after checking out many other places, including Kansas City and Nashville. As time went on, many people moved to join family members already in Lewiston. The city also became a primary resettlement site for new refugees.

As for the moderate Islam I believed most Muslims practice? Jared told me it didn't exist. "The 'good' Muslims people talk about? They're irrelevant. And deluded," he said. "They're not in touch with what the Quran is telling them to do." What does the Quran dictate? "The spread of Islam through whatever means necessary." Islamism is fulfillment of the Quran rather than a perversion, Jared said.

Like Corcoran, Jared zeroed in on the notion of jihad by emigration. He talked about hijrah, Arabic for "migration," which in Islam refers to the journey of Muhammad and his followers from Mecca to Medina. "Look what's happening in Europe," Jared said, referring to nations with large numbers of Muslim refugees and asylees. "That's hijrah. If something's not done soon, it will be too late for some of those countries."

Every argument that countered his—that sharia is subject to interpretation rather than a monolith; that far more Muslims have been killed by Muslim extremists than have people of other religions; that much of the violence in the Quran is less prescriptive than historical narrative; that the Bible contains violence as well—Jared had heard and dismissed them all. He kept dismissing them. "My beliefs just keep getting stronger," he said.

I didn't doubt the depth of his convictions, but I questioned the process by which he'd arrived at them. He took in a lot of information from right-wing, biased sources. And his lens: did wholesale pessimism about Islam predispose him to accept every anti-Islam "fact" he came across? Did Jared and other anti-Islamists ever truly listen to those with opposing views, or did they just try to whack the intellectual ball back across the net? For that matter, did progressives ever listen to *them*? Were people looking to have their preexisting views confirmed? Was I?

In 2014, Maine ACT hired Dave Gaubatz to investigate two mosques out of concern, Jared said, that they were promoting extremist views. Masjid A-Nur was one of them. The measures Gaubatz and two undercover assistants used seemed inexact, but they allegedly addressed sharia compliance, sermon content, austerity of dress, treatment of women, and similarity of the mosque's written materials to those of extremists.

Gaubatz rated Masjid A-Nur as high risk for the harboring of Islamists and for the dissemination of extremist views. "That mosque has been infiltrated," Jared told me, though he wouldn't say by whom, and though religious leaders and members roundly—and in some cases exasperatedly—denied it.

After Gaubatz finished his work, Jared and Frank asked for a meeting with the governor. They carried Gaubatz's affidavits to Augusta and handed them to LePage. He promised to read them and pass them on to law enforcement officials.

Around the same time Maine ACT hired Gaubatz, a former deputy director of the volag International Rescue Committee called for a national moratorium on refugee resettlement. In a letter to the State Department, Michael Sirois said that under pressure to process rising numbers of refugees, the program had deteriorated to the point that it was "a danger to our security and a detriment to our economy and society."

Frank bluntly stated his perspective: "Islam is the single greatest threat Western civilization has ever faced."

Jared felt the same way, as did many of his ACT members. In Lewiston, those who opposed the newcomers often took a more temperate view. "Person by person, I have nothing against them," said a contractor I interviewed in 2013. "I'm not afraid of Islam." He was okay, he said, with refugees and asylum seekers receiving assistance but thought there were too many. "We're saturated," he said. "Lewiston is not a well-off city."

The belief that new immigrants got more than their share continued to echo. In the tree streets neighborhood, a cashier at Dee's Variety also had "no problem with individuals," found them on the whole agreeable. But in processing transactions, she said, she could see amounts available from food stamps—more than $700 in one case. And here, on the other hand, was this older white guy who'd been getting $70, who she knew really needed it, and now he'd lost it. You couldn't prove cause and effect, she said, but overall it seemed newcomers were getting more and longtime residents less.

It was true new immigrants qualified for some loans and programs that others did not, yet there was little evidence Somalis or other Africans preferentially received welfare dollars (beyond the initial eight months for primary-resettlement refugees). "Not true, not true," Phil Nadeau said. "Everyone in this city is on equal footing as far as benefits go." Even so, the narrative persisted: newcomers getting more money—and more help—than people who'd lived in town for decades. The new people got special consideration—whole agencies to look after their wellbeing, business loans, extra attention at school.

In the sense that refugees needed a boost educationally and vocationally to find their way in a new place, there was some truth behind this perception. And at a time when resources were hardly overflowing. Lewiston was still struggling to recover from its loss of industry. Twenty years had passed since the city took possession of the Bates Mill complex following years of tax nonpayment. Some saw it as symbolic. The infrastructure that had supported so many jobs, yielded so much productivity—and given rise to so much pride—had become a liability.

And before that: decades of contraction after a century of grand expansion. One by one, textile mills on the east side of the Androscoggin and shoe factories on the west had closed. With each job lost, so too a family's way of life. Multiplied by thousands. Those who stayed did so out of loyalty or inertia or love of the western hills. Or hope that things would right themselves. The poverty and anomie that took hold as years accumulated was all the more bitter because people remembered such different lives.

I interviewed longtime residents for every story I've written about Lewiston. Those who opposed the new immigrants often didn't want to give their names out of fear they'd be misperceived. Or shamed. They didn't have many facts to back up what they were saying. Mostly it was emotion-laden anecdote. And sometimes it seemed the emotion was resentment looking for a place to roost.

Yet what I sensed overall was longing for an earlier, thriving Lewiston. People wanted Lewiston's glory days, even if they were too young to remember them, even if what they held on to were impressions left by a father or an uncle of a company town where hard work pretty much guaranteed a good life. More than anything, they wanted the pride.

I got that. In the town where my village was, the mill was a friend we visited on school tours, the place where most of the dads worked and earned money to buy snowmobiles and camps on lakes. And the Androscoggin—dirty, yes, but also beautiful, with rapids we canoed and sandy islands we explored. Years later I'd be stung by a description in a fishing guide of my hometown—which to me had seemed thriving and appealing in spite of the mill stacks—as "an odiferous hamlet with little aesthetic appeal."

To me in the 1970s, Lewiston had seemed a hub of self-sufficiency. When my mom and other women combed the racks at Ward Brothers, or Aunt Nell took us to City Hall to visit her neighbor who worked there, the adult world I'd eventually join seemed a solid place. The Lewiston of the '80s and '90s lost that feeling of solidity. The mills were gone, people leaving. Lewiston would not be the same again.

"You can't move forward by going back," Phil Nadeau often says, but I can see why people wished they could. And when they couldn't go back—blame. Some blamed the new residents for whatever felt wrong in Lewiston—lack of living-wage jobs, taxes, generational poverty, dilapidated infrastructure. And in blaming felt, in some small way, united.

But here's the thing: You can view the arrival of Muslim and other African newcomers as part of Lewiston's decline. Or you can see them as the closest thing the city has to a solution.

6

Late Summer–Fall 2016

Carrys, Nasafari, Fatuma, Jamilo

SOMETIMES FARAH ADAN FEELS THE INSIDE OF JUBA HALAL IS the whole world, the air spice-heavy around him. Sunlight slants through the window in the morning, passes overhead, finally drops and turns his sliver of Kennedy Park to amber. Ten hours, gone.

Occasionally he walks down to Banadir for Muna's tea and sambusas. He carries the food back to Juba—past the vape shop and the adult bookstore, past Paul's Clothing & Shoes with Paul plus two collies behind the counter and game heads on the walls, past the gap of torn-down buildings.

At his perch behind the register, Farah sips tea and eats. Wipes crumbs from his fingers and remarks that sometimes he tires of sambusas.

He dusts cans, rearranges shelves of lentils and chori. There are no cigarettes, lottery tickets, alcohol—all forbidden by Islam, *haram*. The customers come, he chats them up in Somali or English. Fires up the saw and carves meat into the bite-size chunks cooks like. Waits for more customers.

His sons, when they help out, don't seem thrilled to be here, Farah says. Be personable, he tells them. Talk with the customers. But often the customers speak first to the boys. How are you today? *Good*. How's school? *Fine*. This store is Farah's dream, not theirs. Who, Farah wonders, will run the place when he gets old? He tries to distract himself by looking at politics on his smartphone. The upcoming election—both candidates so foolish. He's a Republican. He should vote for Trump. But really.

Competition among Somali shops on Lisbon is fierce; new stores opening, others closing. Everyone needs a niche—translation services, money wiring, tax prep, something. Farah knows his is meat—good, halal goat and beef, meat people come back for. But a lot of people on Lisbon sell meat, some cheaper than he. Farah has a couple of things going for him—he's first in the lineup of Somali shops, and he has a loyal clientele.

The door jingles open. Another customer, as proof.

~

SUMMER CLOSES DOWN in Lewiston. In late August, Carrys begins classes at USM. He managed to pay his tuition with his summer earnings plus the scholarship. "I feel very fortunate," he says. He's living off-campus with five other guys. Misses Isaac a lot—they were brothers in that apartment—and his friends at Tree Street. But Portland: Carrys has never lived near the ocean before. Boats on the water, busy Old Port, the lights of the Eastern Prom at night. Free music and art. "Enjoying life to the fullest," he posts to Instagram.

School comes first, Carrys keeps reminding himself. He's used to being without parents, has learned to play that role himself. It works, mostly. Already he's spending long hours at his desk. The small lines forming at the corners of his mouth suggest determination. If it takes two days to figure out the quotient property of logarithms, then it takes two days. Sometimes Carrys stays up to hang out with his new housemates or explore the city, but mostly he's in bed early so he can get up and get at it.

One weekend night he wakes startled from sleep around ten p.m. Isaac sits at the foot of the bed, grinning—"Hey!"

Carrys sits up, blinks at the light coming in from the hallway. Isaac pulls on his arm. "Get up! Let's go have fun." He's driven down from Bowdoin with other students. Carrys grumbles—he was sleeping, he's tired. Isaac persists. "Oh, come on. It's not that late. I've missed you!" Carrys laughs as he pulls on clothes. Only for Isaac.

The boys' asylum situation remains the same. No date, no interview. Carrys tries not to think about it. Occasionally Isaac talks about going back to Congo when he graduates from Bowdoin, to help stabilize and rebuild the country. Carrys can't wrap his mind around something that wide-angle right now. "Actually, I want to stay in the US, finish my education and find a job." He pauses. "And maybe, in a few years, a wife. I would like to have a family." In a few years. The next photo he posts shows him standing with a backpack in front of a USM building.

Nasafari launches into her senior year at LHS. She takes a new job at Lever's Daycare, where her older sister Nabega also works, to save money for college. Nasafari puts in her hours after school. The SAT is scheduled for October 1. This time she feels ready. Sometimes at night she surfs the St. John's website: 1.7 million books in the library; one faculty member for every seventeen students; a subway ride to Manhattan; students from 124 countries. "I know I shouldn't keep imagining myself there already," she says. "I can't help it."

Whenever Nasafari doubts herself, she thinks about Maya Angelou's "Still I Rise," the poem she won second prize for reciting during a school contest. "Just like moons and like suns, / With the certainty of tides, / Just like hopes springing high, / Still I'll rise." It doesn't matter that she's not the top student in her class. Doesn't matter that she doesn't know how much financial aid she'll get. Doesn't matter that New York is a long, long way from Maine and her family—*she's got this*.

The time she spent during the summer working on herself is paying off. She feels more mature, tuned in to those she loves. At home she's helping out more with Moses and Christina, giving her mom a hand with meals. In taking care of others Nasafari is being a good daughter, she says, and also showing she can look after herself when the time comes.

Things with the boy she liked may be cooling off. They're not texting as much. She's not, anyway, going to push the boy or dating on her parents right now. They recently found out that Nabega is pregnant. Her parents are in shock, especially Norbert. Nasafari hopes everything will work out, that even though Nabega's boyfriend, Tyler, isn't born-again, and he and Nabega aren't married, her father's love of family will come through. Nabega and Tyler care for each other deeply—they've been together for years. And the pregnancy puts things into a different perspective. When she spends time with Nabega, Nasafari feels her joy. A new life. Nabega's belly is rounder already.

ON A SUNNY afternoon Fatuma leads US congressional candidate Emily Cain and her aides down Lisbon Street. It's slow going. They stop at every store, and Fatuma—nearly nine months pregnant—moves like a small ship, imperturbable and solid.

Politicians often show up in Lewiston to court Somali business owners. Cain, a Democrat, is running a tough race against incumbent Bruce Poliquin. She spends a lot of time here in the largest city of the second district, which is mostly inland and rural, encompassing the whole state except for the coastal strip of district one. Fatuma wants to make sure people hear Cain's progressive message.

Inside a small grocery, she introduces owner Shukri Abasheikh as "Mama Shukri," a Somali honorific. Fatuma and Shukri are close friends. When Shukri moved to Lewiston, she and her children lived with Fatuma's family. Shukri is a calm, efficient woman, but whenever she talks about that time, she gets emotional. She was in a bad situation in Atlanta—felt isolated and unsafe. Fatuma urged her to come to Lewiston. Shukri's first job was janitor at the high school.

So there's a world between Shukri and Fatuma as they stand together waiting for Cain's entourage to fit themselves into the packed aisles. The store also offers translation services and money wiring. A two-table restaurant in the back serves Somali food.

Diners listen from the curtained-off space while Cain talks about her plans for jobs and education. Out front, Shukri fidgets; she's not used to standing still. She runs a clothing business, too. On weekends, a white woman named Brenda whom Shukri met back when their kids were in kindergarten stitches Somali wedding outfits in purples, pinks, and peacock blue while shoppers squeeze around her. Finished garments pile up in a gauzy heap as the day goes by. Shukri knew she wanted to hire her after Brenda showed up at the school one morning with a carefully stitched pair of pj's for Shukri's daughter, a gift for wear-your-pajamas-to-school day. The kindness of the gesture and Brenda's skill—this was someone for Shukri to respect.

Just before the group leaves the store, Shukri affixes a Cain placard to the register. Fatuma turns to another of Shukri's daughters, who's shelving juice, reminds her to go to the polls. "Young people like you need to come out and vote," she says. "We all need to exercise our rights." Farhija nods, locks eyes with Fatuma. In two months, Farhija will step into the voting booth.

The same day Cain visits Shukri's store, Donald Trump releases a letter from eighty-eight retired military leaders who say they back his bid for the presidency. Trump, they write, is the only candidate who can keep the nation safe. The letter cites the defeat of "our Islamic supremacist adversaries" as a priority. It accuses Hillary Clinton of failing to track down terrorist groups around the world.

That night at LHS, the boys' soccer team plays the Lawrence Bulldogs under the lights. It's the Blue Devils' third game of the season. As often happens, play is mostly on the opposing team's side of the field. Whenever the ball winds up on the Blue Devils' half, they turn it around with the footwork and speed for which they've become known. "Excellence, perfection, teamwork, success!" call the cheerleaders, performing a routine that includes aerials and flips. The cheerleaders are champions in their own right—the number one squad in New England last year.

The Blue Devils score; the crowd roars. Play goes on. National and state politics seem, for this short time, far off and unthreatening. In the stands, Jeannie Martin sits with her husband, absorbed. Their kids graduated from the high school a while ago, but the Martins come to every game. LHS soccer is one of their loves. "Best five-dollar entertainment in town," Jeannie says.

Around the Martins, kids whoop at good plays—"Go, Maulid!" "Nice, Joseph!"—and flirt with one another during breaks in the on-field action. Moms in hijabs take phone videos while younger kids climb the bleachers. People eat food from the Snack Shack. It varies—shepherd's pie, chili, sambusas. Jeannie says she looks forward to dinner on game nights.

Score! The Blue Devils do it again.

After the 4–1 victory, Coach McGraw gathers his players. "The easy games are over now," he tells the kids seated on the grass. Two thirds are African immigrants; the rest are white. From here on, the team should expect the season to get tougher, McGraw says, starting with next week's matchup. "We almost can't mention that name because the rivalry is so big," McGraw says of the Blue Devils' across-the-river competitor, Edward Little High School in Auburn. He goes on: Lewiston will be intense but fair in that game. Lewiston will win.

"Yeah!" someone shouts. The players clap. They stand and cheer. The air is charged, filled with possibility.

Another state championship this year? Maybe, McGraw says later. He hopes so. But in spite of the wins, this team still hasn't quite gelled. It's got the talent, now it needs cohesion. He's waiting for the fluidity and ease that characterized last year's team. Which was special—largely because of the players who'd lived together in Dadaab. They'd formed a formidable core, and many of them graduated in June. McGraw's still optimistic about this year's team. "It's a thing of beauty when they play well together."

Fatuma doesn't make it to the game, but she's a fan. "Mike Mc Graw represents the best of Lewiston," she says. "That team was so important to us all." She often talks about the tail end of last season, when momentum built and the city seemed to respond as one. And that postgame celebration at the Ramada Inn—memorable to her for its joy and inclusivity: "The whites and the blacks, the young, old, women, children, men—all of us were there to celebrate our boys."

By the end of September, Fatuma is more than ready for her baby to come. She's uncomfortable; her feet swell every day. Finally he's born—seven pounds, twelve ounces. Bright-eyed and alert, looks like a tiny version of Muktar. They name him Mohamed.

In his first month Mohamed travels to Augusta, Farmington, several times to Portland, and attends a two-hundred-person conference. Not for Fatuma the traditional forty-day lying-in period, during which the extended family cooks and cleans and looks after older children while the new mom recovers. Like other working women in Lewiston, she can't afford the time. The IRC is pressing to expand into housing and elder care. Pressing to ensure that the most recent round of immigrant women understands their rights and responsibilities as Mainers.

So yes, Fatuma feels tired a lot of the time. But she and Mohamed are on the go.

~

ON THE DAY Donald Trump comes to town, the weather's doing what it often does in western Maine, seasonifying seemingly at will. This October afternoon it's winter: cold wind plus intermittent pelting rain. A few untimely snowflakes.

The rally takes place a mile up the road in Lisbon, in the gymnasium of Open Door Bible Church and Christian Academy. People begin arriving before noon in hopes of getting in early or scoring tickets (no chance), or just to hang out with other Trump supporters and catch a glimpse of the candidate. Despite the weather there's a festive atmosphere, almost giddy—the jubilance of the like-minded. People are clearly relieved to be among those who see things the way they do—that their candidate can win, that he must.

Vendors hawking Trump paraphernalia do a steady business. One customer peels twenties from a wad, puts a red "Make America Great" hat on his head and walks away with half a dozen other hats hugged to his chest. People in prison jumpsuits inscribed "Crooked Hillary" carry "America for Trump" signs. Others wave magenta "Women for Trump" placards.

Protesters from Bates College hoist signs of their own—"Nasty Women Vote," "Love Trumps Hate," "Pussy Power Grab Back." Other than proximity, the candidate's supporters and foes don't really interact. I see little of the spitefulness reported of other Trump rallies.

The crowd grows. A family of five shows up: mom, dad, and three kids wearing Trump T-shirts and Converse sneakers. The dad carries a heap of jackets. Why did the kids want to come? "Because Donald

Trump believes what we believe," says the older of two girls, a preteen. What is that? She ticks off items. "National security. The Second Amendment. Lower taxes." The parents home-school all three kids. Today is a field trip. The boy, the youngest, seems ready to explode with excitement. He breaks in, "He's going to drain the swamp!"

Supporters swarm locations they think it most likely the candidate will arrive—lower parking lot, the stairs to the big church, gymnasium entrance. Secret service agents and police officers keep shooing people back. The 3:00 p.m. start time comes and goes. 3:30, 4:00, 4:15. It rains and stops, rains again. A rumor circulates that Trump's plane landed late at Logan so he got held up at his event in New Hampshire. Now he's on his way.

"Breitbart's carrying this live," a man announces, though everyone already knows. He and others without tickets tune in on their smart phones. "Making history here," a teen in a rain poncho says. Thinking this election may be his first, I ask whether he's old enough to vote. No, but his mother and his brother are—and they're for Trump.

Inside the gymnasium, 1,200 bodies pressed into the bleachers turn the place into a hothouse. People fan themselves with signs, drain water bottles. An older man with a "Vets for Trump" hat hands out mints. The soundtrack, heavy on country, launches into another iteration. Outside, the rain picks up again. People stand shoulder to shoulder under a patchwork of umbrellas, waiting, waiting. Someone shifts—a sudden leak, a gasp as cold water hits skin. But everyone stays put. It occurs to me for the first time, in the middle of this wet crowd, that Trump may win. I've attended many rallies, never one this fervent. Tickets for today's event—hastily planned, practically a pop-up—were gone within hours.

Many attendees don't conform to the rough, undereducated stereotype of a Trump supporter. I meet a pharmacist, a math teacher, a couple who live five months in Maine and the rest of the year in a Miami retirement community. But ideologically, everyone's united.

Ready for change. Aching for it, actually. Ready to shrink Big Government, corrupt and inefficient and run by special interests that don't care about real people. Ready for that immigration crackdown. For tax reform, welfare reform. They believe Trump will do all this. And more intangibly: ready for release from the feeling that liberals get to dictate what everyone else should think.

"I am a proud patriot who loves my fellow Americans," the retired woman, Ellen Bryant, tells me. "But welfare is not the answer to poverty. It makes people more dependent. We need jobs and education that teaches kids how to do things."

Ten minutes later back in the gym—a drumroll followed by the opening bars of "The Star-Spangled Banner." The candidate, here at last. Hundreds of phones rise overhead like zeitgeist periscopes as Trump makes his way to the podium. By way of greeting, he tells his supporters he loves the land here, that they live in "one of the most beautiful places on earth."

His speech hits the usual notes—Clinton's emails, the national debt, drug crisis, trade deficit, Obamacare. He sounds more coherent in person than he does in sound bites. His points on national security get the most applause. He will build that wall, Trump says. He will keep the nation safe. People beam, cheer. They wave homemade signs.

At nearby Dingley Press and Argo, African immigrants are among workers finishing their shifts. On Lisbon Street, stores bustle with shoppers buying halal meat for supper. Jamilo and the kids are watching *Dora the Explorer* because it was too rainy to go to Kennedy Park.

Perhaps intentionally, Trump doesn't mention the state's Somalis this time around. He keeps his comments general: "We allow people to come into our country we know nothing about, what their thought process is, where they come from, what they want to do." Shouts and boos from the crowd—Trump nods solemnly, affirming their outrage. "Hillary wants massive immigration from the most dangerous regions of the world where ISIS operates. . . . We're not going to be a modern-day Trojan horse." When he vows to "keep radical Islamic terrorists the hell out of our country," cheers erupt again.

After it's over, Trumps lingers to sign hats and photos. He seems reluctant to leave the auditorium. Finally outside, he slips into the back of a Cadillac Escalade. Most of the crowd remains in the upper lot, looking down on the doorway where his entourage exited. As the motorcade pulls onto Route 196, Trump presses his face to the glass and waves to the few lone figures on the rain-soaked sidewalk, as if looking for every last vote. Later, in an interview with *Time* magazine, Trump will say in his elliptical way, "In fact I went to Maine four times. Four times I went to Maine, because I had to get one [electoral college] vote."

As far as I know, no Somalis or other African newcomers attend the rally. I see no hijabs and few people of color. But that doesn't mean none of Lewiston's new immigrants will vote for Trump. Many hold traditionalist social views—and he's the Republican candidate. In some ways the newcomers have more in common ideologically with conservative Lewistonians than with their progressive, secular supporters. Nasafari, a self-described fiscal moderate and social conservative, is leaning toward Trump. During primary season she liked John Kasich and—especially—Carly Fiorina for her business savvy and because "she's a strong, intelligent woman." As for Trump: "I like that he's vocal, but he has no filter. He needs to tone it down."

There are conservatives, too, among Somali businesspeople. Farah's politics marry freewheeling entrepreneurship with traditional social views. He's in favor of equal pay for equal work, though, and wary of unbridled capitalism. On balance, his position weighs out on the right; since he's been registered to vote in the US, he's usually chosen Republicans. But months pass, and he still dislikes Trump.

"He needs to learn how to act," Farah says, "and he needs to straighten out his facts about immigrants." Farah shakes his head.

Here's a story: he met Tim Kaine years ago while driving a cab in Kansas City. Kaine was in town for a governors' convention. Farah recognized him from TV. For a $30 cab ride, Kaine gave him $45. "A really nice guy," Farah says. Still, when it comes time, he'll probably vote Republican down the line.

A few weeks after Farah tells me this, I stop in at Juba Halal. A Somali couple I don't know stands behind the register, now repositioned in a corner. Rather than look out at passersby and the sliver of park, the new owners face inward. "What happened?" I ask Farah when I reach him. He decided to go ahead and close the store, he says. His financial situation just kept getting worse.

There's a shrug in his voice, resignation. If a business fails, it fails. There should be no bailouts.

~

IN A LETTER to President Obama just days before the election, Paul LePage announces he's withdrawing the state from the refugee resettlement program. He's lost confidence in the federal government's ability to run it, he says. LePage cites former Freeport resident Adnan Fazeli, an Iranian refugee who died in Lebanon in 2015 after leaving Maine and joining ISIS.

Writes LePage: "Whether the federal government grants refugee status to a current terrorist or to someone who is susceptible to radicalization by virtue of their having come from a nation that either supports or is overcome by terrorism, it is a failure to properly vet entrants and it puts American lives at risk."

The letter appears timed to appeal to anti-immigrant sentiment. He asks the federal government to reconsider "both the quantity and national origin of refugees it resettles and the vetting processes they are subjected to—in order to best protect the safety and the interests of the American people."

LePage's move won't directly impact how many refugees come to Maine. The federal government controls the resettlement program, and states can't prevent people from crossing their borders. Still, it's another sour note for new immigrants. That same day, a Catholic Charities Maine spokesperson tells the *Portland Press Herald* the organization has "complete confidence" in refugee vetting, calling it "one of the most stringent vetting processes for anyone coming into this country."

In Lewiston, life goes on—colder nights, shorter days, kids scuffing through leaves on their way home from school. A few weeks after Aaliyah's four-year-old birthday party at the orchard, Jamilo agrees to a "family night" with her ex-husband, Yussuf (not his real name). She doesn't really want the outing but gives in to pressure from her relatives. So she and Yussuf, Aaliyah and Hamzah go out to eat at Lotus. Usually the smells of sesame chicken and Hunan beef make her mouth water the second she steps through the door. That night she barely makes it through a half-filled plate. Things feel so awkward between her and Yussuf. Forced. Mostly they turn toward the kids.

Jamilo goes home sad—her heart keeps saying no, and no. Yet—though she doesn't think Yussuf treated her with the regard a husband should during their short marriage, she doesn't dislike him. She feels connected with him as Hamzah's other parent; no one will ever love Hamzah the way they do. Yet she doesn't care for Yussuf enough to be his wife. Why, she asks, did they get married in the first place?

But really, she knows the answer. She came back to Lewiston from Massachusetts on her own with Aaliyah, and her family wasn't okay with that. According to the Somali way, she needed to be married. It was a matter of pride and the perception of propriety. Yussuf came from a good family, said he cared for her, wanted children and would be a stepdad to Aaliyah. Jamilo understood how her relatives saw things—the pull of the culture, eyes of the community on them. She felt some of that herself.

So she went with it: big Somali-style wedding at Shukri's hall, two hundred guests, dancing and a feast. A beautiful event. But afterward—she worried right away that she'd never have with Yussuf what she'd shared with Aaliyah's father. She knew what she should feel, and didn't feel.

Then she got pregnant. Throughout the months she carried Hamzah, she tried to convince herself it could work. But her compass, her heart, kept swinging away from whatever rational thing she told herself. And they argued—Jamilo felt Yussuf ignored her, treated her uncaringly. They separated just before Hamzah's first birthday.

Now here she is. In her third-floor downtown apartment, sharing a bed with Aaliyah and Hamzah because none of them likes sleeping alone. On a fall evening they sit together on the living room rug for dinner. Chicken drumsticks, corn with lime, rice, strawberries with chocolate syrup. Jamilo spent over an hour in the kitchen while two preteen cousins watched the kids.

Hamzah is plopped in her lap, the top of his head grazing her chin. She alternates feeding him and herself. He likes the chicken—"More!" Aaliyah keeps playing with the cousins. She's fussier. If she says she's not hungry, Jamilo doesn't push. Too stressful, especially since the pediatrician says Aaliyah is growing well.

Somali meals tend to be more elaborate but less formal than American ones. Things take time to prepare. Once served, the meal can go on and on. Sometimes the kids leave, and adults linger. Or the grown-ups eat then feed the kids. Finally Aaliyah comes over. She and the cousins rinse their right hands in a bowl of water and reach for a handful. Already skilled at scooping from the communal platter, Aaliyah drops barely any rice grains.

Hamzah turns away from a bite of chicken—done. Jamilo sets him on his feet, bumps up the TV volume. He sits in front of it, the hues playing across his face. Finger puppets dance onscreen. *Sister finger, sister finger, where are you? Here I am, here I am, how do you do?* Jamilo and the younger cousin hum along. They've heard this tune, what, five hundred times?

Jamilo and the girls sit back from the platter. "That was really good," the younger cousin says.

Aaliyah nods. "Mmmm."

Jamilo beams. "I'm glad you liked it."

The older cousin to Jamilo: "Granddad doesn't like you." She says it without malice. Matter-of-factly, perhaps seeking to understand why.

Jamilo's face closes in with hurt. Her eyes darken. Her face is mutable; depending on how she's feeling, she looks like a different person. She doesn't respond, gets up after a few moments and carries dishes to the kitchen. Rinses, puts them in the sink. The man the cousin referred to as Granddad is Yussuf's father. What else does he say?

When Jamilo returns to the living room, her face again its open self, the cousins are sitting on the sofa. Jamilo slips in between them. Her shoulders touch theirs. Aaliyah comes and leans against her mom's knees. In that moment Jamilo seems completely adult, the center, emanating everything-will-be-all right.

One of her favorite books is *A Child Called It*, the story of a severely abused boy whose spirit and dreams kept him alive. The boy's mother treated him far worse than Jamilo's relatives treated her, but long after she finished the book she kept thinking about him. How he'd not just survived but thrived. "He made a happy life," Jamilo says. "That's what I'm going to do."

Jamilo sees that people who've treated her harshly have their own traumatic past, stemming from the fighting and instability in Somalia or conditions in the camps, or both. "Almost everyone has suffered," she says—which may be partly why she seems to hold little lasting rancor. That, plus her nature backs away from bitterness. "She has a beautiful soul," someone close to her tells me.

Jamilo credits Allah with her resilience. "When something happens, he's where I go to," she tells me. "I'm Muslim for Allah and for myself."

Jared and Frank may argue that Islam is a political system, an ideology, but Jamilo's Islam comes across less political or doctrinal than practical. Rooted in the affirmative, it reminds me of the prosperity gospel some Christians follow: God as a forgiving father, yet one with expectations. Some days she turns to him actively in prayer. Other times it's as if he's there alongside her.

That moment with the cousins and the remark about what Granddad said? Jamilo felt able, with Allah, to let go of the hurt for the sake of the kids who were waiting for her reaction. For her sake too, actually. She tries to ask, *What would Allah have me do in this situation?* With time she's gotten better at this, Jamilo says. Her feelings of upset sometimes run deep; she's learning to step aside.

She needs all the resources she can muster, because fall brings trouble upon trouble.

One afternoon a sheriff comes to the door with notice that Yussuf is taking her to court. He wants the judge to establish his parental rights, with the possibility of being awarded full custody of Hamzah. The news shakes Jamilo. "Freaking out," she texts. At eighteen months Hamzah needs, she feels, to live with her. And now that she's made it clear she won't go back to Yussuf, some of her relatives shun her, not returning texts and avoiding her on the street. A few of her married friends have also backed away. She tries to understand.

But it's hard. *Yussuf treated her indifferently—didn't others see that?* And after they separated he spread rumors she heard about from friends and sometimes didn't pay his share of Hamzah's care, she says. (When asked, Yussuf said he did not recall missing support payments.)

Jamilo is used to the world being tenuous. People disappear from her life, break promises. Don't follow through. At times she's that way, too. She realizes many view her as having broken a commitment by leaving Yussuf. Yet—is a marriage a true commitment if entered under pressure? She prays for clarity on that.

A few days after the sheriff, the whole family comes down with a tenacious strep throat—first the kids, then Jamilo, then the kids again. Trip after trip to the doctor, a late-night visit to the hospital when Hamzah's fever spikes and Jamilo worries he's having trouble breathing. As they rush to go to the ER, Aaliyah puts on the gauzy angel wings she got for her birthday. They've become a talisman.

At the hospital, doctors prescribe another round of antibiotics for Hamzah. A few days later, Jamilo gets sick again. She recovers physically in a week, but she feels alone like never before. Being surrounded by community wherever she goes yet feeling disconnected only heightens her sense of isolation. Close friends like Binto and Aspen call and come over, but even they can't totally relate. Aspen's not Somali. Binto isn't married.

Jamilo suspects her ex-husband wants to be able to claim Hamzah for tax purposes. And that he's deeply resentful. But what about Hamzah? The way she sees it, too often he winds up at Yussuf's mother's house when he's supposedly with Yussuf. That's okay on occasion—the grandmother sometimes babysits for Jamilo, too—but Jamilo thinks Hamzah's first bonds should be with his parents. Yussuf's hurt doesn't justify his actions, she says. And this time, she's not giving in. She sets up a consultation with a family court advisor, braces for what will come.

Conviction and anxiety show up by turns in her Facebook feed: "Weak people revenge. Strong people forgive. Intelligent people ignore." "Have you ever just randomly started crying because you've been holding in all of these emotions and pretending to be happy for way too long?" "Oh Allah, allow our hearts to be fully devoted to you." "Hold on . . . He will free you from all this misery."

In late October, the web of babysitters she's put together starts to tear apart. But Jamilo needs to work. She lives paycheck to paycheck.

The unsubsidized portion of her rent is due, plus utility and cell bills. Not to mention food, and clothes for Aaliyah and Hamzah, who's already outgrown his 2Ts. Jamilo reaches out to other single moms, patches together care, offers it on weekends in return. At night, exhausted, she sprawls on the sofa and dozes, fatigue a wall that keeps her from going upstairs to bed.

Or, anxious, she sits up and watches TV. This close to the election, it's politics everywhere. Jamilo intends to vote for Clinton. She can't imagine any refugee voting for Trump. A Facebook photo of Somalis at a Minnesota Trump rally upsets her. One man holds a "Make America Great Again" sign. Jamilo hypothesizes: imagine a fellow Somali Muslim born in the United States and thus eligible for the presidency, with views similar to Trump's. Would she vote for "this child of Adam"? No way. "I can only imagine if [Trump] becomes the president. What kind of world will our kids live in?"

On November 8 she walks down to the elementary school and votes. That night she watches the returns. State after state goes red. *Trump can't win. He can't*, she thinks. Around midnight she heads upstairs, settles in with Aaliyah and Hamzah. She sleeps restlessly, dreams, and wakes. The dark thins. The kids sleep on. Jamilo lies there, listening to them breathe.

~

BY MORNING, DONALD Trump has made an acceptance speech. Around Lewiston, it's a different world but the same world. Parents walk kids to school past the stop sign—vandalized weeks ago—with TRUMP spray-painted below STOP. In Kennedy Park, two moms with babies sit together on a bench. What do they think of the election? One puts a splayed hand to her temple—the Somali gesture for outrageous. "No good," she says.

Down on Lisbon, shops open; at Baraka, Mohamed's wife, Ardo, is brewing a pot of shaax. "No one can believe it," Mohamed says. "We live in a democracy and Donald Trump is the best we can do? But even still, it's Wednesday and everybody has to work."

A few towns away, Jared is unsurprised by Trump's win and Clinton's defeat. He felt it coming. The nation needed change, he'd thought, and Trump—while not ideal—would bring that. Sitting in front of the TV last night, he and his wife shared a sense of elation after it became clear that, in spite of the polls, in spite of the money poured into her campaign, Clinton would lose.

In her work cubicle, Jamilo tries to concentrate. Not easy. She wonders how many of her Knox Street neighbors, white or black, voted for Trump? What about her co-workers? Friends and family members in Dagahaley text their dismay—"What's going to happen in America?" Her social media feeds buzz: Trump is going to implement his refugee ban as soon as he takes office. Muslims will no longer be welcome in the US. And then, at noon, while she's in the crosswalk on her way home for lunch, the guy leans out his car window and shouts at her to take off her hijab. Jamilo runs into a nearby health center where people she knows work.

She's not the only one harassed. A few days later in the Walmart checkout line, a woman pulls the abaya of another shopper, tells her "Go back to your country." A high schooler who works in a restaurant is told she'd be "cuter" if she dressed in Western clothes. A Lewiston poll worker reports that on election night a man made a racist remark about Somali voters—one was helping another in a voting booth—and tried to photograph them.

In response to the incidents, Mayor Macdonald releases a statement: The city "will not tolerate the harassment of any members of our community for any reasons."

By the weekend Jamilo manages to right herself, though she puts her phone on camera whenever she goes out. At home that Sunday, she pays bills online while the kids play. Her phone rings—her mother. She's called from Dagahaley three times since the hijab incident. Jamilo switches to Somali. *She is okay, the kids fine; yes, she's feeling stronger now.*

She hangs up, shakes her head. "Everyone there is worried." She notes the irony—her mother even asked whether Jamilo wants to return to Kenya. No, Jamilo said. Guriga waah Lewiston. *Lewiston is home.*

Abdikadir feels the same way—his home, and he wants to preserve and protect it. All week people have been streaming in and out of MIRS and calling him with fears and worries. "I am leaving out this country with my children," someone texted. "Good luck to you guys with Trump." Yet most people are looking for reassurance, a sense of solidarity.

Abdikadir addresses the distress not just of refugees but of many Lewiston residents in a letter that runs in the *Sun Journal*. "We need to come together," he writes. "As community, as we the people, it is our responsibility to fix the divide caused by our political leader." He's heartened, he writes, by the many people who've come forward to offer help, such as legal services and counseling to the city's new immigrants.

He makes a few observations, among them: "[Many Somali refugees] are struggling to understand why Americans would vote for someone to be president who has created a lot of hate." And, "There are some who feel that Americans aren't ready for a woman president, which is sad. Why are we so concerned about women's rights in Arab countries while we have a nation that isn't ready for women to be president?"

Mostly he focuses on ways Lewiston can move forward. The city's Muslims have been looking to the Quran for strength, he says. Like this verse: "'And it may be that you dislike a thing which is good for you and that you like a thing which is bad for you. God knows but you do not know.' Many community members are holding on to this verse as part of healing this painful moment and putting all their trust in God."

At a new-immigrant panel that happens to fall on the Thursday after the election, Abdikadir delivers a similar message. When it's his turn, he takes the mic with the same quiet charisma I've often seen in him. He talks about the election, his hopes that Lewiston will keep growing and the young will decide to stay, his journey from Somalia. He's easy in front of the crowd. His English isn't error-free, but his communication is. It's not the first time I imagine him running for political office himself. Later Abdikadir will say it's not the first time he's thought about it either—and that now, with Trump soon to be inaugurated, it seems more urgent.

In mid-November, my sister and I lead a writing workshop in Lewiston. Four young Somali men are among the participants. Inevitably, conversation swings to the election and the nation's polarization. "Right now we need to listen to each other," a man named Mohamed tells us. "We need to try to understand."

During a writing exercise, Mohamed puts down details of his life before America. His family fled Somalia sixteen years ago on foot to take refuge in Dadaab. Midway there, bandits ambushed them. One pressed a gun to Mohamed's father's head. Mohamed was huddled beside him, terrified, but somehow he found it in himself to reach for his father's hand. "I was trying to comfort him," Mohamed tells us. "I wanted to shield him with my body, but they wouldn't let me move." Ultimately, the bandits let his father go. The badly shaken family continued toward Dadaab. Mohamed was fifteen.

When he received entry into the US, Mohamed got his GED and started a business, then a second one after the first failed. Memories of Somalia lingered; they gave him nightmares and lodged in his body, making him jittery and jumpy. *Don't let yourself get off track*, he kept telling himself. At the workshop, when the conversation swings back to postelection rifts, Mohamed calls for optimism. "There's no place in the world like the United States. We need to focus on keeping this a great country," he says.

The participants begin a final exercise. The room quiets. Whenever I give a prompt, a young man named Ali writes quickly before laying down his pen and picking up his phone. It's hard to tell whether he's engaged.

At the end, people read from what they've written. Ali's response to a prompt that called for a string of words:

Clean
Cartoon
Read
Play
Soccer, basketball, football.
Why hate me?
Why me?
Hope.

Ali tells us he came to the workshop to brush up on writing skills, especially for cover letters. He's just finished a stint with AmeriCorps and is back home in Lewiston, looking for a job.

After the workshop my sister, an ardent Clinton supporter, says she feels better than she has in weeks. I know what she means. I voted for Clinton too and—despite that day at the Trump rally, despite ingesting a variety of news sources, some supporting Trump—his victory surprised and dismayed me.

The truth is that in the election's aftermath, I want to be in Lewiston more than anyplace else. The Muslims I know do worry about what the coming months will bring. But there's a marked lack of bitterness. As Mohamed said at Baraka that first morning, they're getting on with things. They've seen far worse political rancor back in Africa, and far worse abuses than anything Trump has talked about so far. Does surviving so much hardship desensitize people or give them perspective? Both? I'm not sure, but in Lewiston, at least, the immigrant community seems focused less on anger and despair than on building lives. On progress day by day: going to school, taking a college exam, sitting for a job interview, planning a marriage. And on maintaining a sense of humor. Around Thanksgiving, newcomers in Lewiston widely share a Facebook post of a trussed turkey with the ends of the legs for eyes and an orange toupee.

For years I've watched Abdikadir, Fatuma, Zamzam and others reach into a "toolbox" that includes consensus-seeking, de-emphasis on "being right," and listening. Partly the approach is cultural. Partly it's acquired, especially around the de-escalation of conflict. Infighting—between clans, between ethnic Somalis and Somali Bantus—intensified the nation's war. Lewiston's Somalis understand firsthand the costs of conflict.

I stop in at Baraka in late November. When I bring up politics, Mohamed waves me off. *Enough*. He's been thinking about my mother, he says. Can I remind him—how long since her husband passed away? A year, I tell him. Mohamed offers a story. Last summer Ardo and the kids went to Somalia. He stayed in Lewiston. All day he'd tend the store; at night he'd go home just to sleep. Except he couldn't. "It was too quiet... Every little sound makes me wonder, what is happening?" He asks, now that your mom is on her own, shouldn't she move closer to family?

Yes, I tell him, she should. I'm glad he doesn't press for more. It's complicated—whenever I bring up leaving Florida with my mother, she tells me she'll consider it but wants to live independently if she does. My sister and I think she'll need more care. Yet even if we can convince her, she's said assisted living isn't an option, that she's not a "group person." We wonder, could it ever work to have her live with one of us?

My sister and I grew up mostly single-parented by our father. Mom made it for birthdays and holidays, but it was Dad who braided our hair and cooked and drove us to gymnastics.

Dad died eleven years ago. Mom—I talk with her by phone almost every day. Those road trips last summer: she was easy. At the Dunkin' Donuts drive-thru, she'd order dark roast and a glazed. Caffeinated, we'd get out to walk—the beach, the state park, block after block in Lewiston. She told stories, repeated herself, repeated herself again. It was okay. Sometimes it felt as though we were reconciling the past without talking about it directly. That day she commented, "[Maine] will always be my home," I was surprised, but I got it. She lived here thirty years.

On the phone not long after Mohamed makes his comment, my mother tells me, "My mind is beginning to go, you know." Later she misplaces some important documents. We sort that out, but it's clear things are precarious.

~

BY EARLY DECEMBER in Lewiston, winter has edged out fall—nights in the 20s, the first snowfall. It's pretty around town in a bare-knuckled way. Jamilo buys boots for the kids; the three of them crunch through what's left of the leaves on their way to Kennedy Park. No lines for the swings or the slide. Out beyond the river valley, the bare foothills look hunkered down like hibernating animals.

Jamilo stops putting her phone on camera mode when she leaves the apartment—Alhamdullilah, she's encountered no more harassment. But just in case, she and some friends role-play in her apartment. They take turns with the insults, and with responses: "You have no right to speak to me that way." "Get out of here." "I am calling the police." Jamilo starts to ham it up. Words may not be not enough.

How about a karate chop? A well-placed kick where it counts? Everyone cracks up.

Troubles with Yussuf continue. Rather than get more entangled in the court system, Jamilo tries to compromise. Hamzah can be with you on weekends, she tells him. They can figure out child support themselves. It doesn't go well, she says. Jamilo won't return to the marriage? Then Yussuf's in no mood to negotiate. See you in court, he says. Yet again, relatives push her to go back to him. They cajole: Yussuf is starting his own translation company. He could become rich. Jamilo holds firm. He could be rich one moment and poor the next, she tells them, and anyway—as they've heard her say before—she wants to marry someone she loves.

One morning Jamilo wakes up and finds she can't call or text. Yussuf contacted T-Mobile and had them turn off her service, she says. She goes out and gets a new phone, new number. But she's angry: "He wants me scared. I won't be." (When asked, Yussuf said he did not recall this happening.)

For all her warmth, Jamilo has a don't-mess-with-me edge that emerges when she feels she's being taken advantage of or mistreated. An insistence on respect—and pride. She'll get through whatever's going on and more if she has to. Later she texts: "Let me keep it real with you. I'm happy for not going back to him and not listening to what they say."

Not long after the cell phone incident, her babysitting network unravels to the point that she has to give notice at her job. Too often she winds up with no one to watch the kids; because of the situation with Yussuf, she's no longer comfortable leaving Hamzah with Yussuf's mother. She cries at the thought of leaving Community Concepts—she's loved working there. And the money—rent is due and she's only saved $150. She pawns the gold earrings her mother gave her in Dagahaley but still comes up short.

Aaliyah, meanwhile, wonders about Santa and whether he brings presents to all kids who are good. She pores over the Christmas flyers that arrive in the mail with images of dolls and Legos. At the pediatrician, she holds back tears when she gets shots. "Tell Santa I didn't cry," she urges Jamilo, who decides then that there will be presents and she'll deal with credit card payments and the meaning of Santa later.

Mid-December Jamilo becomes less communicative than usual, as she does when under duress. Often it means she's planning something big but isn't ready to say what. They want her and Yussuf to see a family mediator, she eventually tells me, to help them sort through the mess they're in—"they" meaning her uncle and a cousin. She refuses, balks when I suggest it might actually get them to a place where they could parent Hamzah with less discord.

"Not happening," she says. Instead she wants to take the kids and leave Lewiston. "I have nothing here but trouble," she says.

Where is she thinking of going?

Rhode Island, inshallah.

7

Beginnings II

STRATEGICALLY LOCATED ON THE HORN OF AFRICA, SOMALIA has been in international crosshairs since the middle of the nineteenth century, when colonists began to carve the vast territory of the Somaliweyn—Somali people—into parcels. Before that, nomads had migrated their livestock over widespread grazing lands for centuries. The Somaliweyn relied on a complex web of clans for structure and order rather than on a centralized government. Colonizers from Egypt, Great Britain, Italy, Ethiopia, and France maneuvered clan divisions to maintain dominance.

Postcolonization, the Somali people struggled to establish lasting stability. In the 1970s and '80s, first Russia and then the United States backed the Somali military in armed conflicts. The nation was flooded with weaponry. After Siad Barre was deposed as president in 1991, Somalia erupted into the civil war that has yet to resolve. More than 500,000 have died, and countless others have been persecuted. Drought and famine worsened conditions for civilians as danger rose and outside help lessened.

In 2007, the UN declared Somalia the worst humanitarian crisis in Africa. In recent years, al-Shabaab has exploited instability and clan and political grievances to further its Islamist agenda.

Imams and other Somali leaders in the US urged refugees to set aside ingrained divisions. Clan distinctions linger in Lewiston but less so—and much less openly than early on when Hawiyes, Rahanweyns, Isaaqs, Dirs, and Darods jockeyed for position. Then it was, which clan best represents the Somaliweyn? Who could best lead displaced Somalis in their new northern home?

In those early days, Fatuma worked to make a place for all refugee women, independent of clan or ethnicity. She protected United Somali Women fiercely as a proxy for newcomers she hadn't yet reached. USW's creation was not straightforward; although outsiders saw refugees as a single entity, the community was more fractious then—including and apart from clan. While Fatuma sought funding, another group surfaced, claiming itself the true representative of Maine's Somali women. Several fiery meetings ensued. Fatuma took the infighting calmly: She was younger, and she didn't live in Lewiston. (The family moved soon afterward to Auburn.) USW won that tussle, but among the newcomers new disagreements arose over issues like degree of religious observance.

In 2005, when Somali Bantus began to arrive, the situation grew more complex. Some ethnic Somalis (many who consider themselves Arab African) viewed Bantus as second-class citizens more than a century after the abolition of slavery in Somalia. In an unsettling echo of the past, Bantus sometimes did the work of servants in refugee camps. Early on in Lewiston, Bantu kids reported being called *adoon*, the word for "slave," by Somali classmates. And the distinction between jileec (soft) hair and jareer (harder, curlier) persisted—jareer meant Bantu, as did darker skin and compact stature.

But things changed quickly in Lewiston. Actually, they'd started changing years earlier in refugee camps where some Bantu kids went to school and envisioned futures apart from farmer or laborer. In Dadaab, Abdikadir imagined himself a teacher, modeling himself on an instructor he revered.

For Bantu newcomers in Lewiston—more than five hundred by 2007—things ramped up. Here, everyone went to school and anyone who graduated could apply to college. As time went on, many Bantus did. Here, they were equals who possessed ambitions. Who strived and succeeded or failed alongside ethnic Somalis and everyone else.

Catherine Besteman, an anthropology professor at Colby College, lived in a Bantu village from 1987 to 1988. After she reunited with former villagers in Lewiston, she saw the changes firsthand. In Somalia, Bantus were resigned to lower status, Besteman says. Now there was increased awareness of how discrimination had held them back. And a sense of self-empowerment. In a book about her experiences within the Bantu community Besteman writes, "Not only had the Somali Bantus found a collective voice with which to articulate their historical grievances, they also claimed an active role in negotiating a future free from injustice."

For Abdikadir, it came down to opportunity. "You watch for it," he says. But he had to be ready for opportunity, and the shift in Bantu identity helped ensure that. His mother, for instance, a quiet yet powerful woman, in Maine assumed Abdikadir would graduate high school and go to college. Hadn't they left Africa in part so this could happen?

There were challenges for both Bantus and ethnic Somalis, and for other African newcomers—especially from 2008 to 2009. It was becoming clearer that many refugees suffered from PTSD, which took form as severe anxiety or depression, or both. Symptoms suppressed for years while immigrants grappled with basics—food, shelter, safety, work—emerged over time. "We realized a lot of [new residents] were still experiencing the effects of severe trauma," says Fatuma. "People began to understand the importance of mental health along with physical health."

Isolation was another issue, especially for those with little English. Language barriers hindered communication between employers and workers, caregivers and patients, teachers and parents. Most profoundly, parents struggled to communicate with their own children as, with time, kids became fluent in English and adults picked it up more slowly. Even at home, many kids preferred the new language. And the power dynamic seemed inverted. In Africa, parents were strict. Children did as they were told, or else. But things seemed upside down in the US. Sometimes kids talked back, sometimes it was more subtle.

Once when Abdikadir chastised his son Jamal, the boy kept looking up at him: "He's watching me with those big eyes. In Africa you're taught never to look a parent in the eye. It's considered rude. Here it is the opposite. So he's watching and I'm, *Stop looking at me*, but in America you're supposed to give eye contact. We were both confused."

Qamar Bashir and her husband raised three children in the US. She remembers them always asking *why*. "'Why are we doing this? Why do I have to? Why?' It sounded like they were talking back. In Africa, children were always 'Yes, sir' or 'Yes, ma'am.' Here they were taught to question things." Kids struggled—and still do—Qamar says, with accommodating two identities. "Their parents saw them as not Somali enough, their friends saw them as not American enough."

There was conflict, too, around material possessions. New-immigrant parents weren't used to buying many toys or electronic games—now children pleaded for them. More searingly, parents wanted their kids to care about African things—their genealogy, for instance. In a lot of African nations, children learn their kinship back several generations. Here, many didn't seem interested. And some didn't care about learning a language other than English.

The stakes were higher with teens. New-immigrant kids knew their way around Lewiston, literally and figuratively; many parents did not. A void developed, the teen tendency toward group self-reference going unchecked. As parental control waned, a handful of newcomers made bad choices. High school suspensions rose. So did the dropout rate. Some boys embraced hip-hop culture, looking and sounding like the inner-city stereotype. There were a few muggings and thefts and, especially in the tree streets neighborhood, fears that gangs might form. Educators worried struggling kids would internalize and fulfill a view of themselves as troublemakers.

Parents were even more distressed. Had they come this far only to lose their children? New-immigrant community leaders called for a series of meetings to sort out what was happening—hours during which people talked about what to do. Health-care professionals, teachers, and police took part too. The kids were *daqan celis*, people agreed, out of touch with traditional African values and at odds with positive American ones. They needed firmer parenting and redirection.

New partnerships formed—adults reached out to kids in and out of school, through the mosque and sports. Around this time, Tree Street Youth opened its after-school programs. By late 2009, many of the kids were back on track to graduate. A couple joined the soccer team. And according to Lewiston police, the crime rate, which hadn't increased despite persistent rumors, continued to decline.

Through the end of the first decade and beyond, Lewiston's African immigrant population kept rising—3,500 by late 2007, 4,200 by 2011, 5,000 by 2014, according to Phil Nadeau. As Bantus arrived, so did more ethnic Somalis, along with Sudanese refugees and asylum seekers from Chad, Djibouti, and Congo drawn to the city's African diasporic community. Some refugees were coming through primary resettlement, but many still relocated by choice, part of an historic twenty-first-century micromigration.

It was a singular time. After decades of population loss, large numbers of people were forging lives in Lewiston. "In many ways, it was really exciting," recalls Nadeau. "Suddenly we were a place where thousands of people wanted to be." The National Civic League designated Lewiston one of ten "All-America Cities."

Yet even as graduation rates rose and newcomers found jobs, there were unsettling moments. New clashes between new-immigrant youths and white Lewistonians living downtown occasionally flared up, particularly in Kennedy Park. These were uncommon, with seasons typically passing between incidents—and few involved arrests. But in 2018, when new-immigrant teens are involved in the assault on Donny Giusti, the death will be held out by some as evidence the newcomers cannot coexist peacefully in Lewiston. Among city leaders, it will prompt another round of soul-searching.

THERE WERE OTHER echoes of earlier times. In 2014, twelve years after Raymond's letter, Mayor Macdonald sent his own letter to Portland mayor Michael Brennan asking him to stop recommending asylum seekers relocate to Lewiston. That year the city's budget exceeded $100 million. Lewiston spent about $800,000 on General Assistance, a little over $100,000 of which went to asylees. Meanwhile, the wait period for those seeking asylum was rising, along with the processing time for work permits. Asylees lived years in limbo, unable to qualify for loans, often relying on money scraped together from families abroad.

Norbert and Kamakazi considered themselves fortunate. By 2014, the family had lived in their Lewiston condo for a decade. Nasafari, who was five when they moved in, was a high school freshman. Baby Christina had turned two. Apart from her and eight-year-old Moses, Norbert considered their gray-sided townhouse the family's greatest new blessing in America.

They'd worked for it. In 2003, Norbert had begun to think about buying a house. Was it possible? At Barber Foods, he placed the ham and cheese on Chicken Cordon Bleu, loaded frozen meals onto pallets. Between paying rent and utilities, and keeping three growing girls fed and clothed, he and Kamakazi didn't have much left at month's end. But rent—this felt like tossing money out, the dollars just gone. Norbert preferred the idea of a mortgage, ownership increasing bit by bit. Kamakazi agreed. So they scrimped and saved and put together a small down payment.

The idea was that Kamakazi would stay home with the kids while Norbert worked. But the real estate agent Norbert approached told him the family income wouldn't qualify for a mortgage on any currently listed homes.

"After your wife has a job, then maybe you can buy a house," she said.

Norbert: "But my wife is caring for our children."

Realtor: "I'm sorry."

The same grit that had gotten Norbert through fourteen months of imprisonment took hold. If Kamakazi wanted to stay home with the kids, then she would stay home.

He went to another real estate agent—no. And another, no.

Then Norbert came across an agent named Corky Gray. Corky thought she could help. "We'll find you a home," she said. By now, Norbert was doubting himself. Who in the world would give him a mortgage?

Norbert and Kamakazi and Corky started looking in places outside Portland—Biddeford, Westbrook, Old Orchard—more than a dozen towns altogether. So many nice homes, everything too expensive. Norbert learned a new phrase: "Not in our price range." Finally they found something that seemed affordable. The numbers worked on paper. But then Norbert realized he hadn't factored in something.

"We can't buy this house," he told Corky.

"Why not?"

Norbert explained—his family back in Rwanda depended on the money he sent. He told Corky, "I don't want to live in a nice house if my family is in need in Africa." The amounts he wired weren't large—$50 or $100 every month—but his parents and stepsiblings needed them. And on Norbert and Kamakazi's budget, $50 meant they couldn't move forward with an offer.

They kept looking. One day Corky mentioned Lewiston. At first Norbert and Kamakazi didn't think it would work—too isolated, too far from Norbert's job. "Too much country," Norbert said. Corky convinced them to take a road trip. They drove north on a summer day—toured the schools, the parks, the downtown stores plus Shaw's and Hannaford supermarkets. They crossed the Androscoggin into Auburn, then back again. *Sister cities. I like that,* Norbert thought when Corky told him.

The next time they went to Lewiston it was to look at a specific place Corky found—a brand-new condo with a porch and a backyard deck, three bedrooms, bath and a half. $80,000. Downtown, a few blocks from an elementary school. The place was part of the city's affordable housing plan. Lewiston would pay the $25,000 down payment, which the family would have to reimburse only if they left within ten years. Norbert thought it an extraordinary offer. "Very generous," he recalls—more evidence to him of the American Dream.

The family moved in a few days before Christmas 2004. A storm dropped a foot of snow the night before the closing. When they arrived at the new house, Norbert shoveled a path through the drifts, up the stairs and to the door.

~

AROUND THE TIME Jared and Frank delivered Gaubatz's affidavits to Governor LePage, Fatuma's eldest daughter, Nafisa, began her sophomore year at Georgetown University, and the first Somali elected to office in Lewiston was eight months into his school committee term. "As a father, it is my duty to serve the school system," Jama Mohamed had told the *Sun Journal* before the election. "Education is the most important thing."

Abdikadir put it almost identically: "We value education more than anything," he told me during our first interview, and many times after that. He and Jama and another Somali man cofounded the organization that would become MIRS with sports equipment and a van. Their idea was to teach kids to apply the intangibles gained through athletics—perseverance, discipline, team building—to schoolwork. They offered tutoring and mentoring and soon branched into leadership training.

"Education is freedom. You have to take it seriously," Abdikadir said. He means it.

In 2015, his youngest brother slipped during his senior year at Lewiston High School. He slacked off on homework; his grades dropped. So Abdikadir confiscated his cell phone and video games. The brother fumed. Abdikadir didn't budge. "Focus on your schoolwork. Get your priorities straight," he told him. His brother made it, graduated that May and went on to the University of Maine at Machias, cell phone back in his pocket.

Abdikadir sees education, for kids and for adults, as the bridge to self-sufficiency. After a couple of years, MIRS grew to include services for adults—ESL, parenting and health classes at first, money management and counseling later. "We realized that to help the kids you need to help the parents," Abdikadir said. The skills adults gained propelled them forward, too. Now among the largest private nonprofit social service agencies in the state, MIRS operates out of three locations. More than five hundred people have gone through its citizenship program, which has a 99 percent pass rate.

More and more the newcomers have taken over responsibility for their own adjustment to life in the US. They run agencies, prioritize goals and advocate for themselves, compete for grants. Self-sufficiency means having the ability to handle issues within the community. The competition for funding that has Fatuma scrambling to expand IRC's services results from a strong web of outreach from new immigrants to newer immigrants.

Yet the very qualities that seem to best serve the city's newcomers—initiative and self-reliance—continue to be viewed darkly by some. Time and again I've been told previous generations of immigrants behaved differently. They gave up their old ways, and within a short time the core of their identity was American.

But the notion that previous immigrants assimilated quickly—or that longtime residents easily accepted them—is a myth. French Canadians, who defined Lewiston's ethnic character for more than a century, faced decades of prejudice when they began to immigrate in the late 1850s. So did the earlier wave of Irish immigrants who helped build the city's mills and dig its canals.

Then, as now, it came down to religion, culture, language. And numbers: animosity toward newcomers spread with the surge in French-speaking Catholics emigrating from Canada. Fear and anxiety mounted with every trainload of newcomers disembarking at Grand Trunk station: there were too many of them, many Lewistonians felt, and they had too many children. The city's Irish Catholic population already had climbed, as families fled the Great Famine that killed more than a million people in Ireland. Nativists believed that if Catholics got political power, they would answer only to the pope, undermining Protestant values and American civil liberties.

Fear of a Romanist conspiracy factored into the rise of the American Party, which began as a secret society and became commonly known as the Know-Nothing Party because members were told to "say nothing" when interrogated. In 1854 Know Nothings tarred and feathered a Jesuit priest in Ellsworth. That same year they burned the Old South Church in Bath, where Catholics worshipped.

The Know-Nothing movement lasted only a few years in Maine before dissolving over lack of leadership. But discrimination persisted.

In Lewiston and other parts of the state, French Canadians generally were relegated to the lowest-paying jobs. Protestant-run hospitals and schools sometimes didn't admit them. Nor did some social clubs. Maine voters passed a law in 1919 mandating English-only schools; teachers punished kids who lapsed into French and rewarded students who tattled on them. Some Franco parents adopted English-sounding surnames and stopped speaking French at home to help their kids fit in.

In the postwar isolationism of the 1920s, thousands of Maine residents joined the Ku Klux Klan. Photos from that time show Mainers marching the streets in white robes and hoods. Crosses were burned in several towns, including Lewiston. The goal of the Maine Klan was similar to that of the Know Nothings—to preserve nativist ideals in government and prevent Catholics from holding political office. It was a peculiarly New England subtype of Klanism that took form in lectures delivered in civic halls on the marriage of KKK beliefs with the Protestant ethic, but sinister nonetheless.

Despite ongoing discrimination, Lewiston's new Franco residents managed to maintain much of their Quebecois or Breton culture. A weekly French-language newspaper, *Le Messager*, circulated for more than eighty years. Newcomers opened stores throughout new Franco neighborhoods, including on and around Lisbon Street. The Institut Jacques Cartier bought property and constructed new civic buildings for the Franco community. Near the turn of the century, residents began work on a cathedral in hopes of relocating the Catholic diocese from Portland. The diocese didn't wind up moving, but the cathedral—redesignated the Basilica of Saints Peters and Paul in 2004—dominates the city's skyline and serves as its most prominent landmark.

For decades, Catholic schools taught students in French; many people retained French as their primary language. Long before Paul LePage became governor, he convinced Husson College to consider admitting him despite his low verbal SAT score. College founder Chesley Husson Sr. asked LePage to take an achievement test in French. When he aced it, Husson told him he was in. LePage had grown up in Lewiston, one of eighteen children born to a mill worker and his wife—a scrappy boy who lived on the streets for two years after fleeing his father's alcohol-fueled abuse.

Through the mid-twentieth century as the Franco population grew (and the pope did not take over), relations between newcomers and longtime residents eased. The first Franco American was elected mayor in 1914. And the city's economic base kept expanding. By the late 1930s, mills were pumping out shoes by the thousands and bolt upon bolt of fabric. Times were good. Newly middle-class families began moving to tract homes on the city's outskirts and in Auburn. By now Lewiston was known as the state's Franco capital, with restaurants, theater, and music that drew crowds on weekends. This was the busy, vibrant Lewiston I knew when I went there to visit Aunt Nell and shop or to take ballet.

But even as the city's Franco residents prospered, wounds healed slowly and memories lingered. When Larry Raymond wrote his 2002 letter to Somali newcomers, earlier times came flooding back for some.

"Call it déjà vu or history repeating itself," said Mary Bedard (not her real name), the granddaughter of Franco Americans who'd arrived in Lewiston almost a century earlier. "Too many people, too poor, too many babies. That's what my grandparents' generation heard," Bedard told me. "Wrong language and wrong religion." By the time Bedard started school in the late '50s, circumstances had improved—but her mother told stories of having her hands smacked by a teacher for speaking French. Bedard herself remembered feeling uneasy when Protestant friends heard her grandmother, who lived with the family, speaking French at home.

"It definitely brought things back," says Phil Nadeau. "The church burning, KKK, priests accused of having orgies in convents with nuns, and on and on and on." At the public forum six months before Raymond released his letter, Nadeau watched with amazement and horror as residents—Protestant and Catholic—stepped to the microphone to disparage the newcomers. "It was like, don't you realize what you're saying? We've been here before."

Somalis shared discrimination with the French Canadians who preceded them and happier things too: a dense community of relatives and friends; a future-oriented outlook; the hope of upward mobility for themselves and their children; strong faith. Yet Somalis differed in fundamental ways. They were black, and Muslim, while the earlier newcomers had been Christian and white. And most Somalis arrived as refugees, with histories of dislocation and extensive trauma. These differences made adjustment to life in the US more fraught, and often more difficult.

The Lewiston to which Somalis arrived also was a profoundly different place from the one that awaited generations of French Canadians. There were no textile mills or shoe factories, little in the way of economic expansion. Jobs, yes, but often minimum- or low-wage, not the kind that would easily support a family. It was, in fact, not just a different Lewiston but a different America—no longer a land of seemingly limitless resources and wide-open opportunity. A lot of longtime Lewistonians were trying to figure out how to navigate it, too.

Many still are.

8

Late Fall 2016–Winter 2017

Fatuma, Jamilo, Abdikadir, Nasafari

TRUMP'S SOLE ELECTORAL COLLEGE WIN IN THE NORTHEAST comes from Maine's second congressional district. (Like Nebraska, the state does not conform to winner-take-all; Clinton gets three votes—one for District 1, two for taking the state overall.) In Rumford, where I grew up, Trump bests Clinton by 9 percentage points. It's an epic flip-flop; in 2012 Obama won about two thirds of the area's vote.

Many in the second district saw it coming. The buoyancy at Trump's rally in Lisbon was a harbinger, not a fluke. Even longtime Democrats felt a shift—some were moved to go along. Mary Theriault, a former cook who lives in Auburn, was one of them. "You didn't hear too much, then Trump was everywhere," she says. Theriault got caught up. She can't remember the last time she voted Republican—"twenty years or longer"—but Trump got her vote: "Jobs, the economy, I didn't want Hillary. The same way everybody felt."

It seemed like that to Theriault, yet Lewiston is actually one of the only places in Androscoggin County where Clinton did well. Two months after the election, her supporters are still awash in unreality. Yes, they'd seen the Trump yard signs and the bumper stickers. Heard the talk in checkout lines and read sunjournal.com comments. Still.

As winter descends, there's trepidation among new immigrants about the coming four years along with a sense of wait-and-see. As Jamilo puts it: "I didn't vote for him, but he's going to be our president. Let's hope he's better than everyone thinks he'll be."

On the whole, the city's Muslim refugees are still holding off to gauge whether Trump's actions will match his harsh words, says Abdikadir. They're operating according to the Somali adage *Belayo ka sii jeeda layskuma soo jeediyo*: If trouble is showing its back, don't force it to show its face. Abdikadir does know two families that left for Canada and one that returned to Africa. Most are staying put. "People are worried, they don't know . . . what this president will mean for their families or Muslims around the country. But you can't focus on that. You keep going."

That's easier some days than others. Twenty-four hours after the inauguration, an emotional Fatuma Hussein steps to the podium at the women's march in Augusta. Elsewhere around the nation, the day is unseasonably warm. Here it's winter. Outside the State House, wind lifts Fatuma's hijab as she says, voice unsteady, "I'm from Somalia."

Long pause. She begins to speak again, chokes up, stops. Her eyes well up. She tries to smile through tears. So many people. So much kindness and support amid the fear. Yet here she is again, having to dispel the myth of the Muslim extremist. Here she is again, embodiment of the ideal refugee. It's a lot to carry.

A woman calls out, "You're welcome here!"

Fatuma, hoarsely: "I know!" She wipes her eyes and nose with a tissue. Stands silently, composing herself. People applaud and cheer. Cowbells ring. The crowd at the rally, a sea of pink pussy hats and protest signs, is later estimated at more than six thousand.

Ten seconds pass. She takes a deep breath, pushes back her shoulders.

Better now. Fatuma begins again, tells the short form of her story of coming to Maine a decade and a half ago. For refugees like her, she says, the United States represents safety, hope, a bright future for their children. "Yet—we have a very long way to go because that future, that bright light at the end of the tunnel, is threatened by a few." She doesn't mention Trump by name but condemns any leader who "gives the permission to let racism, discrimination, and isolation continue... In this day and age, we are one people. We are one Maine." The crowd erupts. More cheers, more bell-ringing.

A man who's just joined the crowd asks the woman beside him, "Who is she?"

"One of the refugee leaders," the woman says.

He nods. "Powerful."

"Make sure intimidation doesn't get to you," Fatuma says. "Make sure that you stand up for the vulnerable... [oppressed because of their] age, sexual orientation, gender, religion, background, culture. We shall say no to all of those discriminations."

After Fatuma finishes, a woman with a toddler in a backpack rushes forward to hug her. Fatuma holds steady in the embrace. *Mashallah, an important day*. Her two oldest daughters are at the Washington, DC, march. Her five-year-old, Amina, stands in her ruffled red coat near Fatuma, taking everything in. The two are very close, partly because of temperament, partly because Fatuma fretted over Amina for years while the child struggled before her celiac diagnosis.

Later, Amina will have questions: Why were you crying, Mommy? How come so many people were there? What is "inauguration"?

~

JARED'S FRIEND FRANK leads his ACT for America chapter from the home in a Portland suburb where he lives with his wife. The Atlantic rolls onto shore half a mile from his book-lined office. Lewiston is thirty miles up the road and a world away.

Frank grew up blue collar. His dad was a firefighter, his mom worked at Sears. His grandfather emigrated from Quebec's Gaspe Peninsula to take a job in a Maine textile mill. Frank got lucky and grew a couple of successful businesses. He and Jared have been friends for nearly twenty years. At first, golf connected them. Now the counterjihad movement does. They have different styles. Jared sums it up—"Frank is calm and cool, I'm feisty and emotional." Sometimes they tussle. Frank says, "We go back and forth on which one of us is Master Po and which is Grasshopper." But ideologically, they're one.

"I believe Americans are being duped," Frank says. "Liberals think of refugee resettlement as a humanitarian value. I can understand that. But the migration of Muslims is ultimately a conquest." And Islamism—he sighs. "Hijrah and jihad are intertwined. Jihadists are doing what the Quran and Islamic doctrine tell them to do."

Frank got to the same place as Jared by a different path. In the '70s Frank and his then wife lived a year in Afghanistan as Peace Corps volunteers. He rode his bike back and forth from their small house to his job teaching English at the University of Kabul. A karate expert who'd later create cardio kickboxing, he offered after-school classes in martial arts. They'd gone to Afghanistan, Frank said, to counter the stereotype of "the ugly American, the militaristic warmonger. To show another face." And to help reconstitute the country after decades of instability.

The couple left Kabul with a lesser view of Islam. Things accumulated, Frank says: the second-class status of women; the dog they adopted that Muslim acquaintances didn't treat well; an atmosphere of oppression. One day at the university, Frank offered Darwin's theory of evolution as an example of the concept of scientific theorizing. "Two students went ballistic. They stood up and started yelling that I was insulting their religion," he says. A dean stepped in and defused things, but the incident lingered in Frank's mind.

Nasafari in her government class at Lewiston High School.
(CREDIT: AMY TOENSING)

Girls with instructor in the dance room at Tree Street Youth.
(CREDIT: AMY TOENSING)

Fatuma at home in Auburn. (CREDIT: AMY TOENSING)

Jamilo (on phone) with Aaliyah and friend Binto at Mogadishu Store in Lewiston. (CREDIT: AMY TOENSING)

Abdikadir (center) at home with (L–R) Ikran, Samia, Jaseem, Jamal, and Siham.
(CREDIT: AMY TOENSING)

Skateboarder in downtown Kennedy Park.
(CREDIT: PORTLAND PRESS HERALD / GETTY IMAGES)

Jamilo and Aaliyah in Kennedy Park. (CREDIT: AMY TOENSING)

Fatuma and U.S. congressional candidate Emily Cain talk with voters on Lisbon Street. (credit: Tom Williams/Getty Images)

Carrys at work at Argo, a marketing company on Lisbon Street. (credit: Carrys Ngoy)

Carrys at home. (credit: Carrys Ngoy)

LHS varsity boys soccer try-outs in September 2016.
(CREDIT: PAT GREENHOUSE, THE BOSTON GLOBE/GETTY IMAGES)

Aba Abu works with women at Trinity Jubilee.
(CREDIT: CHRISTIAN SCIENCE MONITOR/GETTY IMAGES)

Abdikadir and Ikran prepare dinner. (CREDIT: AMY TOENSING)

Nasafari between classes in the hall at Lewiston High School.
(CREDIT: AMY TOENSING)

Men share a meal at Masjidul Salaam Mosque in Lewiston.
(CREDIT: AMY TOENSING)

"It was discouraging," he says. "After a while we felt we couldn't make a difference, that there was an entrenched eighth-century mentality that would never change."

South Korea, where Frank and his wife transferred, was different—"more tolerant, more open." The couple traveled to India, Pakistan, Japan, and Malaysia. Frank arrived back in the States with a new appreciation for American democracy. He'd always been a big reader. Now, what had been a hobby took on intention. What about the US had made him so grateful that he actually knelt and kissed the ground when he and his wife got home?

Frank bought dozens of new titles for his home library: history, economics, philosophy. Tipped toward libertarianism by *Atlas Shrugged*, he also felt drawn by Milton Friedman in *Free to Choose* and F. A. Hayek's arguments in *The Road to Serfdom*. As a Catholic-turned-agnostic who'd attended a Jesuit-taught school before college, he was also interested in the juncture between spirituality and science. He liked Carl Sagan. He examined the histories of Judaism and Christianity. Then Islam. Or, as he decided after a few months of reading, "the problem of Islam. Not just radicals but the core of the religion itself."

A series of texts convinced him: the Trifkovic book; Bill Warner's monographs on sharia law, the Quran, the Hadith and the Sunna; Robert Spencer's *Did Muhammad Exist?* Frank read *Reliance of the Traveler*, a reference of Islamic lifestyle guidelines. Eventually, he came to believe that freedom and choice lie at the heart of human happiness, and that Islam threatened both. That ocean down the street from Frank's study? The nine-foot tide rises and ebbs. But what if, year by year, it rises a little higher? Say a steep shore means you don't notice much until one day seawater washes over the tableland and the whole town floods. If that sounds like climate change, it's also radical Islam, according to Frank's view: slow net gains and then a deluge.

Much of what Frank now reads addresses what he considers "the West's looming crisis." More than a hundred books in, plus dozens of DVDs and films and seminars he attends around the country, he's become a proselytizer. "The careful consideration of Islam should not be a political issue. It shouldn't divide into conservative or liberal, Democrat or Republican," he says. "The West needs to get educated on the doctrine of Islam. Now."

Frank and Jared ride the incoming Trump tide. Republican representatives in the state legislature agree to sponsor two pieces of legislation Maine ACT wants passed. Heidi Sampson picks up an American Laws for American Courts (ALAC) bill, and Heather Sirocki takes on a measure to criminalize the female genital mutilation (FGM) of minors. It's Maine ACT's third attempt to see an ALAC bill enacted, its first on FGM. Other pending bills unrelated to ACT include one holding resettlement agencies accountable to the state and another requiring Maine to sue the federal government for failure to comply with the Federal Refugee Act.

Interest in laws regarding Muslim refugees and immigrants hasn't been this high since 9/11, Jared says. It's time to safeguard the nation. His lion is in full force. He's up early, often at his desk by seven a.m. He fires off emails to chapter members. "Ladies and gentlemen, I hate losing and it's important to our state and country that we win. For far too long the left has had their insane way with things. It's our time, but it won't happen without courageous effort by all of us."

Reach out, Jared urges members. Step aside from political correctness and make clear the issues. LD 903 references "foreign laws" rather than specifying sharia, but Jared tells people to spell it out in their letters to editors and calls to legislators, and in-person testimony at the state house. He calls sharia the "really big elephant in the room." Another tactic, popular among conservatives: remind legislators of their oath to uphold the Constitution.

He circulates a note from Dave Gaubatz advocating the inclusion of strong anti-Islamists on Trump's national security team. Gaubatz writes, "Mr. Trump is on the right path to fully understanding Islam, but listening to the false advice [of those who believe the religion has been misused by extremists] will put him and our country at grave risk." Gaubatz says the new president's advisors must persuade Trump that "America is at war with Islam itself."

Jared sends out a few more admonitions: "Do not waver. Do not snooze. Do not let the left prevail."

~

HIS NAME IS Mustafa. It's another inevitability, as much so as Jamilo's first love with Aaliyah's father and her leaving Lewiston to be with him, as much so as her return to the city with Aaliyah and the subsequent arranged marriage. The relationship with Aaliyah's father ended four years ago, and it's been two years since her marriage with Yussuf broke up. Even now, in hard times, Jamilo pulls people into her orbit. She shines. Of course someone would come along.

Mustafa is the reason for Rhode Island. He grew up there as a boy named Dean, son of a white mother and Cape Verdean father. Converted to Islam twenty years ago.

Jamilo wears her faith easily, instinctively; Mustafa's seems more effortful. Before he and Jamilo get together I know him as the big guy in a white kameez who sets up a sidewalk table stacked with Qurans. Passersby stop, or they don't, and if they glance toward the table Mustafa says hello. He may initiate a chat. Offer a free Quran. Stay, and he'll talk about how Islam changed his life—made him put others before himself, helped him be a better father to his five-year-old twin sons. If he comes across with a convert's zeal, his eyes are sincere.

Jamilo and Mustafa were friends before she married Yussuf. They'd see each other on the street, smile, talk a little. Mustafa admired her exuberance. She is filled with Allah's spirit, he says. To Jamilo, Mustafa is older, experienced, trustworthy. And this fall and early winter, with the sheriff's notice and people turning away, and the election, Jamilo needs steadiness. Needs to feel someone cares. On nights when the kids are with their dads, Mustafa's warmth draws her like a fire. He makes her feel as though she can get through anything, do anything. He believes in her. Loves her.

She finds herself caring about him, too. At first she doesn't tell anyone. Then she lets in Aspen and Binto and a few other friends. No one in her family, though they'll hear soon enough. Nothing stays private for long within the community. Jamilo doesn't care. Let people approve or disapprove. Mustafa is a committed Muslim with a big heart. Her nickname for him is Polar Bear. Their kids are close in age. With Allah, they can build a life.

Elsewhere problems mount. An acquaintance Jamilo found to babysit while she's at work needs a place to stay. Somali-style, Jamilo lets her sleep on the sofa in return for childcare. A few weeks later, Jamilo receives a letter stating she's violated her lease, which permits only her and the kids to inhabit the apartment. Jamilo calls the landlord's office and protests: the woman is there temporarily to help out with Aaliyah and Hamzah.

The landlord sends an eviction notice. Why? Jamilo and the babysitter suspect Yussuf of stirring up trouble. The babysitter moves out but keeps taking care of the kids. The landlord refuses to rescind the eviction. Jamilo feels sure there's a misunderstanding. And she doesn't want anything like an eviction on her housing record: "Somalis can have a hard enough time finding a place to rent without that on top of it." She wonders aloud whether the landlords want her out so they can rent to someone white.

One afternoon Jamilo and the babysitter zip the kids into their coats and go to the landlord's office to explain what's happened. No one there seems willing to listen. As Jamilo gets the kids ready to go back outside, the babysitter argues with office staff. She curses. A manager calls her abusive. A few days later, Jamilo sends the landlord a letter apologizing for the babysitter's behavior. She gets a letter back:

The eviction stands. To fight it means more court on top of the battle over Hamzah.

"I really need to get out of here," she tells Kim Wettlaufer, a go-to when she has problems. He says she should stay and work things out. This is your community, Kim tells her. You'll miss it if you go. He suggests she get a lawyer, offers to go with her to the legal aid clinic.

Kim doesn't know about Mustafa, though. Mustafa wants to leave Lewiston, too—wants distance from his ex-wife and the chance to start over with Jamilo. He keeps talking about Rhode Island, where much of his family still lives. There's a Muslim community, and without traffic it's just over three hours from Lewiston. Mustafa has joint custody of his twins; they can go back and forth with Aaliyah and Hamzah. Rhode Island, Mustafa tells Jamilo, is where they can both begin anew.

They drive down to look at rental places. The house Mustafa likes is outside Providence. Three big bedrooms, a park where the kids can play. Jamilo likes it, too. She prays for guidance—should she stay in Lewiston or go?

Go. Things move quickly. First, a *nikah*—a Muslim marital contract. Their union won't be legal under US law, but Mustafa wants it Islamically sanctioned. After the contract is witnessed and signed, Jamilo packs clothes and a few furnishings; they'll finish clearing out her apartment on weekends when she brings Hamzah to Lewiston to see Yussuf, before her eviction takes effect.

Mustafa buys an L-shaped sofa that will hold the six of them. Tufted, in burnt orange. The Providence house awaits.

~

JANUARY 27, 2017—DONALD Trump issues an executive order suspending the resettlement of Syrian refugees and banning citizens of seven predominantly Muslim countries from entering the United States for ninety days.

The order takes effect immediately, generating confusion and protests at airports and prompting legal challenges. In Lewiston, Muslim residents looking for reassurance again stream to MIRS and the IRC, to town hall and the mosques. Another difference between Lewiston's new and previous waves of immigrants: for all the discrimination earlier immigrants faced, they weren't subject to a president who singled out their religion so directly.

Around the same time, Mayor Macdonald goes after asylum seekers again. He meets with Governor LePage, later telling Maine Public Radio of the city's asylees, "We're being overrun by these people. . . . And the money we're having to spend is phenomenal." The mayor does not quantify the impact other than to say that most of the more than $400,000 spent by the city helping new immigrants resettle in the first part of 2016 went to asylees.

Macdonald doesn't point out that after two years, refugees no longer qualify for General Assistance, that federal law prohibits asylum seekers from working for the first six months, or that the city's total budget exceeds $100,000,000. Of the sixty asylees with appointments for assistance, Macdonald says, "They may be victims over there but what's happening here is . . . they're making the taxpayers of Lewiston, which is one of the poorest cities in the state—we are the victims."

Carrys, at the start of the new semester at USM, frets about fellow asylum seekers in Lewiston. "What can people do? They come here because of danger in their countries. And, when they get here, they have to wait a long time before they can work, and there's a lot of hostilities."

He's heard that the asylum process has slowed even more since the election. For now, he tunnels into his classes—he managed mostly A's last semester despite the distractions of worrying about his family in Congo, worrying how much thinner he could stretch the money he made at Argo. Ziti and rotini, it turns out, are even cheaper than ramen if you buy supersize packages. Boil the pasta, dress up tomato sauce with a pound of hamburger—you've got dinners for a week.

Now for Carrys there's the added strain of the election results and a new president he senses may not want him in Maine any more than the governor and Mayor Macdonald do. His studies provide respite in the form of a well-written proof or immersion in Gauss's law. Or in the larger ponderings that Carrys lies in bed at night considering: "Actually, I'd like to conduct a study," he says one day. "What makes people who hate math dislike it? Why do others love it?"

Outside the United States, people continue to feel the aftershocks of Trump's travel ban. In Kenya, Somalis who made it through the UN resettlement pipeline—some who'd even booked seats on flights to the US—get the distressing news they'll not be leaving. Instead they must return to Dadaab. Thousands of people around the world face similar uncertainties.

On February 3, a federal judge issues a ruling that blocks the president's order. Twenty thousand visa holders and green-lighted refugees rush to rebook. But most don't manage to do so.

Pressure builds to keep Dadaab open. After announcing it would close the camp by year's end, Kenya has extended the deadline to May 2017. Ongoing fighting in Somalia combined with a lack of basic resources continue to make repatriating refugees difficult. A few thousand have relocated from Dadaab to Kismayo, a port city in southern Somalia where food is short and al-Shabaab remains a daily threat. Of those families who do go, many wind up coming back. Now, Trump's order intensifies pressure on the United Nations High Commissioner for Refugees (UNHCR) to figure out where people can go. Even with overseas family members helping, like Jamilo with her parents, prospects look bleak.

On a late January morning in Lewiston, members of Masjid A-Nur show up at dawn for prayers and find a broken window. It's a small pane in the rear door, no graffiti or other evidence of vandalism. Still, there's a hole in the glass—and no way to explain how it got there. The news spreads on social media. Someone proposes a vigil, but people seem uncertain. Was the act intentional or not? If an accident, does a vigil send the wrong message?

A few days later, Heidi Sawyer steps forward and suggests a community potluck, "Breaking Bread, Breaking Barriers," to bring together new and longtime residents. She's wanted to do this for a while; now feels like the time. She blasts emails, posts on social media, calls almost everyone she knows in L-A. Once the date is set, she gets businesses to donate raffle items.

On a night so cold the air seems breakable, Lewistonians pick their way across the icy parking lot of the middle school into the cafeteria. Mostly white people wind up coming, some Somalis, a few other Africans. Tables laden with lasagna, Swedish meatballs, Somali-style rice, and several kinds of salad line two walls. A huge sideshow of pies and cakes.

People stand around in animated little clumps. Superintendent Webster is here. So are teachers, coaches, a minister, a *Sun Journal* reporter and dozens of others. Heidi bustles around, hugging, beaming—*This is Lewiston at its best.*

Abdikadir comes through the door carrying a tray of chicken drumsticks that Ikran made. She's home with the kids, he says.

Later, back at their townhouse, Ikran will be grumpy she didn't get to go—and she'll show it. Baby Jaseem's grin as he's passed from lap to lap will contrast with her frown. "I told you I wanted to be there," she says pointedly to Abdikadir, who looks chagrined; Ikran's big personality delights him—except when she's upset and it's directed at him. He equivocates: he didn't realize it was important to her, he stopped at the potluck only briefly. Ikran shakes her head, not buying it. But her displeasure sweeps through like a squall, and then she's herself again. She loves Abdikadir, even if sometimes it seems she does more of the work. Loves him especially when he acknowledges that.

At the potluck, people mix and chat: the deliciousness of the food, the weather, the 2016 boys' soccer team—which played well though ultimately didn't win the championship the way everyone had hoped. The few new immigrants are magnets. People lean in and listen closely to them in a way that's both heartening and a little awkward.

Heidi announces a game, divides the room into groups according to age and gender. Now, to underscore commonalities—*Step forward if you've ever been bullied... Step forward if you were an A student in school... Step forward...* After the dinner—not one of Ikran's drumsticks left—raffle winners come forward to collect their prizes. Conversation peters out. Heidi thanks everyone for coming. Later, she says she's not disappointed but does wish more new immigrants had showed up. She'll try again next year. In the meantime, if a couple of friendships result from tonight, then everything was worth it.

It may turn out the Trump climate actually helps efforts like Heidi's and Abdikadir's to integrate the city. Postelection, particularly post–travel ban, everything in Lewiston feels heightened. Trump has emboldened those who oppose Muslims, but his actions also have angered and energized supporters—and prompted some who previously were holding back to step forward. It reminds me of what happened when white supremacists announced they were coming to town in the aftermath of Mayor Raymond's long-ago letter; some who before might not have taken a stance were moved to do so.

In February a man rapes a sixteen-year-old girl in a motel in southern Maine. Social media and reactionary websites claim the man arrested, who was black with an African name, is a Somali Muslim refugee from Lewiston. The man does live in Lewiston, but he's actually Sudanese and Christian. A couple of days after it happens, I'm at a place where I sometimes go for lunch a few miles from the city. Several of us are sitting at the counter. A woman brings up what happened, and how this shows why the Muslim ban is necessary. A man looks up from his plate. "He isn't Muslim," he says. The woman stops talking. The man goes back to his lunch.

After the woman leaves, I approach him—a bearded guy in his forties. Tell him I'm writing about Lewiston. Does he have Somali friends? No. But they aren't being treated right. "Getting a bad rap," he puts it. Beyond that, he doesn't really want to talk. But he has spoken.

Apart from the election, the city continues its two-steps-forward-one-step-back progress. In February, the ACLU of Maine files a complaint against Lewiston for failure to meet the needs of students of color and those with disabilities. Citing several federal violations, the complaint charges the city with failing to identify students of color as having disabilities, retaining English Language Learner (ELL) students in classes that don't count toward core requirements, and disciplining students of color and those with disabilities in ways that impede learning.

ACLU legal director Zachary Heiden says older ELL students are particularly set apart. He urges the city to upgrade its ELL program for them, and to bring their learning space out of the high school basement. Writes Heiden: "No one believes that learning English as an older student is easy, but it is precisely because it is so challenging that the district needs to pay extra attention to it."

He also cites what others have pointed out as a shortcoming: a near-total lack of black teachers and staff.

~

IN MID-FEBRUARY, DURING one of her nightly calls from Florida, my mother says, "I've been thinking about that man in Lewiston."

"You mean Mohamed?"

"Not Mohamed. The man outside the store." This is how she talks these days, pointed and vague, both.

Does she mean Abdikadir? No. Shukri's husband? Not him either.

"The man who talked about elders."

Oh—we'd stood on the Lisbon Street sidewalk one day, looking at fabrics in a storefront. Mom admired the array. She stepped closer to better see the shimmering orange and magenta. A man standing nearby smiled. "This is my brother's store," he said.

They started talking. Mom brought up that she was eighty-six years old. (This is new, too. Her age has gone from something she concealed to a point of pride.)

"Mashallah," the man said. He told us Somalis look to the old as a library, full of information and resources. "We don't have many counselors or therapists. If we need help, usually we go to an elder."

"I like what he said," my mom says now on the phone. "That they view the old as having wisdom."

She doesn't ask, "Do you view me as wise?" If she did, I'd say yes—but being among Lewiston's newcomers has made me reconsider values I grew up with.

One of my family's core messages was that individual attainment leads to happiness. Especially from my mom, my sister and I learned early that approval hinged on A's, sports wins, accomplishments. Among most new-immigrant families I know, ambition and achievement take a backseat to relationships. Education does matter; parents want their kids to do well in school. But achievement is a means to an end—the support of people you love or contribution to a community.

On the phone, I ask my mom, "Now that you're in your eighties, what matters to you most?"

She doesn't hesitate: "Family." I'm not surprised. She's been telling my sister and me for a while that once Florida lost its appeal—tennis, bridge, gardening—she'd be "coming home to family."

But what if growing up, and watching our mother's example, we'd learned family and community came first? We weren't bereft; our dad provided much affection, and Mom showed us a woman could have a career—and told us we could, too. But there was a lack of larger context and connection. I saw that, too, among other achievement-oriented families, or among acquaintances whose families also had broken apart or moved away.

That night on the phone, I don't say I sometimes wish for what I see in my Somali friends—their community and the big, rangy families that dole out love and sometimes pain and day to day are simply there.

And faith. One Sunday a few weeks later I find myself in the same church I've attended occasionally for years. Nondenominational Christian—a place I first stepped into in my midthirties during a time of struggle.

Inside the sanctuary, a band plays. People sway with arms outstretched. The church is gentler than I'd imagined from stereotypes I'd absorbed about evangelicalism as a left-leaning New Englander. I've found it a place of caring and support, yet one where I don't quite fit. Politics are part of it, an assumption of shared views that often aren't mine. And disbelief that there's only one way to God. My lens includes religious ambivalence, though I understand why Jamilo and others in Lewiston feel sustained by Islam; at times faith has supported me, too. I've felt heard when I prayed. That morning in church, I sense the Holy Spirit as I have often there before.

Reading the Quran to better understand Islam has rekindled my interest in the Bible. But why church now, after more than a year away? I don't know. Still, I drive home happier than I've felt in months. The next week I go back.

~

THE SUN FLITS across the sky, emerging after seven a.m. and gone by four if it appears at all. For Nasafari, one day gives way to the next without much definition. Not that she really minds. Her applications are in: Mercy College, Husson University, Trinity College, University of Maine at Augusta, and of course St. John's. She didn't wind up applying early decision because her application wasn't ready. Her SAT retake came in with better scores, thank goodness. But she wanted to perfect her essay about taking part in Maine's Youth in Government program at the state capitol. Those three days marked a turning point.

In the essay Nasafari describes her dream of becoming a prosecution attorney—and her reticence about public speaking. She writes about how learning to stand up and speak in the House chamber, "knees shaking and palms sweating," helped her realize "the only person who can put me in a corner is myself." Instead, she writes, she "chose from that day forward to let my voice be heard."

Now, college process over, she waits. For the first time in two years she feels relaxed; it shows in calm eyes and a quicker smile than I'm used to seeing. Even her speech has slowed from a year ago. Nasafari has done her part. "It's kind of a relief to have things out of my hands. Now it's up to them," she says.

Weekends, she kicks back a little—scrolls through Facebook or catches up with the Forresters on her iPod. On Sundays she and her dad watch football. They're both die-hard members of Pats Nation. If the Patriots aren't on, then soccer.

Her sister Nabega waits, too, in her ninth month, for her baby to come. A girl: Azaleah Ella-Jean. In September Nabega did a gender reveal: a small pumpkin painted pink, inside a larger white-painted, scooped-out one inscribed "It's a..." Tyler lifted the lid of the larger pumpkin and made the discovery. Hundreds of people liked and loved the Facebook photos that showed him holding the pink pumpkin and beaming.

A few weeks ago, friends threw Nabega a baby shower. Kamakazi and Nasafari were there—even Norbert went. How could they not? Throughout her pregnancy Nabega has been so happy she seems lit from within. Her parents see this. They may wish Tyler were born-again. They may wish the two were married. Norbert, especially, still talks about his upset that Nabega moved in with Tyler without her father's permission, much less Tyler asking to marry Nabega. Still, a new baby means new beginnings.

Births, weddings, graduations, birthdays, holidays—all offer needed lightening of the weight the family carries. Oldest daughter Antoinette still lives in Arizona with another family; the reason has to do with Norbert's strictness, though it's rarely talked about. As for Kamakazi, she feels tugged back by Congo and Rwanda, her friends and family there. She struggles with English—now Moses has taken it upon himself to teach her. *School*, he gently tells her when she tells him to get ready for *iskooli* in the morning. *Breakfast. Milk. Shoes. Backpack.*

Norbert doesn't feel pulled toward Africa as Kamakazi does. He wouldn't want to live anywhere but the US. What worries him most about the election is his sense that people didn't see Trump's absolutism. "It seems like some Americans are sleeping," he says. "It's scary. Where we come from, it looks like the wrong direction."

Still, Norbert values democracy, even if in this election he thinks it went awry. Rwanda may be doing okay under its own new president, but with insufficient checks and balances, people's lives remain precarious. He does miss some things—wishes, especially, that his kids could know his mother. Norbert grew up close with her—he was her first living baby, and his last name, Rwambaza, translates to 'Now I have someone who can help me.' It saddens him that she lives six thousand miles away, that she's never met Moses and Christina.

And there's Norbert's past, which crops up at seemingly unlikely times. One afternoon the family watches soccer on the big screen—Norbert, Christine, Kamakazi on one sofa, Moses with his Game Boy on the other. Norbert offers up a story: In the second jail, the one so crowded that prisoners slept sitting with their heads on their knees, people were dying of dehydration. Wherever you moved, you had to step around the dead. Moses looks up when he hears this, lays the Game Boy on the sofa. His round eyes look into his father's.

Norbert continues: someone in the cell found the end of a pipe sticking out of the wall. The prisoners took turns sucking and spitting out the brackish liquid that came out. Finally the youngest among them—a boy, really—sucked hard and clear water ran. It seemed a miracle, says Norbert: the cool, clean water, the boy who saved them all.

Moses leans forward. "How did the water taste?"

"It was very good."

"There were dead people in the cell."

"There were."

A mild day, the TV soccer score zip-zip. Moses gets up, announces he's going out to ride his bike. He takes the story of the boy and the miracle water with him.

~

AFTER TRUMP'S INAUGURATION, Jared and Frank go full bore ahead but ACT as an entity seems to moderate. ACT president Brigitte Gabriel fires Texas chapter leader Roy White for refusing to cancel a meeting about how to shut down mosques. ACT is "not in the business of shutting down any place of worship based on what religion it houses. We are in the business of making sure no house of worship incites violence in the name of religion, nor harbors or supports terrorists who wish our destruction" reads a statement.

Gabriel warns members: "In no way does our organization advocate or tolerate bigotry, or threats of violence toward anyone, especially because of which God they may choose to worship." Members who espouse bigoted views will be expelled, she says.

It's a curious turn, given the group's hard-core stand against Islam in the past and given that Gabriel previously had lauded White. Has Gabriel nudged her organization away from hard right because the Southern Poverty Law Center named ACT a hate group and she wants to disprove the designation? Does she hope to attract members by broadening ACT's base?

I ask Jared what's going on. He's not sure. A few weeks later Gabriel posts two photos on Facebook. She's in Washington, DC, at the White House, giving thumbs-up in one and seated with an unidentified staffer in the other. A caption reads "Very productive day at the White House."

9

Early Spring 2017

Nasafari, Jamilo, Abdikadir

ST. JOHN'S SAYS NO.

The ripped-open envelope, letter in her hands. Nasafari's heart plunges. St. John's doesn't want her? This is so not what she expected.

But by the time she messages me—"I got denied"—she has, Nasafari-like, already begun to right herself. I've seen her do this before, buoy back up to the surface—yet never with a disappointment as big as this. Within hours, she's reframing things to lighten them, the same way Norbert and Kamakazi do. Is it a trait acquired of hardship or inborn?

There's no way to find out why St. John's didn't take her. Okay—Husson said yes. So did Mercy, also in New York, and the University of Maine. All three offer paralegal studies, so she can stay on track. And Husson really wants her, gave her a scholarship then upped the amount when she still wavered. These are good things.

A few weeks later, Nasafari makes a turn-around decision. She'll attend Central Maine Community College (CMCC) in the fall—on a full tuition scholarship plus a stipend for books—and live at home. She will buy a used car with the money she saves. In two years, with an associate's degree, she'll transfer to St. John's. From there she'll continue on her way to becoming a paralegal and, not wavering here, a JAG.

Her decision to go to CMCC pleases Norbert and Kamakazi—particularly since Nasafari came to it on her own. Why the sudden shift? Nasafari can't say, exactly. Partly because she still just wants St. John's. Partly because of money; for schools that weren't her first choice, Mercy and Husson cost a lot even with financial aid. Partly because of family—for all her self-directedness, she's very close with them. It makes her happy everyone's getting along again, that she no longer has to serve as the bridge between her parents and Nabega.

Azaleah was born ten weeks ago. Nasafari's huge love for the baby surprises her. She expected to care about her, of course, but not quite so consumingly. Her favorite part of every day is being with her. Where does such love come from?

On a May evening, she pushes open the door to the condo carrying her niece in her arms. Nabega comes in, too. The sisters still work at the same daycare. Many nights now, Nabega drives Nasafari home and stops in for dinner. The two are very close—a testament to their bond because Norbert has held Nasafari up as an example of how to do things right.

Before the sisters even sit, everyone crowds around the baby. KamakaziNorbertMosesChristina—all are Azaleah's people. She smiles a big *O* of delight. Casts her baby spell. As one, everyone smiles back. Azaleah wears a shirt embroidered with her name. Her hair is combed up into a tiny pouf. After the family settles into their spots on the sofas, she gets passed from person to person for inspection and admiration, finally winding up with Kamakazi, who keeps her.

"The baby is getting big," Norbert says.

"Yes, she really is," Nabega tells him—eleven pounds at her last doctor's visit. Father and daughter are cautious with each other, finding their way toward a new, better place than where they've been the last two years.

Outside, the city that was gray for months finally has greened up. The last mounds of snow have disappeared. Spring—it makes Norbert aware of how quickly seasons pass. Makes him nostalgic, he says. Christina was small like Azaleah a short time ago. Before that Moses, and before that Nasafari and Nabega. And Antoinette. Wow, he says. They grow up, but they're always your babies.

Once when Norbert was a kid in Africa, he was visiting his grandmother's house. His uncle—her son—arrived late for a big meal. Everyone else had eaten, but the kids were still clamoring for more. Norbert's grandmother brought a filled plate from the kitchen for the uncle, only. The kids protested: You told us no, but you had some for him! Grandmother lifted her chin. That's for my baby, she told them. The kids: But Uncle is grown! Grandmother didn't budge. It doesn't matter, she said. Uncle smiled and ate.

Kamakazi calls everyone to dinner. She lifts pot lids—stewed goat with cassava, beans, rice, and fufu, which is cooked semolina and corn flour. Steam thickens the air. At the table, Norbert says less than usual. His eyes take on the hooded look they get when he's preoccupied. Later he'll again say he's glad Nabega comes by with the baby, but he does wish she and Tyler were married. And Antoinette, still in Arizona—he wishes she'd move back home.

He rolls a piece of fufu into a grape-size orb, indents it with his thumb and uses it to scoop up stew, lifting the construction carefully to his mouth. Then repeats the process with the next bit of fufu. Kamakazi casually mixes her food in a way that differentiates their natures. Both keep an eye on Christina, who spears beans and ignores everything else.

Moses takes advantage of the lull, turns to Norbert. "You paid eight cows to Mom's father when you got married, right?" He's looking less to confirm the information than to open a back-and-forth. Moses likes to talk about Africa, each conversation a thread that weaves with others into whole cloth.

Yes, Norbert tells Moses. It worked like this: her father gave back two cows right away so Norbert and Kamakazi could start their own herd. He gifted a third to Kamakazi to buy furnishings and staples for her new household. Then, after Kamakazi got pregnant, her father sold another cow to help prepare for baby Antoinette. And by then, Norbert and Kamakazi's herd had multiplied.

Moses considers. "I would pay two cows for a bride," he says. Everyone laughs.

"In Africa, they would say you are a very cheap guy," Norbert tells him.

"Okay, four."

Another lull. Nabega and Azaleah have headed home to Tyler; he works on a paving crew, so the three of them go to bed and get up early. Nasafari excused herself and went upstairs to do homework. Norbert rolls more fufu.

"Dad, we're Tutsi, right?" Moses has an eleven-year-old's persistence. He finds his way to answers. For efficiency, his parents try to provide them sooner rather than later.

Norbert looks up. "What?"

Moses repeats the question. Norbert nods. "Yes, we are Congolese Tutsi. There are also Congolese Bantu."

Moses watches him steadily. "Uhuh, but we're Tutsi." It's a matter of identity to him, a fact, like he's Christian and has four sisters. But Moses knows a little about the origins of the discord in Congo, too, from overhearing things. His eyes flicker with uncertainty. Should he ask more?

On this, Norbert will hold out against his son's tenacity. The Tutsi-Bantu conflict lies at the heart of how Norbert got separated from his family during the cattle drive to Lubumbashi. Why he was imprisoned. Why the family has reconstructed a life in Lewiston. For now, the simple explanation will have to suffice: *Yes, we are Congolese*

Tutsi. Moses doesn't need to know the extent of the suffering. Of the division—especially since Lewiston has Africans of many ethnicities. Including both Bantus and Tutsis from Congo. During the day, Kamakazi babysits Congolese children whose parents work. Some of the toddlers have dark skin, some lighter.

"The kids at school think I'm Somali." Moses holds out a plump arm, peers at it. "My skin is light."

"Mm-hmm," Norbert says.

Some Somalis in Lewiston are quick to claim Tutsis from Congo, Burundi, and Rwanda as similar to themselves. One day at Baraka, I share with Mohamed a magazine piece I wrote that includes a photo of Nasafari's family. He taps the page. "Yes, I know these people," he says. "Like Somali Tutsi." The city's Africans make many ethnic distinctions among themselves—more so at home in private, and the older generation, more—centuries-old categorization by skin color, facial features, texture of hair, height.

Norbert notes something about the city's Congolese that echoes what Abdikadir says about Somalis. In Lewiston, what binds Congolese immigrants is greater than what separates them, Norbert says. They share a homeland, languages, history. And loss.

There's also growing recognition that the differences aren't so clear-cut, in any case. There are lighter-skinned Bantus and darker ethnic Somalis. And genetic analyses have shown Rwandan Tutsis and Hutus to have virtually identical DNA.

"No game-playing until you finish your food," Norbert tells Christina. She glances up from the iPad in her lap, protest on her face.

Kamakazi says something in Kinyamulenge, points to the child's nearly empty plate and drained milk glass.

"Oh, so you are finished," Norbert says. Christina nods, goes back to her game.

Norbert has no thoughts of anything like bride price here. It's an old-country custom—even if his brother paid fifteen cows when he married last year in Kigali. In the US, Norbert's expectations and hopes have shifted. He focuses on the kids' education, on bringing Jesus into their lives, on providing his family with comfort. In return, he looks for a modicum of gratitude, and harmony. Yes, it does bother him that Tyler didn't ask him for Nabega's hand, and that Nabega no longer goes to church. Still, the baby is healthy and happy. And, at least for now, Nasafari will stay in Maine for college.

Compromise. Nasafari started kindergarten not speaking fluent English. Her teacher reached out, offering after-school language lessons, sometimes taking Nasafari shopping or on other outings. Accepting the help tweaked Norbert's pride, yet he went along. "It made a big difference to Nasafari," he says—got her off to a good start. When another teacher made a similar offer to Moses in kindergarten, Kamakazi and Norbert again agreed. They'll do the same again if someone reaches out to Christina when she goes. Saying yes—this is part of how they make sure the kids become American.

~

HOW DO JARED and the ACLU guy wind up in the same elevator? Jared had checked his jackknife with security, pushed his leather bag into the X-ray machine. Walked through the metal detector and tapped the elevator button. Waited.

The doors slide open. Jared steps in, the ACLU lawyer right behind him. Where did he come from? Zach. That's how Jared knows him. Tall, dark-haired young man who testifies at the State House almost every time Jared does. Zach does not figure among Jared's favorite people. Comes across as smug, Jared says. And worse, he doesn't act in the best interests of the citizens of the state of Maine.

Inside, the elevator smells of coffee and fried takeout. The men ascend in silence.

Despite the inauspicious start, Jared feels optimistic about today's hearing on ACT's anti-sharia measure in front of the legislature's judiciary committee. President Trump recently issued a second travel ban for citizens of six Muslim-majority countries. Like the first, this one has been court-challenged. Jared still thinks things are headed in the right direction. Last week during a town hall meeting, a moderator asked the president whether he trusted American Muslims. Trump equivocated—some he did, some he didn't. Then, with Trump bluntness: "We have a problem, and we can try and be very politically correct and pretend we don't have a problem, but...we have a major, major problem." Jared's position, exactly.

Jared feels confident, too, about the tenor of the bill Maine ACT got representative Heidi Sampson to sponsor. The gist reads, "The Legislature finds that it is the public policy of this State to protect its citizens from the application of foreign laws when the application of a foreign law will result in the violation of one of the following fundamental liberties, rights and privileges guaranteed by the United States Constitution or the Constitution of Maine: due process, equal protection, freedom of religion, freedom of speech, freedom of the press and the right to keep and bear arms; and any right of privacy or marriage as specifically defined by the Constitution of Maine."

If the measure passes, Maine will be the thirteenth state to enact ALAC legislation. Anti-Islamists claim current statutes regarding foreign laws are an easily overturned patchwork. ACT's position: some judges factor Islamic beliefs into decisions on domestic cases involving Muslims, especially with respect to divorce and child custody, and Muslims place sharia above American law.

Inside the hearing room, Jared chooses a mid-row spot in a gallery that soon fills to capacity. Zach disappears into a side office; a couple of reporters stand by a wall. Legislators settle into the horseshoe of desks, readying to hear testimony. They'll recommend passage or not to the full Senate and House. ACT supporters have already flooded the committee with emails and letters.

First come hearings on an Equal Rights Amendment (ERA) to the Maine Constitution and on a proposed bill for sanctions against companies that deny climate change. Jared nods vigorously at testimony from a University of Maine professor on the climate bill: "The suppression of free speech fosters polarization, not consensus." Why, the professor asks, do we not have "a marketplace of ideas, in which the most valid, the strongest, and the most competitive prevail?"

ALAC's turn—Rep. Sampson steps to the podium to introduce it. The United States affords unique opportunities and privileges, she says—and she wants to protect them. She's lived in the Middle East, witnessed disregard for human rights. Still, "this bill has nothing to do with fear of other cultures." Instead, says Sampson, it's about safeguarding rights set forth in the Constitution.

Jared makes his way to the front. A stop clock is set for three minutes. Despite the tick-down, he's measured. He tells the committee he's a navy vet, former Maine Conservation Teacher of the Year, a grandfather, and leader of an ACT for America chapter. ACT is responsible for this necessary addition to Maine law, he says. What will happen if the measure passes? Effectively, nothing. State policy will be clear, though, and no foreign law will ever impact Maine citizens. What if it doesn't pass? Probably not much right away, Jared says, but give it time. He pauses for effect. Seconds pass. 1:42, 1:41 . . .

The legislators' expressions reflect Republican attentiveness and Democrat skepticism. Jared continues: Without ALAC, the mores of other systems will arise in US courts. Judges who refuse to allow such arguments could be seen as biased. Jared mentions marital rape and the valuing of men over women in child custody disputes. Foreign laws have been brought to bear in cases around the nation, he says. "This bill protects our own laws and excludes only those others that are contrary . . . I implore you to vote 'ought to pass.'" Zero seconds—he steps away from the podium. Over so quickly.

Another ACT chapter head comes forward. "You know how they put up the stoplight after the fatal accident?" she asks. "Can we put up the stoplight now?" It's fitting that the committee heard Maine ERA arguments today, she says, because ALAC also concerns women's rights. Two women who testified for ERA glance wide-eyed at each other.

Another woman reads a letter from someone who has worked in Lewiston's Muslim community. She has Somali friends, the letter-writer says, and among the city's Muslims sharia is followed. Women face inequality. Some people practice polygamy. A representative in a maroon shirt leans forward, intent. Later he'll say he wishes the writer had been there to take questions.

Then comes the opposition, solely Zachary Heiden. The ACLU legal director's testimony is succinct. The notion that people can get away with things because of sharia law is false and preposterous, he says. It does not happen. The maroon-shirted legislator asks for outright assurance that sharia is not an issue.

"There are no concerns," Zach says.

Dissent washes over the gallery—most of those who remain are pro-ALAC. Jared exhales exasperation. He expected this; the ACLU colludes with Islamists and leftists, he believes, for reasons that originate in a shared dislike of unfettered democracy. But, still.

Committee members schedule a work session to explore court cases in which foreign law may have been considered. The hearing breaks up. Factions gather in the hall outside. Zach, high-ranking Democrats, and other ALAC opponents stand together. Jared and ACT members along with a handful of conservative legislators form a smaller, tenser cluster. If the hall were a school lunchroom, Zach and his group would be the cool kids—they joke and scan the room.

Afterward Jared says he thinks the hearing went okay. He thinks Zach may have erred tactically in not responding to arguments made by bill proponents. Already Jared is crafting a rebuttal to Zach's brief remarks. He may also send the committee a booklet of cases of sharia incursions on the US legal system.

Later he emails me the booklet. In it, I mostly find rulings that involve enforcement of foreign custody decisions from Islamic-governed nations and legal arguments incorporating cultural defenses, like the case of a Muslim man who claimed the woman he murdered had dishonored him by ending their engagement. (He was found guilty.)

I ask Jared whether he considers these cases evidence of sharia invading our court system. Look, he concedes, sharia isn't such a big issue yet. But it's coming. Take what's happened in England, where Islamic tribunals exist alongside British courts.

Jared knows some people view him as a hater—the cost, he says, of standing up for unpopular, un-PC beliefs. He's braced for what's coming: negative press on ALAC, and a judiciary work session to which an ACT lawyer likely won't be invited.

Then there's the hearing two months from now on the bill to prohibit female genital mutilation (FGM)—among the most contentious measures of the legislative session. Jared realizes he's seen as an unlikely champion of women's rights. Sure, he wants the cultural issues around FGM out there for people to grapple with. But listen—he has granddaughters. What about the rights of girls? He's determined the bill will pass.

~

THE SOMALI WORD for mother, *hooyo*, describes the relationship as much as the person. Jamilo and Aaliyah are hooyo; so too Jamilo and her mom and any mother-child relationship. "Mother love" approximates the feeling, but not the complexity. To nurture is to be nurtured, and the converse. Islam teaches the centrality of mother. In the Hadith, a man asks whom among people he should honor most highly. Muhammad answers, "Your mother." The man asks, "Then who?" "Then your mother." The man: "Then who?" "Then your mother." "Then who?" "Then your father."

After she moves to Providence, Jamilo drops out of sight for a while. She deflects texts, parries attempts to visit her. Her Lewiston friends say she's out of touch, too. I chalk it up to her being busy, out of state, wanting privacy in her new life. In the end it turns out to be all these but also something else—hooyo.

Jamilo needs time to figure some things out. She does care about Mustafa; he's the first person she's trusted her heart with in years. But she loves Aaliyah and Hamzah first. And, searingly, Aaliyah is struggling in their new life.

Jamilo has sensed her withdrawal for a couple of months. Now Aaliyah doesn't want to leave her grandmother's home in Boston, where she stays when she visits her father. She dislikes the back and forth from Providence to Lewiston to Providence to Boston to Providence. Hours and hours in the dinged-up but serviceable Nissan Versa Jamilo bought to drive the kids around.

At the new house, Aaliyah plays alone. If she plays. Mostly she wants to watch TV. She gets angry with Hamzah and Mustafa's sons if they're rowdy or they pester her, which happens a lot. Every morning when she wakes, the smile she used to wear much of the day passes across her face and disappears.

It's killing Jamilo. She likes the house, the peaceful setting, the space for all the kids. She likes the big living room where she'd imagined happy domestic scenes. Imaginings that have been slow to materialize. The twins are a handful, more active than Aaliyah and Hamzah. Jamilo takes care of them while Mustafa works, and then everyone's exhausted at night. She tries to rationalize to Aaliyah: It takes time to adjust, things will be okay. The boys mean well—they're just a little rough. Aaliyah listens, nods sadly. When can she go back to Grandmother's?

Two weeks pass. One night Jamilo asks Aaliyah whether she wants to go for a ride. Just the two of them. "Yes." They leave the boys with Mustafa, head out in the Versa. It's dusk, quiet, the thrum of the engine around them. Jamilo glances into the rearview. Her daughter's almond-shaped eyes stare back.

"Aali, tell me what's the matter."

Jamilo waits. Aaliyah's face reflects the cabin's amber lights.

Finally: "I don't like it here."

"Why not?"

Tears slide down Aaliyah's cheeks. "I miss my old room. And my bed." A pause. "I don't like the twins. I don't hate them, but I don't like to be with them. They're too wild." Jamilo feels torn—she cares deeply about Mustafa, and the twins are his. Just little boys. She pulls the car over. Closes her eyes, a quick prayer.

Hooyo. She feels pulled toward her daughter, that huge, elemental love. Aaliyah, who is observant and particular and loves unicorns. Who is powerful in her quiet way. The two of them have woken together on more than a thousand mornings. Jamilo can't compromise her.

Incredibly, Mustafa understands. When I talk with him three months from now, he'll say someone older and more experienced than Jamilo might have been able to make it work. Someone with less damage to heal. Still, he loves her and always will. He says it again: "She has a beautiful soul." And, more—Allah holds both their lives in his hands.

So Mustafa doesn't try to keep Jamilo in Providence. But if she goes, he tells her, it's over. By late April, Jamilo is back in Lewiston with the kids. If she feels embarrassed to have returned so soon, she doesn't say so. Doesn't say Kim Wettlaufer was right, that she made a mistake in going. To the contrary—she says she's glad for the time in Providence, happy she spent those months there with Mustafa and the twins. But she made the right choice in coming back, she says. Aaliyah was so unhappy. Already she seems better.

And, now that they're in Lewiston again—how can Jamilo put this? Mustafa's boys needed discipline. Aaliyah and Hamzah can act up, sure, but mostly Jamilo knows how to manage them. Plus, there's only two of them. In Providence, things often felt as though they were tilting out of control. And then—this wouldn't have been a reason for leaving Providence, but she likes being a working woman. Thinks of herself as one, and has for years. In Providence, not having a job made her uneasy, she says. As did Mustafa's preference that she stay home.

The Knox Street apartment no longer belongs to Jamilo, and she gave away much of her furniture when she left. She and the kids move in with relatives. It's crowded: the family of eight plus Jamilo's three. Jamilo sets out to find a job. Her resilience: what would overwhelm others, Jamilo handles. Others see this. Binto, who's known her since fifth grade, puts it this way: "No matter what happens, she gets up and keeps going. She's always been like that."

Binto sees Jamilo's time in Providence with Mustafa as a major misstep. She's just glad to have her back. Others feel the same way. Aspen, especially, is happy and relieved—Jamilo's her compass, the one who helped her through her pregnancy after the baby's father left. They've been friends for more than a decade; Aspen calls Jamilo her role model. Sometimes she posts homage on Jamilo's Facebook page: "This girl right here is my everything, my best friend, my other half. She's the reason I am who I am."

Soon Jamilo, Aaliyah, and Hamzah are back hanging out with the other moms and kids at Kennedy Park. While Jamilo waits for the job interviews she's lined up, she babysits for friends. She still has the Versa, so she drives people to appointments and to work, takes them to Sam's Club or to St. Mary's to visit relatives in the hospital. Someone texts; she loads the kids in the car and goes. A no-charge Uber. "I like doing it. I know what it's like to be without a car," she says. In turn, people invite Jamilo and the kids for dinner. Or buy her gas. A corollary of biil: Help those in need, and in turn be helped.

It surprises me the Somali community accepts Jamilo back so unquestioningly. She and they seem to take it as a given. Does kinship supersede all else? And what about sharia, and claims by anti-Islamists that Muslims skirt US law and follow practices antithetical to human rights? According to that view, Jamilo would have been punished for leaving Mustafa and before him, Yussuf, and for getting pregnant with Aaliyah. Yet nothing dire has happened. She returns to the community, even if some disapprove.

Jamilo's self-direction does sometimes come at a personal cost. It can drive her forward in ways that don't serve her—or Aaliyah and Hamzah. Leaving Providence may have been right in the long term, but returning to Lewiston without an apartment lined up results in instability for months. Jamilo always keeps the kids well clothed and clean, hair styled—but it's challenging without a place of their own. At bath time, a cousin needs the shower, then an aunt wants to handwash an abaya. Piles of the kids' clothes tidied one minute get strewn around the next. A boot disappears, turns up days later. And her kids can't keep toys there because there's no room.

Aaliyah, sensitive and private, begins to struggle again in the crowded space. After a few weeks, Jamilo realizes living there isn't going to work. She returns one day from grocery shopping and finds Aaliyah outside on the steps with an older cousin. "Uncle wants me to get out," Aaliyah tells Jamilo, and whether that's actually true or a misunderstanding, Jamilo decides they're leaving.

For a while, it's hard to know where she and the kids will be at night. Eventually they wind up with an acquaintance named Fatummah who lives in a triple-decker in the Knox Street neighborhood off Kennedy Park. Another tight fit—Fatummah has three kids, a fourth on the way. Jamilo has little money and no job yet. She gets $300 monthly from Aaliyah's father and the state of Maine combined, and about the same amount from Yussuf. At Fatummah's, instead of paying rent, Jamilo pitches in for groceries and drives the family wherever they need.

But the stress of not having one place to call home accumulates. Hamzah begins throwing daily tantrums. They intensify after Fatummah's baby girl is born. Hamzah wants to be on someone's lap. If he can't, he kicks and cries. When I admonish him one day for tugging the baby's curls—not hard, but enough to furrow her brow—while Fatummah isn't in the room, he asks, "Baby going away, Cynthia?" And Aaliyah's sad a lot, still longing for her bed at the old apartment. Even if she usually slept in Jamilo's, she liked having it as a safe space. Aside from clothes, she has little of her own at Fatummah's—everything is stored. But Aaliyah is not a tantrum thrower. She grows quieter, a little petulant.

One afternoon while Jamilo goes to an interview, Aaliyah comes with me to the Lewiston Mall, a semi-occupied strip of stores whose heyday was the '70s. At the nail salon, she chooses pink with sparkles. I pick black. Aaliyah says she wants black, too. Thinking she may not like it, I tell her okay, but it's a color mostly grown-ups wear. Seemingly from nowhere she says, "Grown-ups are supposed to keep kids safe."

Hooyo matters more than anything to Jamilo, but her trauma has left her with deficits the kids in turn feel, too. Sometimes she's impulsive, sometimes short with them. Like a lot of young moms—especially those without their own mothers in their lives—she's learning as she goes, a better parent month by month. Still, the kids' lives feel at times haphazard.

And yet—the tenderness. One day Aaliyah twists her knee badly enough that the ER doctor bandages her leg from midthigh to calf. He tells Jamilo to keep her immobile for two days until her follow-up with the orthopedist. Jamilo scrambles—finds someone to take Hamzah, asks whether she and Aaliyah can stay on at Fatummah's. Yes.

That night Aaliyah lies ensconced on the sofa, leg elevated, a bag of frozen peas on her knee. It hurts, and she's upset that Fatummah's daughter said the fridge, packed with food and cold drinks the kids all covet, does not belong to Aaliyah and Hamzah. "She said it was only theirs. That made me feel sad."

Jamilo smooths her daughter's hair, kisses her forehead. They'll have their own fridge soon, she promises. They'll fill it with treats for everyone!

As always, Jamilo's buoyancy lifts everyone else. Slowly the mood shifts. Fatummah's son pats Aaliyah's leg while they watch *Arthur* on TV. She smiles. Everyone eats some ice cream. Fatummah's toddler gathers the extra spoons, clacks them together. Aaliyah brightens—the bag of peas makes her knee feel better, she says. And vanilla is her favorite. A little while later, she drifts off.

Jamilo looks worn out. She's not sleeping well—waking early, anxious about her situation and mulling over the past. Knowing what she wants for Aaliyah and Hamzah—a stable home and family, good education, an understanding of Allah—is one thing. Getting there is another.

Recently a temp agency sent her out for a job. She knew little other than it was the night shift at a packing plant. Her GPS led her to a beer-brewing facility. She rang a bell to be let in. A man came to the door and asked her inside. Jamilo explained why she was there. He picked up a phone, said to someone: "There's a little black girl here to see you." He asked her to have a seat, not unkindly. Jamilo felt pretty sure he hadn't meant what he said the way it sounded, but still: the comment, the beer smell of the place, the dark outside. She got in her car and drove away. The next morning she told the temp agency what had happened. A manager apologized, said they'd find another position. Jamilo's still waiting for the call.

Inshallah, things will get easier soon. She stares at the TV, thoughtful. Aaliyah starts pre-K soon, the summer session; Jamilo has to figure out how to get her a backpack. Aaliyah needs the same things the other kids have.

Suddenly Jamilo laughs—"Ahahahhah, they shouldn't have that on a show for kids!" Rhyming words that end in *eed* have been rolling across the screen. Now, *W- E- E- D*. "Weed," the TV voice intones invitingly. "Weeeeed."

Jamilo keeps laughing, contagiously. Fatummah's kids crack up too, even though they don't get the joke. Aaliyah sleeps on. Her eyes scroll behind their lids—she's dreaming, face relaxed. Jamilo settles into a corner of the sofa across from her daughter. "I do bounce," she texted me once, and it's true. Jamilo and the kids bounce back.

Soon after, it happens again—some of Jamilo's relatives try to push her into a relationship. Even from a distance they sense her vulnerability—no job, no home, little money. This time it's not a marriage, exactly; call it an arranged, long-term commitment. They've given up on Yussuf—that tune's been sung now that he's announced, to Jamilo's relief, that he's seeing someone. Jamilo's relatives have shifted their focus to a Somali man who lives in western Massachusetts, she tells me. A man who has a wife. Jamilo finds the development astounding. Again? To a married man this time? They can't be serious.

They are. The union would be sanctioned by some in the community. Islam allows a man to have up to four wives; some Somali women, particularly Bantus, arrived in the United States as second or third wives unable to claim their marriages under US law. Early on, some moved to Lewiston to try to reconfigure their families. It's much less common for a Muslim man to marry a second woman in the US, and if he does, both have to go forward legally as though she's his mistress rather than his wife. Jamilo's family's argument: the man would take care of her, and he'd help out financially with the kids.

None of that matters because Jamilo won't have anything to do with the proposal. *Mai-ya!* she tells her uncle and aunt. Hell no!

Still they pressure her, even convincing her one night to prepare a meal at their house after the man shows up in person because she's blocked his phone number. She fixes rice and beef—he's someone she knew during high school, a nice enough person, actually—but she doesn't have romantic feelings for him, won't marry him, and in any case doesn't want to become a second woman, no matter whether the first agrees. "I'm number one or nothing!"

Jamilo's food is the best he's ever tasted, the man tells her, to which she just says, "Thank you."

There's even an attempt at what feels like bribery while he's still in town. The man will rent an apartment for her and the kids if she'll be with him, her uncle tells her, to which the suitor nods. Mm-hmm, Jamilo says. No thanks. After persuasion fails, they try disparagement. "You know, I'm the devil's child . . . Karma is doing this to me," Jamilo says. "But they don't understand. I hear what they say, but I don't listen to it. I'm going to find an apartment for me and the kids. And I'm going to get a job, soon."

She's right about the job. A few weeks later, she's offered a position as a home health aide for people with developmental disabilities. The six-week training starts right away. Jamilo chooses to work hands-on with clients, both new-immigrant and longtime Mainers, rather than in support—"otherwise I'd just be in people's kitchens, translating documents." She comes home to Fatummah's from the first training excited. Likes her co-workers, loves being back in the workforce. And $9 an hour: far from riches, but inshallah she'll soon have money of her own again.

With her first paycheck she heads to Walmart, buys clothes for the kids and food for her family and Fatummah's—eight people altogether. She pays her cell and credit card bills. Sends $50 to her mother in Africa. Banks a few dollars. A new plan is forming in her mind: find an apartment away from downtown where the kids can play outdoors. Some trees and grass. By summertime she'd like to make it happen.

~

FOR NEW IMMIGRANTS in Lewiston, gender norms differ from those in Somalia and elsewhere in Africa. Here, women do come closer to equality with men. There's little tolerance for early-teen marriage, polygyny, and domestic abuse under American law. Fatuma's IRC and other nonprofits educate women about their rights and try to see that they exercise them. (Fatuma's take on polygyny: Permissible in the Quran, yes. But only under specific conditions—a wife's infertility, for instance, and the man must have the means to support both households—and illegal under US law in any case. And: "I'm a feminist, so of course I see it as unequal. If a man can have several wives, why can't I have several men?" She laughs. "Not that I'd have time.")

Also in Maine, girls attend school as a matter of course, graduate, go off to college or take jobs. In Somalia, a single mom like Jamilo would live with her family, or the children would be awarded to her husband's family.

"I'm amazed by the strength of refugee women in Lewiston," says Aba Abu, the single mom from Atlanta who's now a caseworker at Trinity Jubilee. "They're doing the kids, they're working, they're doing the work at home. They're balancing everything. Many of the men don't take responsibility." Aba views this darkly. She takes adult-ed classes in her free time, doesn't want to get remarried: "I am not raising a grown-ass man."

At Masjid-A-Nur, an instructor named Aliya sees things through a religious lens. "Men are not assuming their God-given roles," she says. "In Somalia they took care of their families. Here they cannot or they do not."

City leaders say men's adjustment has been more difficult than women's. Many men lost their land and their livelihood while women caretakers continued in their roles. Women raise children and run the domestic realm. Often they're the ones who navigate complex social and health-care services on top of holding jobs. Besteman, the anthropologist, says one challenge going forward is how to replace men's lost status in ways that empower them without compromising women.

Many men do work, of course. A lot of businesses and nonprofits in Lewiston were founded by men and, according to Phil Nadeau, the younger generation of new-immigrant women and men are about equally represented in the workforce.

Gender relations among the city's newcomers are complicated. Women may sometimes seem in charge, but the Quran grants higher status to men, and inequities remain. I know a girl who underwent a nikah at age fifteen; now twenty-one, she has four children.

Safiya Khalid, who works on a boot-making machine at L.L.Bean, was accepted to the University of Maine at Orono. She was excited about living on campus and studying psychology. Then her mother, who is disabled, asked, "Who will take care of us?" Safiya had a brother right behind her in school, but the assumption was she'd look after the rest of the family while he went off to college. So now Safiya commutes to nearby USM as a day student. "I work full-time, go to school, pay bills, that's it," she says. "I love my family, but that's the double standard for men and women in my culture."

New-immigrant girls and boys, especially Muslims, internalize different messages from the time they're small. About modesty, for instance: at Tree Street Youth on summer days, boys play outside in water bare-chested, wearing shorts, while girls have to get wet in their long skirts and hijabs.

Yet I see, too, that women and girls sometimes insist on rigid roles. Control of the domestic realm is power. One night at Jamilo's apartment, her half brother came in saying he was hungry. Two girl cousins, around twelve, looked at him and then at each other. They got up from the sofa, went into the kitchen and came out with a slice of bread spread with jam. Not Somali food. They cracked up, handed it to him. He sat holding it and scowling. They giggled some more. Was it a joke or a power play? Finally they brought out some chicken.

Adjusting to new norms can create conflict in a marriage. Some couples navigate more easily than others. Abdikadir and Ikran, for instance—they view each other as equals, mostly, though Ikran does more of the work at home and occasionally calls out Abdikadir for taking her for granted. On big decisions, they partner. Ikran wants another baby, their fifth. Abdikadir doesn't—at least not now. All right, Ikran waits. She lavishes her baby-love on Jaseem. During the rare dinner out alone with Abdikadir, she might bring up the topic, to gauge how he's feeling. "We have learned how to negotiate," she says.

It comes down to trust. She believes Abdikadir wants her to be happy, as does she him. He'd like to run for political office? Ikran opposed the idea at first. Although an extrovert, she's private—doesn't enjoy having reporters or photographers around. But seeing that "it really means a lot to Abdikadir to serve," she's relenting. "The next Barack Obama," she jokes whenever the topic comes up. Abdikadir smiles, reddens. Ikran: "Okay, then go for VP first."

The differences between them show up every day. One afternoon they're out riding in a friend's motorboat. The two oldest kids are with them. The friend asks whether Abdikadir wants to drive. He does. He eases forward on the throttle. Gently the boat rides the waves. "Faster!" the kids cry. Abdikadir goes a little faster. Ikran's hijab flutters in the breeze. "What about my turn?" she asks. Abdikadir laughs. "Oh noooooooo," he says. Ikran drives. Her hijab flies. The boat planes out, the kids squeal.

They balance each other, Ikran says later. A decade into marriage, they've mostly come around to letting each other be. A good marriage is less to do with chemistry, she says, and more to do with the kind of person you want to become. "I've matured and I've grown." She laughs. "More than Abdikadir. No, I'm kidding. We are good partners together."

It's hard to imagine two people deeper into a life. Ikran works from eight a.m. to four p.m. in shipping at L.L.Bean while Abdikadir's mom watches the two youngest kids. Then Ikran comes home and cooks and cleans and supervises homework. Abdikadir puts in his ten-hour days and makes an appearance at pretty much every community event. Weddings or funerals, the balloon festival, a juvenile justice seminar, potlucks and city council meetings and summer film night—likely he will be there.

Nighttimes, he comes home to Ikran.

10

Badbaadiye (Survivors)

Spring 2017

Fatuma, Jamilo

WORLDWIDE, MORE THAN 200 MILLION WOMEN HAVE UNdergone female genital mutilation (FGM), also known as female genital cutting. Almost every girl in Somalia is subjected to partial or total excision of her external genitalia sometime between age four and eleven. A higher percentage of Somali girls are cut—estimates range from 95 to 99 percent—than anywhere else in the world. More than half undergo FGM's most extreme form: infibulation, which includes excision of the clitoris and most of the inner and outer labia. What's left of the labia is stitched together, leaving only a small opening through which to urinate and, later, to menstruate.

Jamilo's infibulation took place when she was five, or maybe six.

Fatuma founded United Somali Women in part to raise awareness of FGM's dangers and long-term health consequences. She and most health-care professionals say FGM doesn't happen in Lewiston. Years ago, working earlier stories, I heard rumors about families sending girls to Africa for the procedure but rarely hear them now. Women do experience complications related to earlier infibulations—painful scar tissue like Jamilo has, difficulty delivering a baby, urinary tract infections.

Many Westerners view FGM as a Muslim practice, but it comes down to culture and tradition. (FGM predates Islam by centuries.) Historically, Somali marriage represents more than the union of two people; it merges two lineages and strengthens interclan relationships. Female circumcision indicates not just a bride's virginity but also fidelity to her family and clan—as well as her future loyalty to her husband, his family, and his clan.

Because a female elder typically performs the cutting, some argue that women themselves choose to perpetuate circumcision as part of Somali tradition. Seen from this perspective, a girl becomes ready to assume her rightful place among the married, adult women of her community only after she's undergone the procedure.

But FGM is rooted in patriarchy. In Somalia, a virtuous woman is one who has been circumcised to preserve her virginity and to curb her sexual desire, making her less likely to "wander." Somali boys are circumcised, too, though this procedure just removes the foreskin of the penis and is not intended to keep boys chaste or inhibit desire. And the fact that most men refuse to marry an uncut woman means considerable pressure on families to allow the procedure on their daughters. Parents see the financial and emotional gains of marriage as outweighing the trauma of cutting.

Not so in Lewiston now, Fatuma says. Through the education of women and community leaders—particularly female elders—Somali newcomers learn that circumcising their daughters is not only illegal according to federal law, but also doesn't carry the social imperative it did in Africa. "Parents want to secure the best future they can for their daughters," Fatuma says. "Here, what matters is education, what matters is opportunity. It doesn't take long for parents to see that things are very different and that girls are better off uncircumcised."

No aspect of Somali culture is more fraught. To some in Lewiston, the fact that almost every Somali girl in Africa undergoes FGM—and that any female who arrived in the US after age nine likely has been cut—suggests a vast divide, even if the practice doesn't occur here. "I know that cultures differ, and respect is important," says a nurse who used to work at a Lewiston hospital. "But I have a hard time thinking anyone would do this to little girls, no matter the circumstances." Infibulation is an extreme rite of passage by Western standards, not analogous with other initiations Americans are familiar with—First Communion, for instance, or Catholic confirmation. Or the circumcision of newborn boys. For some, the practice of FGM in any form makes Somalis seem unreachably foreign.

In part, Jared and Frank are counting on that sense of foreignness to carry LD 745—"An Act to Prohibit Female Genital Mutilation"—through to passage. Mainers may feel they can coexist with Islam, Jared says. But who can relegate FGM to a matter of cultural relativism?

Federal 18 U.S.C. 116 already prohibits genital mutilation; LD 745 backers want a law so state prosecutors can pursue a more specific charge than aggravated assault. If the measure passes, Maine will be the twenty-fifth state explicitly to ban FGM.

Renee, the Lewiston woman whose pro-ALAC letter was read at the judiciary hearing, has told Jared she believes FGM continues. On the May morning the measure comes before the legislature's criminal justice committee, she sits with him and other supporters of the bill on one side of the hearing room. Opponents, including more than a dozen African immigrants, sit on the other. It's one of the few times I've seen anti-Islamists and Muslims together in the same space.

LD 745 is modeled on a recently passed South Dakota statute. It makes it a felony to cut the genitals in any way of a female under age eighteen or to take a minor out of state for that purpose. No religious or cultural custom can serve as justification. Now is the time, Jared says. Less than two weeks ago, police in Detroit arrested two doctors and one of their wives and charged them with performing FGM on young Dawoodi Bohra Muslim girls. And in March, an Ethiopian man convicted of excising his two-year-old daughter's clitoris was deported after finishing his prison term.

In-favor testimony begins. Bill sponsor Heather Sirocki tells legislators Maine has the highest per capita concentration of Somalis in the nation, and Somalia has a long history of FGM. In Maine 1,603 females are at risk of it, Sirocki claims. It's a human rights issue. The bill would make the procedure a Class B felony for the cutter and Class C for parents.

A spokesperson for the Maine Prosecutors Association takes Sirocki's place. She also advocates passage, calling FGM a barbaric practice bearing no resemblance to male circumcision. "We want clear statutes, without guesswork," she says.

Jared's turn. He makes a similar introduction to the one from last time: grandfather of nine, retired schoolteacher. Imagine, he asks the committee, "You're five or six again, playing peacefully... You are brought into the kitchen of your home by your elders—parents, aunts, possibly your grandmother." They place you on the table, Jared says, they take off your clothes and restrain you. Without anesthetic, a razor is used to remove your genitalia.

A male committee member winces visibly. Jared continues, addressing the female legislators. "You are thusly 'protected' from wanton desires of sexual pleasure in later life, and thus you've become a better and more trustworthy wife-to-be." He finishes—little ethos or logos to his argument this time, just this uncomfortable pathos. "Having imagined this just for a moment, please tell me how you can vote not to criminalize this practice with severe penalties.... How can you justify a vote of 'ought not to pass'?"

Others step forward in favor. A woman urges, "Take a spotlight and shine it on this horrendous procedure," and the head of an antiabortion group says her organization stands against anything that endangers or debases human life, and that "[genital mutilation] debases girls."

Renee takes the podium, tells the committee she learned firsthand about FGM from refugee friends. Renee doesn't come out and assert the procedure is being done in Lewiston, though later she'll say she knows personally of girls sent to Africa. She says she's seen the complications in women, asks, "How many times did I bring someone to the hospital?"

Now the opposition: A Democrat legislator argues for an alternative to LD 745 that would emphasize outreach and increase spending on education. Criminalization is "not the right way to go," she says. Passage of the measure as it stands could be stigmatizing; the issue should be approached within the sphere of public health. Others opposed include a health-care professional who calls the bill a framework that accentuates cultural and racial differences. She distinguishes genital mutilation from genital cutting, saying the latter carries less shame.

In her seat, Renee mutters. A legislator reprimands her. "Absolutely no comments. We listen to everyone with respect here."

A Somali man who runs a Portland social services agency takes the podium. Ending FGM requires three *C*'s: cooperation, cultural sensitivity, and community-driven education, he says. The current bill is "a rush to legislate" without those necessities.

Two more Somalis step forward—an older woman and a younger one serving as her translator. The woman says that in the community, some people think of cutting as a decision made to assure a child's future. It's not done with intent to harm. Criminalizing the practice may make women avoid interactions with health-care providers or cause people to feel ostracized. She, too, urges amendment to shift the focus to education.

ACLU legal director Zachary Heiden isn't in the hearing room today. Another lawyer speaks for the organization, in opposition to criminalization. The ACLU sees no evidence that FGM is occurring in Maine, she tells committee members. Renee shakes her head, keeps shaking it but remains quiet.

Pro and con testimony concludes. The committee chair calls for anyone who wishes to speak generally about the bill, neither for nor against.

Fatuma Hussein comes forward. She slipped in just after the hearing started, with Amina at her side. Now they stand together in front of the legislators. Fatuma's hand rests on top of her daughter's head, lightly, so she won't dislodge the peach-colored bow in Amina's hair.

Three minutes on the clock. Despite the microphone, Fatuma's voice sounds soft. She has eight children, she says, including two daughters in college and two at home. Her agency provides services to immigrants and refugees. She pauses. Her face crumples. She fights back tears. Seconds pass. The legislator who proposed the alternate bill, Rachel Talbot Ross, gets up from behind her desk, comes and puts her arm around Fatuma.

"I am a survivor of this horrendous procedure," Fatuma tells the legislators. "The worst form, where they take away everything you have. Your legs are tied together so you cannot walk." She was eight years old when it happened, she says, her younger sisters six and five. The women who performed the procedure weren't medical professionals.

The emotional toll was enormous. "It takes your innocence away," Fatuma says. And the physical side effects—she missed a lot of school when she got her menstrual period because of pain from blood that backed up. She's known women who lost babies midpregnancy from FGM complications and women who suffer chronic urinary tract infections.

The stop clock has run to zero. No one interrupts. The proposed bill is misguided, Fatuma says. Culturally specific services are the right approach to preventing FGM in Maine. "My four daughters are not mutilated because of the education and support I received as an informed parent."

She looks down at Amina. Her voice drops again. She's struggling. "I stand here with my daughter, six years old, with a very bright future in front of her. Amina is strong in math and very curious about the world." Fatuma pauses, gathers herself. "My daughter will not go through my horrific experience. Amina stands in front of you as a symbol of hope and prevention."

Throughout the gallery, people wipe away tears. There's silence after Fatuma finishes. She takes Amina's hand, turns to leave. Later, she'll say it was necessary to share her story publicly "but very, very hard."

Downstairs in the cafeteria after the hearing ends, Jared sits quietly, absorbing what transpired. Renee is there too, nursing a cup of coffee. "Fatuma and her little girl—" Jared finally says. He looks upset, shakes his head. "It's sad. They're following a false religion."

Usually I don't counter what Jared says—it too easily devolves into argument—but now I say genital cutting is a cultural practice, not a Muslim one. He eyes me. Islam is a religion that oppresses women, he says, and FGM is an extreme form of oppression practiced around the world mostly by Muslims. Dishes clatter in the kitchen. Steam rises from Renee's cup.

When the committee meets again next week for a work session on the bill, Jared will approach Fatuma and introduce himself. She knows his stance on the measure, but he'll come across as sufficiently warm that she'll ask him to come see the IRC and Lewiston.

In an email Jared sends to chapter members, he writes, "We actually had a great discussion. She had tearfully testified about the horrors vested upon herself with FGM, but that she thought penalizing/criminalizing was the wrong approach and that education was the answer.... We debated this, and I got an invite to visit with her and get to know her community better. I think I'm going to take her up on it."

Later, when Jared contacts her, Fatuma doesn't reply. I tell him she's very busy, sometimes overcommitted, and he should reach out again. He doesn't.

Now, sitting across from Renee, Jared says little as she talks about her experiences in Lewiston and lunchtime diners come and go. "I've seen a mesmerizing spirit fall over some people," Renee says. "Among the supporters, there's a glamorized view. 'The new immigrants add diversity. They're colorful. Their food is exotic.'"

Renee wants to reach out to the city's Muslims and draw them to Christianity. In this way she differs from anti-Islamists who take their positions politically. Jared may be Christian, but he's not much of a proselytizer—he stays away from religion with nonchurchgoing relatives and friends. Far more than religion, ideology underpins his sentiments.

"Renee is a zealot," Jared says with affection after she finishes her coffee and hurries off to put a roast in the oven for dinner. It's true she's a force—biblically absolute, and convinced liberalism is the wrong path. On the way to the cafeteria, Renee stopped partway through the atrium. "Look!" She spun Jared around by his shoulders. The view was an inverted reflection of the statue atop the State House dome—wisdom goddess Minerva. "How's that for a symbol of the upside-down justice in this place?" she demanded.

In the cafeteria, Jared says testimony against LD 745 felt slight. "Go ahead and add the education component, as long as it doesn't kill the bill," he says.

He muses over what he'd like to have said to the Muslims gathered upstairs. Something about Islam being a corrupt system, something like what he might have said when he went to a hearing in Auburn to oppose the opening of a Turkish-modeled charter school believed linked to a controversial imam by its opponents. But Jared, as convinced as he is, knows he's unlikely to sway Muslims. Instead, he spoke that night about taqiyya and why he believed Muslims who wanted the school were obfuscating.

Taqiyya—despite the fact that its meaning varies among religious scholars (as does its application)—Jared and Frank view it as emblematic of Islam's incompatibility with Western values. They're still pushing for ALAC, even though the bill got tabled three weeks ago after the work session. Frank emailed a woman on the judiciary committee a day later, offering his view of sharia: Under this doctrine, he wrote, "there is no freedom of religion. There is no freedom of speech. There is no freedom of thought. . . . There is no freedom of the press. . . . Justice is dualistic, with one set of laws for Muslim males and different laws for women and non-Muslims. . . . Our constitution is a man-made document of ignorance (jahiliyah) that must submit to Sharia." He didn't hear back.

Prospects for the committee recommending the bill's passage don't look good. Still, state rep Heidi Sampson told Jared it might come back, so he hasn't given up. At the moment, though, he's trained his sights on LD 745. He'll be "deeply worried about the future of this country" if it fails.

Others worry equally about what happens if the measure passes. Upstairs in the hearing room, where the committee heard testimony on other bills after FGM, emotion still runs high as the session breaks up. Talbot Ross says Fatuma's story will stay with her: "With each sentence, I experienced what she went through. I not only saw it in my mind's eye, but my body took it in." Talbot Ross tears up, remembering. FGM is "a heinous practice," she says, "but if we only think about it from a criminality perspective, we've failed. [The measure as written] amounts to pulling out a community, sensationalizing the brutalization."

That night Heather Sirocki messages Jared, thanking supporters for their letters and testimony. She includes links to the only three

New England publications that ran an Associated Press story on the hearing. "The media blackout on LD 745 is interesting," she writes. Jared thanks her profusely for sponsoring the bill. Her presentation of it, he writes, was so persuasive that "we just have to get a majority 'ought to pass' if not unanimous."

What neither of them knows is that the battle over LD 745 is far from over. It will continue much longer than next week's work session, through May and well beyond, becoming a fight over the soul of a state.

~

THE NINTH MONTH of the lunar calendar, Ramadan begins ten days earlier each year. In Lewiston, a handful of the most devout move into Masjid-A-Nur for the duration. Mostly men—but this year one woman is joining them. She'll help lead the nightly prayers and break out refreshments after salah is over and the imam has finished that evening's portion of the Quran. Each night he reads one-thirtieth.

Jamilo makes it through the fast during the second day. Yesterday she didn't drink enough before sunrise, when each day's fast begins, and wound up so thirsty from chasing the kids around that she gave in and gulped water. That meant she'd broken sawm, which calls for Muslims to abstain from food, drink, sex, profanity, and smoking from dawn to dusk. Today she succeeded: sawm as well as the requisite five salah times.

By the time she and the kids get to the Auburn IHOP around 8:30 p.m., she's hungry and very, very thirsty.

"Look the moon!" Hamzah says on the way inside. "Is a bird!" He's recently discovered sentences and practices them all day long, with exclamation points.

"No, not a bird, Hamzah," Aaliyah tells him. "And it's too far away for us to go to." She pulls the sleeve of Jamilo's baati. "What if the moon asked us, 'Do you want some money?'"

"I'd say, 'Yes, I definitely do!'"

Inside, Jamilo orders quickly and drains the ice water the waitress sets in front of her. It tastes sweet, she says, the way water does when you've been thirsty for hours.

Quesadillas at IHOP will be her iftar, the meal shared with others after the sun goes down. Ordinarily she'd join relatives, but that won't often happen this Ramadan when, yet again, they're all but estranged. As the month goes on, she'll meet up with Binto or Aspen or cook with Fatummah at the apartment. Tonight she treats Aaliyah and Hamzah to breakfast-for-dinner.

Across town, Abdikadir, Ikran and the kids sit down with family inside his mother's apartment. Fatuma won't fast because she's still breastfeeding Mohamed, but she'll cook for iftar—usually waiting to eat dinner with family members observing sawm. (Pregnant and nursing women, the sick, preadolescent kids, and the elderly don't fast.)

Since winter, some of the city's Muslims had worried Trump's orders would keep them from following through on plans to travel and spend Ramadan with family. Mostly that didn't happen. Before the month began, people drove or flew to New York, Ohio, Minnesota, London. With anticipation that stretched on for weeks, turning her usual reserve to cheerfulness then outright joy as the time came, Shukri flew to Kenya. Her parents and brothers run a store in Nairobi a lot like hers. She couldn't wait to see them. "Things here won't be like I would make," she said of leaving Mogadishu Store in the hands of her husband. "But I am going. I will go."

Was she worried about what might happen when it came time to return? No, Shukri said. "I am American citizen. Why I should be afraid?"

At IHOP, Jamilo and the kids wait for the food.

There are trips to the bathroom and to the empty side of the restaurant to let the kids count chairs. Back at the table, Aaliyah squeezes lemons into her water and mixes in one packet of sugar. Tastes it, adds another. "That's enough," Jamilo tells her. Aaliyah sips, "Mmmm, good lemonade." Hamzah keeps reaching for the syrup—"Have some shaax!" he offers, trying to pour everyone a cup. Jamilo tells him no, and no, and no, finally threatens him with time-out in the booster seat he doesn't want to use.

Relief shows on her face as the food arrives. Before the first bite, she murmurs to herself, *Bismillah* (in the name of Allah). She takes quick bites of quesadilla, hands Hamzah fries to go with his pancake.

In her fastidious way, Aaliyah cuts her egg and bacon into even pieces. She's quiet, contained. Is it hard to be the self-possessed daughter of a free-spirited mom, sister of an irrepressible brother? She spears a piece of bacon—turkey—pops it into her mouth. "Oooh," she says, unenthusiastically, before moving on to eat her eggs, with a few fries dipped in strawberry sauce. Jamilo has long since polished of her quesadillas.

Her view of Ramadan: a time of devotion to Allah and his principles, and of restraint. She'll do her best to observe sawm. She'll scrimp and send whatever little money she can back to Dagahaley. She'll work and try not to let fasting lessen her focus.

Dinner is over, the waitress paid and tipped. Kids jacketed. Outside again, Hamzah points a plump finger skyward. "Look the moon," he murmurs, but he's sleepy now, eyes half-lidded and head on Jamilo's shoulder.

"You're tired." Jamilo hugs him close. "Oh Hamzah, I'm so glad you're tired!"

Buckled inside the Versa, they head back to their small room at Fatummah's. So Ramadan begins.

~

ALAC FAILS TO make it out of the judiciary committee. Members vote to recommend "ought not to pass" to the full legislature. No real surprise to Jared and Frank, considering the committee had tabled it. But at 7–6, the measure came closer than two earlier attempts (8–1 and 9–3). They'll try again next year.

They zero in on LD 745, the FGM measure. New argument—Massachusetts and New Hampshire also have FGM legislation pending. If this bill doesn't pass, Maine could become a "vacation cutting" destination, as they believe Michigan may have for Minnesotans. Does Maine want to wind up like Michigan, they ask, passing an emergency measure after an arrest is made?

They circulate this and other tacks to their rising number of supporters. New people are seeking them out—hard to say whether it's ALAC and FGM themselves or the effect of Trump in office.

A friend from my hometown who lives in New York messages me. She's been hearing "a lot of not positive stories" from people about Lewiston. She doesn't mention the pending bills, but says someone told her Somali boys have targeted whites and beaten them up. "So I'm not sure how positive I feel about the Somali effect in Maine. I'd like to think the best, but I live in a dark world these days," she writes.

I tell her what I know—that in spite of a few isolated incidents, police say the crime rate has dropped in recent years, violent crime in particular. Later I wonder, with ALAC and the anti-FGM measure surfacing on social media, are old stories recirculating?

In Augusta, eyes are on LD 745, too. Heather Sirocki has become its crusader. She knew almost nothing about FGM until Jared approached her about sponsoring the bill. The more she learned, she says, the more urgent it seemed. Now Heather burns with what she sees as the hypocrisy of Democrats' refusal to sign on. Politics come into play with every bill—but her colleagues' refusal simply to make FGM illegal? To her it doesn't add up, especially since most Democrats strongly advocate for women's rights.

And the insistence on education alone doesn't ring true to her, either. FGM education has been occurring for years through agencies like the IRC and Maine Access Immigrant Network, she says. It should continue, but not as part of legislation. A fiscal note could kill the measure. Enact a statute to outlaw FGM in Maine, period. Codify what's already federally illegal so state district attorneys can prosecute.

She doesn't hold back from rendering public judgment. "[FGM] is CHILD ABUSE . . . It is SEXUAL ASSAULT," she posts on Facebook.

She and Jared consider angles. Heather wonders, would it help or hurt the bill's chances to bring Islam into the argument? Probably the latter, she decides: "If the perpetrators can lay claim to basing this on religion, the concern is that prosecutors will lose cases . . . as they have in the past, [because of] claims of freedom of religion."

In mid-May, the criminal justice committee votes 6–5 in favor of LD 745 along party lines. Then, after more discussion, three Democrats agree to flip if the measure includes the education amendment. So the bill moves on to the House 9–2 in favor.

Jared permits himself an exuberant email to supporters. "I will tell you that after three successive losses on ALAC this is super sweet. . . . Tons of people have taken part and contributed to this so far. . . . Thank you all." He can't help adding, "We're not done. We need to contact the House representatives, all of them. . . . Take nothing for granted and take no prisoners!"

Later he sends a follow-up. The representatives "should fear non-reelection—public outrage—if they won't protect little girls . . . Educate all you want for sure, but criminalize and get the word out in the great State of Maine that FGM is an abomination."

The machinations continue. LD 745 passes in the Senate 25–10 with strong bipartisan support. Then it fails in the House—twice. The senate majority leader collaborates with Heather to amend the bill and try a third time. That version, which reduces the severity of the crime, passes unanimously in the Senate but fails again in the House—by one vote. Heather amends it again.

Jared goes into full lion mode. "EMERGENCY ACTION REQUIRED," he emails supporters. He lists representatives who might be swayable, asks "Anyone who can contact the media and get them un-silenced?" He pleads with people who know medical professionals to seek additional testimony from anyone who may have seen evidence of FGM.

He writes to House holdouts himself: "It's time to do what is right for Maine and the country and join the other 24 states who have made this crime a crime. It's simply the righteous thing to do—and you know it."

~

BOWDOIN COLLEGE—FATUMA SITS onstage with author Anthony Doerr, musician Chuck Leavell, and Hanna Holborn Gray, president emeritus of the University of Chicago. All four are receiving honorary degrees at Bowdoin's 212th commencement. They marched together on this chilly May morning, led the college's 2017 graduates across the Quad, past rows of jubilant families, past Fatuma's own assemblage of friends and relatives. The ones on the aisle reached out to touch her hand.

The commencement gown Fatuma wears over her dirac helps her stay warm. Even so, she keeps dabbing her nose with a tissue, partly from emotion, partly from the cold she's been fighting. Her family's faces beam at her—19-year-old Safiya, 15-year-old Isaaq, 13-year-old Ilyas, 11-year-old Idris, and Muktar with Amina on his lap. Amina wears a dress that matches Fatuma's and clutches a purse containing Chapstick. The youngest kids are home with the babysitter.

Later, Isaaq will distill his mother's qualities: "determined, aware, loving," he'll say. "Brave," Safiya adds.

Yesterday in a precommencement talk to the Bowdoin community, Fatuma told a story about Isaaq, at five, coming downstairs to complain, hand on hip, that his sisters wouldn't clean his room. Fatuma set him straight, sent him back upstairs to do it himself. Now Isaaq is the tidiest of them all, she said.

Doerr won the 2014 Pulitzer Prize for Fiction. Leavell is keyboardist for the Rolling Stones and an award-winning conservationist. Gray is the first woman to become full president of a major US university. The other recipients' achievements make it all the sweeter when Fatuma—an "agent for change" whose organization "helps families navigate a complex landscape…so that the talents and abilities of Maine's immigrant community can best serve the common good"—stands for the conferring of her Doctor of Humane Letters.

Phones and cameras click and flash. People cheer. "So proud, so proud, so proud," murmurs Kiin Issa, one of Fatuma's oldest friends, beside whom I'm seated in the audience.

Tears trickle down Kiin's cheeks. "A good heart, I will love her always," Kiin says. Another close friend, Asmo, is here in spite of an illness that limits her mobility. Fatuma called her at seven a.m., asked, *Are you sure you should come? It won't be too hard for you to sit that long?* Asmo was coming. "Of course I had to be here," she says. Among them, the three women offer a glimpse of what Lewiston's future can hold. All their children over age eighteen attend or have graduated college. Asmo's daughter Rakiya—here with the others this morning—is a dual biochemistry and African American studies major.

Yesterday during her talk, Fatuma posed a question. "If you have a government and you're safe and you can actually drive to Dunkin' Donuts and get a cup of coffee without your car being blown away, if you can go to school and be whatever you want to be as long as you work hard, if you can be a little girl who has a right to her body, what else do you need?"

11

Madadaalo (Celebrations)

Late Spring–Early Summer 2017

Jamilo, Nasafari

AMID FAMILY TROUBLES, MONEY TROUBLES, MAN TROUBLES, Jamilo finds fun where she can. She settles in at Aspen's for Doritos-and-candy movie night or roams the aisles at Sam's Club, laughing as she piles twenty-pack soap and supersize shampoo into her cart. On warm afternoons, she takes the kids for a splash at Sabattus Lake.

Weddings—she loves them, the way they transport her for an evening. The way they hold out the possibility of happily-ever-after. In Lewiston, every other weekend seems to offer a Somali wedding. Jamilo goes to a lot of them—lavish events that can last days. Guest lists grow so big the bride and groom sometimes don't know everyone who comes.

In May Jamilo gets ready for a Somali wedding reception at the Gendron Franco Center, formerly St. Mary's parish. The gothic-style church was built in 1907 after parishioners overflowed St. Peter's. For decades St. Mary's thrived in the city's Little Canada. By the 1980s it was struggling: the city's population decline compounded a national drop in churchgoing. St. Mary's closed in 2000. Residents hoping to preserve the city's French Canadian heritage bought the property and turned it into a Franco American museum and cultural center.

The Gendron has become an important gathering place, especially for Lewiston residents with Quebecois roots. Paul LePage showed up here, back in the town of his boyhood the morning after his 2014 reelection as governor. The center's board hasn't limited it to Franco events though. They host concerts, plays, private parties. And they've pointedly reached out to the rising population of new immigrants. "Weddings: All Are Welcome!" a Center pamphlet proclaims. Program director Richard Martin says Somali and other African weddings have become important sources of revenue. Receptions are held in a venue called Freedom Hall.

On the evening of the wedding, Jamilo and Binto stop by their friend Mariama's apartment in Auburn. A lot of Somalis get their makeup done by Mariama for events; she's worked as a cosmetics consultant and posts YouTube how-tos. Tonight six women lounge in her bedroom, along with Aaliyah and Mariama's toddler daughter.

"Mmmm, smells nice in here," Aaliyah says—a mingling of perfume, incense, and coffee. She settles on the rug with paper and a pencil.

Jamilo lies on the bed while Mariama works on Binto. The tabletops and dresser hold more makeup than some cosmetics counters, including thirty shades of eye shadow and foundation in every skin tone. Beneath Mariama's hand, Binto transforms into another version of herself, all cheekbones and smoky eyes with gleaming fuchsia lids.

"Looking good, sister," another woman says.

Binto, a college student who usually wears little makeup, smiles wryly. "Thanks."

Aaliyah adds a tongue to a snake in a field of flowers. She erases, redraws it. Done. She sets the drawing aside and watches Mariama's magic. Auntie Binto looks so pretty!

Mariama starts on Jamilo. Aaliyah picks up a sponge and pretends to dab on foundation. In the mirror, she tilts her face left then right. "Looking good," she sings out. "Looking good good good good good!" Everyone laughs.

"Do you ever do her makeup?" someone asks Jamilo.

"Oh no, she's waaaaaay too young for all that."

Mariama burnishes Jamilo's cheeks. Colors her lids and lips. She chooses tones that go with Jamilo's yellow-and-black dirac. Yellow is this year's color at African weddings. Lisbon Street shops are selling a lot of it.

Jamilo muses over whether to wear a head covering. Sometimes women don't at weddings. She tries a black scarf, then brown, finally yellow. "How's this?" she asks. "Honestly?" another woman says. "It makes you look dark." Jamilo stares into the mirror, adjusts the scarf and wears it anyway.

Mariama turns to me. "Want me to do your makeup, Cynthia?"

I'm already wearing makeup, such as it is. A little rouge and lipstick, some eyeliner. I tell Mariama. She laughs. I'm used to being plain among Somalis, a style-bound New Englander applauded whenever I do something different: hair worn up or bright earrings—any deviation from my black-gray palette.

Tonight there's my dress, at least—voile streaked with purple and gold, a dress I didn't have this morning. I wasn't invited to the wedding, but Jamilo is close with the bride and wanted me to come. She got a ticket. Later, she handed me a bag. Yards of voile slid into my hands when I opened it. A gift, Jamilo said.

There were mere hours to turn it into a dress. Downtown, a Somali tailor shook out the fabric, gauged it between his fingers and nodded. He could work with this. Jamilo and another shopper held the voile against me. By committee it was decided I'd wear a Somali-style saat, with an underskirt. The tailor would sew both. He said something in Somali. "How long do you want it?" Jamilo asked. I pointed to midcalf, but the shopper and a clerk shook their heads. Floor-length plus, they said. With a short train.

It was fun to be getting dressed up for the wedding. "Does he need to measure me?" I asked. "No," the clerk said—"he knows." I could come back in an hour. I wouldn't have believed it, except that I'd seen another tailor sew a kameez in minutes and watched garments stack up beside Brenda's machine at Shukri's.

Ninety minutes later I was back in my room. The saat, when I tried it, was a foot too long. Women adjust the length by tucking fabric into the waistband of their underskirt, often storing a wallet or phone among the folds. Not easy—I tucked and gathered but couldn't make it work. Eventually, I used a long necklace as a belt. So much for the train.

At 7:45 p.m., as they're leaving Mariama's, Jamilo tells Aaliyah she's dropping her off. "Where, Mama?" Aaliyah asks. At Aspen's, Jamilo tells her. Aaliyah says she wants to stay with Jamilo.

"Aspen's waiting," Jamilo says. "It's only for a night."

Aaliyah keeps protesting, but mildly, in the way of someone who knows no matter what she says it will happen anyhow. She and Hamzah get moved around a lot.

Outside it's so quiet you can hear the nearby Androscoggin on the rocks. Dark, too—forms on a nearby porch materialize as people only after someone stands and stretches. The hilly neighborhood feels isolated compared with other parts of L-A. Binto hurries to Jamilo's car. "Oooooh, come on. Let's go!"

Aaliyah settles into her booster, pulls a blanket over her lap. Sleep comes quickly; by the time her mother rounds the corner and pulls onto Main Street, Aaliyah is gone.

Jamilo announces there will be a short detour on the way to the wedding. She tunes the sound system to Somali pop, Bluetoothed from her phone, and unrolls her window. Besides bringing Aaliyah to Aspen, she needs to stop at Yussuf's to loan Binto a dress from clothes stored there. Will he be home? Will he mind that she's coming? None of that worries her much tonight.

She drives down Main Street, windows wide to the warm night. Jamilo and Binto are close, old friends—no need for talk. They've known each other since "before boobs and periods," Jamilo says. Ease flows between them.

Over the years Jamilo has earned a reputation for generosity among her friends. What she has, she gives. Now, as she struggles, they're reaching out. Binto and Aspen, especially, help her a lot. Next month for Eid, knowing Jamilo is broke, Binto will take her to Portland to get their nails done. The next day Binto will spend hours putting braids in Aaliyah's hair.

We coast past the always-lit antiques store with its Roseville- and Tiffany-filled windows, across Androscoggin Great Falls, white-foamed in the moonlight. Then a right along Lincoln to the Franco Center. The reception has already started. Jamilo dashes inside to check whether we need tickets in hand to enter. Yes. So she heads across town to the bride's family's house beneath the spires of the basilica, where Congolese and Djiboutian Catholics boost attendance at one of the state's last remaining masses in French.

On her way out of the triple-decker, tickets in hand, Jamilo sidesteps a crew of neighbors drinking beer and smoking. "Hey, hey, can I ask you something?" a man calls out. Jamilo smiles, keeps moving. Back behind the wheel she nudges up the volume of the music, a cross between techno and scaled-back Bollywood. Aaliyah sleeps on.

The Versa flies out of the city and into the woods. The chirp of spring peepers comes through the open windows during the quieter parts of songs. Jamilo drives uphill and out to Yussuf's apartment in Tall Pines. She's doing this for Binto, who could wear something she owns but prefers not to show up in a dress she's used before.

Driving to Yussuf's brings up his name. Did I know that the woman he's seeing was at the makeup party? I did not. Yep, Jamilo says, the woman with the iced coffee. Her family and his are encouraging an arranged marriage. She shakes her head. Binto, not a big talker but direct, remains silent for a while. Then says quietly, "He likes the ones who don't really like him back."

I ask, Then why is he with her? The elders set it up, they tell me. The woman's mother says her daughter is just shy. The love will grow. And honestly? Jamilo's just glad it's not her they're focused on right now.

Talk turns to Jamilo's time in Providence. "I never wanted her to leave Lewiston, but she just had to," Binto says.

"I'm glad I did," Jamilo says.

Binto shrugs. After their decade-plus of friendship, she's used to Jamilo's independence and to her sometimes impulsive decisions. But also, Binto has said: "Caring and loving, energetic, positive. Always there when you need her."

Yussuf's not home—Jamilo's relieved. She and Binto run inside. I stay with Aaliyah, who's still asleep. Light from the streetlamp angles across her booster. Bits of glitter from the makeup party fleck her face. Then they're back, Binto dressed in a floral saat she chose from among Jamilo's things. We cross the outskirts of town to Aspen's apartment. Jamilo's been close with her since elementary school, too—she rarely loses a friendship. Aspen was her first white friend; now they're like sisters—two single moms raising kids and in touch every day. Aspen converted to Islam a few years ago; it's clear she looks to Jamilo for how to be Muslim in Maine.

Jamilo cradles Aaliyah up the steps and hands her to Aspen at the door. Behind the wheel again, Jamilo grins. Bumps the music up some more. "Now for some fun!"

They get to the reception in time for the salad course, stopping for selfies in front of the Franco Center on the way inside. Freedom Hall is done up in pink and white: tablecloths, balloons, garlands of little lights. A pink bow adorns each chair, all two hundred-plus of which are filled. The place might be even more crowded if the couple were Bantu; in Lewiston, at least, Bantu weddings often don't require formal invites. News of the wedding travels by social media and word of mouth. Guests dress up and show up.

On a platform at the front of the room, the bride sits on a throne-like chair, relatives and friends alongside. Tradition calls for the groom to arrive later. This part of the wedding is the aroos. It celebrates the bride and groom plus—and perhaps more important—both extended families, who occupy several packed tables. The nikah, during which the couple actually wed, took place earlier, Jamilo says. The bride's father gave final consent, signaling the family's merger with the groom's. An elder drew up a marriage contract. The groom recited vows from the Quran in front of witnesses, and the elder blessed the union.

The marriage wasn't arranged—"She married for love," Jamilo says approvingly, longingly—but getting to this night required a lot of effort.

The groom and members of his family visited the bride's parents and asked permission to wed their daughter. The family considered the proposal, said yes. The daughter already had agreed, Jamilo says—but because Somalis view marriage as having major financial and social implications, parental approval matters a lot. Few marriages go forward without it. Both sides negotiated how much the groom's family would pitch in for the wedding. The bride's family planned the events for months.

Even after the aroos, the wedding won't be over. There's no post-reception whisk-away for a honeymoon—tradition calls for something else. The bride will return to her family for several days, while community members stop by to congratulate the new couple. Finally, after that, they'll get their first night alone.

Binto and Jamilo squeeze in at a table, embrace friends, take another round of photos in various permutations. The rest of dinner is an American-style buffet. Jamilo eats a little, drains a glass of fruit punch. She's here to party—without alcohol—not so much to eat. Noise and heat levels rise. Dressed-up kids run around, reaching for balloons until parents rein them in.

Someone loves Jamilo's dirac, a couple of others the yellow headscarf. She smiles, vindicated.

A musician in a bow tie and top hat sings to the bride. Jamilo translates: "I hope Allah blesses you with a lot of children.... That you have money and a comfortable home.... I hope you stay together forever." He's a Somali-style crooner—meant for the cross-generational appeal called for by weddings. From Minnesota, he emcees a lot of events around the country and is famous enough that most Somalis know of him.

As soon as the music starts, Jamilo gets up and joins other women on the lighted floor. Binto and I stay seated. It will be another hour before I trust my dress not to loosen from its cinch. Some women will beckon me to dance with them in a loose circle. The dress will swish and flow, no mishap.

Jamilo steps into a cluster of friends, gives someone a hug and lets go into the music. Now the night has begun for real. A fog machine exhales. The music picks up. A woman lets out a long trilling ululation. Another woman echoes her, then a third. Women dance in pairs and in groups that expand and contract.

A few men lean against the big bartender-less bar in the back of the room, sipping from water bottles or holding cups of tea or punch. A couple of them sway a little to the music. None looks too excited. Some men sit at reception tables but mostly women occupy these. So far, no men are on the dance floor.

After a few songs Jamilo returns to the table, face flushed from the exertion. She nudges Binto. "Go dance!" Binto does not. Jamilo wonders aloud: "Where is the groom? Shouldn't he be here by now?" Ever-attuned to drama, she conjectures that he and the bride may have had an argument. Everything's probably fine, Binto tells her. He'll be coming soon. Jamilo nods assent. She pours water, gulps it, heads off to dance again.

The emcee intersperses aroos traditions. A unity dance brings together both newly joined families—everyone else clears the floor. In a ceremony known as shaash saar, all the married women symbolize welcome of the new wife among them by each passing a scarf over her head and gifting it to her.

Still no groom. Late in the evening the bride disappears too—probably just to put on a new outfit, says Binto. At Somali weddings, brides often change several times during the evening. She'll be back, Binto says. Jamilo dances on.

The music pauses again. People stop talking, look around—what's next? Jamilo returns to the table. At last the groom appears, from the entryway, the bride beside him. She's traded her diaphanous guntiino for a white wedding gown. She carries white roses, her eyes cast down and lips parted in a slight smile. The two make their slow way down an aisle between the tables. Guests raise their phones, keep them aloft in a universal cell salute until, a thousand photos later, the couple reaches the front.

Jamilo shakes her head, mutters something under her breath. Then, audibly: "She's supposed to look like she's shy for this part. I don't like that."

It does seem puzzling—the suddenly diffident bride, the contrast with her earlier ebullience and the power of the ululating women who surrounded her. Women have exuded strength and joy all night long while men stood on the periphery. When I made it to the dance floor, it was like being in a sea of energy.

Years ago, during early interviews with refugees in Lewiston, I anticipated passive, subjugated women and girls. Everything I'd absorbed about Islam suggested this. But in Lewiston, at least, that didn't hold. Many Muslim women worked; some, Muna and Shukri among them, ran successful businesses. Within a short time, girls routinely graduated from high school and went off to college. And women who stayed home often seemed to head their families.

At times I wondered whether strong Somali American women pretended men were the leaders to maintain a semblance of cultural convention. But then I'd think that couldn't be true. Almost every Somali I knew strongly identified as Muslim, and the teachings of the Quran and the Hadith call for separate, highly gendered spheres. Women manage the household, yet place below men in almost every other way. Is an event like the aroos dominated by women simply because they planned it? Because it represents a pinnacle of the domestic realm?

I'm still not sure what to think. In Lewiston, the power of Somali and other Muslim women is not illusory. Fatuma, for instance—her agency has remained among the most visible nonprofits in Lewiston for years. When she speaks, people pay attention. Yet, in mentioning how Muktar sometimes takes care of the kids while she works, Fatuma says this isn't something they talk much about among other Somalis. And Jamilo still tells the story of the day Mustafa reprimanded her on the sidewalk outside a barbershop. She had smiled at the barber and asked him, in Somali, to give Hamzah a great haircut for his birthday. Mustafa, who doesn't speak Somali, said he felt humiliated.

At the reception, men finally join the women on the lit-up floor. The music drives harder, the dancing gets more sultry. Couples dance together, lines form and break. Jamilo shimmies alongside other women.

Abdikadir has shown up late, alone, as he was at Heidi's potluck, at Refugee Day and film night—appearances that increasingly seem as political as they are social. He doesn't dance. Wherever he goes now, he strikes me as envoy—between Bantus and ethnic Somalis, between Somalis and whites, between the new-immigrant community and longtime Lewistonians. Always he sidesteps questions about when he's going to run for office, and for what. A local position? Abdikadir, diplomatically: "I wouldn't want to compete with people I know who are already doing a great job." So, state? He'll smile, shrug. Not ready to say.

At the aroos, he greets people, congratulates the bride's and groom's families, and then goes home.

The music ends. The aroos is over—a success. But when Jamilo climbs the stairs and heads for her car, she walks into the middle of a fight. It turns out the woman Yussuf is seeing loves Jamilo's younger brother—actually her cousin, but they grew up together and so, in the fluid Somali way, she calls him brother. He and the woman were in a corner of the parking lot, talking. The woman's sister saw. The sister took off one of her high heels, started hitting him with it. Now she's shouting at them both. Guests exiting the wedding look away or circle closer, depending on their taste for spectacle.

Jamilo tries to break things up. "Go home, now!" she commands her brother. The sister curses. Jamilo curses back. It's the angriest I've ever seen her. She's not even that close to him she'll later say—he's sided with the aunts and uncles in pressuring her—but "family is family."

"Go home, please," Jamilo begs. And again. He doesn't budge. Jamilo retreats to her car. She drives me back to my room, telling herself the fight didn't ruin the aroos; it was still a good party and the bride and groom, when they finally got together, seemed happy. Later she'll circle back to the parking lot, find her brother and take him with her to McDonald's for a burger. She can't control his heart, she knows, but she urges him: For everyone's sake, stay away from Yussuf's woman!

On Monday she's back in her routine—looking after the kids, training for her new job. Out of a sense of urgency, she meets with Fatuma Hussein's assistant to get help finding an apartment. "Well, I guess this means I have a caseworker now," she tells me afterward, without enthusiasm. Assistance is one thing, the oversight that comes with it another.

The help turns out to be unnecessary. In the end, as with so many things, Jamilo advocates for herself. She goes to an apartment complex in Auburn where a couple of her friends live. Close to Walmart and IHOP and Sam's Club. She really needs a place for herself, her daughter, and her son, she tells the woman who manages the complex. And she needs it soon. She has $1,100—enough for first month's $800 rent and part of the deposit. Is there any chance she could pay the rest of the deposit in installments?

The woman says yes. Jamilo can move in a month. It's a nice place, two bedrooms and a deck, a kitchen with a dishwasher. And outside, a tree-shaded yard with a sandbox. Now she just has to get through the next few weeks.

~

THE FIRST SOMALI Bantus graduated from LHS in 2009, one girl and three boys, Jamilo's ex-husband Yussuf among them. "I have never dreamt myself to be one of those graduates from high school, because there was no Somali Bantu who ever graduated from high school in Maine," Yussuf told a *Sun Journal* reporter a week after commencement. He'd lived in the US for four years.

Ethnic Somalis had graduated from LHS before. But most Bantu kids arrived in Lewiston below grade level, with little English. Still, the focus on education was fierce. Many parents pushed their kids to learn English quickly so they'd place out of the ELL classes that granted no core credits toward graduation. Abdikadir coached or tutored all four of the 2009 graduates. "The parents knew, and the kids figured it out, you need education to make it in the United States," he says. Integration and education—these are Abdikadir's refrains.

The LHS Class of 2017 holds sixty-one African-immigrant graduates—from nations including Somalia, Congo, South Africa, Burundi, Sudan, Rwanda, Angola, and Djibouti. Twenty other students are shy a few credits and during the coming year will be "superseniors" slated to graduate next June. According to Superintendent Webster, the new-immigrant graduation rate now exceeds that of the student body overall. This year Zamzam Mohamud, who arrived in Lewiston sixteen years ago with $40 and two young children, will give the keynote address.

On graduation day, Nasafari's house flurries with preparations. Kamakazi orchestrated everything—cleaned and ironed and cooked while Norbert worked his shifts at Pioneer. Savory smells overlay the house's usual lemony scent. Plantains Kamakazi fried earlier cool on the counter. Fufu and beans sit on the stove. Chicken wings in the fridge. Norbert just got home from work, with a stop for dish soap along the way and orange soda for those who'll come by later. No caffeine or nicotine or alcohol in this house, but the family is still known for throwing a good party.

Where did the time go? Nasafari needs to be at graduation in twenty-five minutes, the rest of the family shortly after that. Upstairs, Kamakazi pulls out dresses and shoes, fixes Christina's hair. Christina squeals as Kamakazi combs and clips. Kamakazi murmurs in Kinyamulenge: "Come now, Christina, it doesn't hurt that much."

Moses dashes in and out of the house, announcing to passersby that today his sister graduates, before coming back inside to see who's ready yet. He ferries lotions and brushes to her sisters and his mother, gives progress updates. *Christina is dressed... Mom's in the shower now... Nasafari is almost ready; she's putting on her cap and gown.* A cousin visiting from Rwanda nods and laughs from her seat on the sofa; her English isn't fluent, but the excitement transcends language.

Today happens, too, to be Moses's birthday. He's turning twelve. His celebration will come tonight, after the ceremony at the Colisee—the city's largest venue, the same place Ali knocked out Liston—where almost all the three thousand seats will be taken.

Moses likes to keep track of things. He's worrying about who has the tickets—a coveted ten per student, in many cases not enough for the extended family—when Nasafari descends the stairs. She wears high heels, makeup, and a crimson dress bought with money she earned at TJ Maxx.

Her eyes go straight to her dad, sitting on the sofa with the cousin. The past and the future merge into this moment. Norbert stays quiet for a few seconds, looks as though he might cry. "Wow" is all he says. During the coming evening he'll twice remark that Nasafari was just a little girl Christina's age when they bought this condo. And here she is, grown up.

He remains silent a few seconds more, then speaks to Nasafari in Kinyamulenge. "What about the gold makeup you're wearing around your eyes? Will it rub off and hurt you?"

Nasafari laughs, the moment over. "Don't worry, Dad, it's fine," she tells him—she's got to go or she'll be late. "See you there," she says before leaving with her friend Ada, who's already graduated and came over to help.

On the girls' way out, the next-door neighbor crosses the shared deck, blond toddler propped on her hip. "Ohhhh congratulations, Nasafari!" She'll be at the party later, she says. The two families are close—the woman's husband is Norbert's best friend and the guy he got to take over as condo association president when Norbert grew too pressed for time.

Forty minutes later the family finally is seated at the Colisee, in a row Nabega arrived early with Azaleah to save. Norbert heaves a sigh. Perspiration dots his forehead. They made it—after the processional and the principal's welcome, but in time for the national anthem. He looks around, takes everything in. "Wow, those are beautiful," he says of the balloon arches, of the gowned graduates and dressed-up families around them. Nasafari is there, among her classmates. Their backs are to us; it's hard to tell whether she's the girl near the front or the one in the fifth row.

The ceremony brings the mix of joy and tedium that typifies graduations. But this is Lewiston, rebounding from decades of population drain, now home to one of the highest new-immigrant concentrations in the nation, so the messages of opportunity and hope resonate differently.

School superintendent Webster tells the graduates how important they are to the city. Maintain contact with us, he urges. "We look forward to your coming back." He doesn't say, "to live here for good"—but that seems implied. Later, Webster tells me that's exactly what he hopes. Lewiston needs these kids to put down roots, lifelong Mainers and new immigrants alike.

The class advisor, urging graduates to reach out for help and avoid "going it alone," calls on a student to translate her remarks into Somali. Then the class president begins her address. "Hard to hear," Norbert says—a subpar PA system and chattering kids in the section next to ours. There's a hissing sound in the seats behind. "Someone needs to shut those kids up," a woman says.

Her harshness makes me turn around. She's white, as are her seatmates; the kids who are talking are Somali. "They're so disrespectful," another woman says. If Norbert and Kamakazi hear the comments, they don't show it. Some Burundian friends show up. Kamakazi points out a few available seats, above, and the family climbs to take them.

The ceremony continues. The chatter from the adjacent section rises and falls. The people behind mutter. Finally it's the keynote. "It is not where you start, but how high you aim," Zamzam Mohamud tells the graduates to loud cheers and applause. It's still Ramadan, so many here are fasting, but that doesn't dim the enthusiasm. The graduates will face challenges, Zamzam says, but "you will get better at it every time life throws you a curve... Be hopeful, be grateful, be respectful, and be proud of yourselves."

The heat in the Colisee keeps rising. Another speaker replaces Zamzam. Moses and Christina fidget. Moses asks, "Dad, can I get a drink?"

"No." Instead Norbert amuses the kids by showing them how he's teaching Azaleah, on his lap, to baby-high-five. He puts his palm out, she pats it. They laugh. Again. They laugh. It gets hotter.

At last it's diploma time. Student after student ascends the stage. Nasafari's friend Sadio receives hers, as does one of Jamilo's cousins. So do kids who went through the Tree Street Youth program—more than fifty, all of whom got a college offer or found a job.

The people behind us cheer wildly when their graduate's turn comes. "Okay, let's go," one of them says after the boy sits down again. The whole group gets up and leaves as names continue to be called.

When at last Nasafari's is announced, the normally quiet Kamakazi rises from her seat. She stands and claps, keeps clapping. This is her moment, too. In Congo, Kamakazi got to attend school for only three years. Now her daughter is graduating from high school and going on to college. Two seats down, Norbert leans forward and watches her, his face opening like a flower. Nasafari descends the stairs, too far to really see her family. She waves in their direction, blows a kiss.

Afterward, against a backdrop of reddening sky and the outline of the basilica, the family groups for photos. All of them together, the kids, women only, extended family and friends, Nasafari diva-like in pose after pose with classmates. The sun sinks to the horizon and lingers, as if reluctant to go. Jamilo's here, checking in with her cousin and a few younger friends, and so is Abdikadir. Pretty much the whole new-immigrant community turns out for commencement; everyone knows at least one graduate.

Dark finally comes, the photos grainy now. A few last hugs with classmates, and Nasafari heads home with Ada and her best friend Farhiya. Upstairs in her room, she hangs up the crimson dress, changes into sweats and a T-shirt. Formality over—now it's family time and Moses's celebration.

Downstairs, the doorbell keeps chiming. Half the kids eating pizza with Moses around the dining table are black, the rest are white. The next-door neighbor who congratulated Nasafari earlier sips an orange Fanta; her husband stayed home with their sleeping kids. Other family friends crowd close as Norbert positions a birthday cake in front of Moses.

Meanwhile, at Sadio's family's apartment on Knox Street, relatives are sandwiched into the sofas and seated on the floor. Everyone is hungry and very thirsty, especially after the effort of cheering their way through graduation. Sadio's mom fried sambusas the minute she got home. People drain water bottles and pass the food. Apart from the murmuring of a baby, it's mostly quiet. This is how iftar goes: a concentrated silence as people fill their bellies, then socializing into the night.

Tonight's gathering is bittersweet, the happiness of Sadio's successful graduation dampened by the knowledge that her mom has decided to go back to Kenya, at least for three months and possibly for good. She misses Africa—she single-parented three daughters to adulthood in the US, but Lewiston has never really felt like home. She struggled to learn English, never adjusted to the cold. Sadio has, she says, a sense of "facing my future on my own" in spite of the fact that she'll still live with a sister.

At ten p.m. Sadio stands up. She's going out, she tells her family. A cross-country teammate who graduated last year came back to Lewiston just to see her get her diploma. Now they're going to meet up with other graduates. It's Sadio's Somali self making way for her American one.

"Happy birthday, dear Moses, happy birthday to you," everyone sings at Nasafari's house while Moses looks down, clearly thrilled and suddenly bashful. Norbert hands him a knife, tells him to cut the big cake. Flanked by Ada and Farhiya, Nasafari watches, gold makeup still aglitter.

12

Summer 2017

Fatuma, Jamilo

AFTER FOUR TRIES, THE FGM BILL DIES IN THE HOUSE. DURING the months supporters kept it going, it gained traction on social media. Wherever news of it posted, reaction was visceral. Comments by people who likely weren't aware of the bill's context or its association with ACT piled up: "I'm mortified that anyone would not support this... Breaks my heart." "Can't believe this keeps failing. What is going on at the State House?" "The bill must pass if there's a chance of FGM happening in Maine."

Actress and former Mainer Kelly Carlson rebuked the ACLU. "Shockingly," Carlson said in an online video, "the American Civil Liberties Union opposes the bill, stating... 'The risk of mutilation is not worth expanding Maine's criminal code.' Well, I couldn't disagree with that more."

"People are so angry that this bill failed," Heather will later say in an online interview. "I've never seen anything like it. I have never had so many phone calls and emails as this."

In Lewiston, most refugees didn't know about LD 745, but those who did opposed it. For months no one really thought it stood a chance. One day I was eating lunch with Fatuma at a restaurant near her office. The tricounty district attorney stopped by the table. "That bill is going to die," he told her. Not to worry.

But by the end, Fatuma and others were worried. After weeks of uncertainty—*Can Sirocki get those last few votes? Will the bill get pushed through the House?*—Fatuma can relax, for now.

Jared believes Democrats falsely cast LD 745 as a hate bill, and that's why it failed. He and Frank console each other; the vote couldn't have been closer. The next round will be a win. Because Heather can't submit the same bill in 2018, they mull over alternatives: an appeal to the governor in hopes he'll put forth the measure himself or maybe, Jared says, "a referendum that would draw in the media and expose the hypocrisy of the Democrats."

Heather, who tells people she now carries the issue of FGM "close to my heart," says she would help with the ballot initiative. "I won't give up on this," she says.

My perspective on the bill has shifted. In the beginning, I was opposed. Immigrant-run nonprofits do much to educate women about their rights—and their daughters' rights—to physical and emotional well-being. FGM, newcomers are told, fundamentally violates those rights. That seemed to me the best approach. In recent years I'd heard nothing about FGM occurring in Maine. Earlier rumors of girls being taken or sent to Africa had stopped circulating.

Then Jamilo mentioned a conversation she'd overheard in Kennedy Park. A newly arrived refugee mentioned FGM and was told it was illegal, period. That countered opponents' education-only argument that legislation might push the practice underground. The fact that the Maine Prosecutors Association favored codification of a state law seemed relevant, too.

Around that time, the bill's supporters presented MaineCare data showing providers had sought reimbursement in eight instances under three FGM-specific codes—although it wasn't clear for what and could have been treatment of long-term complications. Also, the Maine Department of Health and Human Services had sent out a memo reminding mandated reporters that FGM was child abuse, and as such must be disclosed. Why, if there was no chance of it occurring?

By June I'm torn about the bill—don't want the Somali community hurt but don't want any girl hurt.

Jamilo has a hard time saying no when Aaliyah asks for shoes. There's a reason for this. Jamilo wrote about an older cousin trying to help her after she was infibulated: "She got warm water. Without touching my pained area, she poured the warm water. Felt so much pain. Tears down my cheek! I just want to be a girl and would love a pretty white dress once I heal and shoes that fit better than the ones I wear! They have holes in them."

Aaliyah's many shoes are lined up in a cubby of their apartment—pairs of sneakers, flip-flops and jellies, boots and slippers, patent leathers. She will have what Jamilo didn't, and she will be protected.

~

MY MOTHER COMES to Maine, partly to visit, partly to figure out where she's going to live if she leaves Florida. Her memory seems a little worse, but she resists going to a neurologist. At the first assisted-living place she agrees to look at, she fumbles when the director asks who's president. "I know I don't care for him," she says and then, "I see that orange hair." Later in the parking lot she'll be embarrassed, and affronted that the director quizzed her. "Of course I know who Trump is. But that man put me on the spot."

Before we even get into the car, she dismisses the place. "Just not for me," Mom says. And thanks, but no need to check out anywhere else. She pulls herself up to her full four feet ten inches. Her white bob shines in the sun. She's ready, she says, to go to lunch.

My sister and I aren't crazy about the place either. As nice as it is, with big gardens and vaulted ceilings, it still feels institutional. But if not assisted living, then what? We both have full-time jobs and, in spite of what we might wish, living year-round with Mom in one of our homes seems unlikely to work out, unless we're willing to do things her way. Yet—for the second summer in a row, she does seem mellowed. Staying with me, she invites the cat onto her lap, even though he sheds a lot. She's more open, less critical. When we go to Lewiston, instead of complaining about the air-conditioning in the café where she works her crosswords, she finds a sunny table.

One afternoon we stop in at Baraka. She and Mohamed take up where they left off—the beaches they love: his Mogadishu, hers Sarasota. Warm climates. She asks about his family. Watching them, I marvel. She's usually not that outgoing, and for the first two years I knew him, Mohamed didn't have a lot to say. Such is the nature of chemistry.

"Are you hungry, Mom?" he asks.

"I think I might be," she says. Another first—she's a fussy eater, rarely agrees to a new restaurant, especially one that might serve her something spicy.

We settle into a table in the back. Beside us three teenaged boys consume one of Ardo's platters of food. My mother smiles. "You were hungry!"

One of the kids laughs. "Yeah, we basically inhaled it."

While Ardo prepares food, Mohamed joins us. "So how have you really been," he asks. "How is it for you in Florida?"

My mom looks at him a while. "I love it there, but I wish my girls were nearer. It may be time for a change." My eyes sting. So true, so complicated. When I pray, this is something I pray about. I've forgiven her for leaving us those years ago, but all the lost time—and the fact that she can be difficult—means I'm not as close with her as I was with my dad.

"I do have a home in Florida. Where I lived with my husband," my mother says.

"Yes, but it's not good to be too much alone." Mohamed taps his head. "Not good for the mind. You know?" He tells the story of Ardo's mother, who languished after a stroke until they moved her in with Ardo's sister. Now she's talking and laughing, "because she has so many people around her. She can help a little. She feels useful."

The platter arrives, sautéed beef with cardamom-spiced rice and salad dressed in Ranch. My mom digs in. Loves the rice—best she's had, she says. The beef disappears, the salad. Mohamed orders tea for all of us, keeps talking. "You know, Mom, you had a life in Florida, and you could have a new life in Maine." She listens, nods. He leaves the table to ring up someone's purchases.

When Mohamed returns, she says, "I think you're right. It's time to accept that I need more help, even if I don't really want to."

I'm stunned—it's the first time I've heard her acknowledge this.

"That's right," Mohamed says. He pulls out his phone. "Let's get a selfie, Mom." They're both beaming in the photo he takes.

On the way out, he waves away my credit card. "No money," he says. "You and Mom are family."

A few days later when I see Mohamed, my mother isn't with me. "Will your mom live with you when she leaves Florida?" he asks. There it is, finally. I hesitate. I tell him I don't know.

"Somalis don't put our parents in a home," Mohamed says.

It's not the first time I've felt vaguely judged by the city's new immigrants—and self-conscious—about my Western ways. *Why does my son live in New York, far from the rest of the family? Why do Americans need homes with so many rooms? Why do women wait so long to have children?*

For a couple of weeks I fantasize about my mother living with us. She could garden, help out in the kitchen, visit with her grandchildren.

But she doesn't remain the way she was early in the visit. The chicken I grill one night is dry, the next morning's oatmeal lumpy. And the cat, actually—can't we do something about his shedding?

My fantasy evaporates. Mom's back to her old self. And she keeps resisting change. She doesn't need help, she says. And in any case, assisted living is out—she will not live in a place with people she doesn't know. With people who depend on those around them. She's going to stay in her home in Sarasota—that's where she's happiest.

When she goes back to Florida at the end of the month, I miss her but also feel relief.

~

DOWNTOWN LEWISTON FEELS different during Ramadan. Some of the Somali stores close, so it's quieter during the day. The streets come to life at nightfall. Kids on bikes swoop down Lisbon Street, past women out picking up a few last items for iftar. Later, people head to the mosque for the special prayers of tarawiy, believed more powerful when offered in congregate. On warm evenings, families linger in Kennedy Park. Kids pump the swings, higher, higher, toes almost touching the Milky Way until their mothers call for them to give it up.

One night Jamilo winds up having iftar at her uncle's house. She goes over to pick up Aaliyah and Hamzah—her childcare situation is dicey enough that she's been asking her family for help again. The adults have just started eating. Hospitality means she's invited to join without being asked. Good manners mean she should.

She sits down with them on the living room rug. Drains a cup of water, eats some stewed goat.

Wallahi, it's uncomfortable. Usually conversation rises in the relief of slaked thirst and a full belly. But tonight no one says much. No one, in fact, says anything directly to Jamilo unless she speaks first. Right now, this is as good as it gets.

The kids, meanwhile, seem oblivious of the tension. They ate earlier. Seven of them race around the house—some version of chase. Aaliyah comes in breathless and laughing, leans against the wall. She's wearing a flowered skirt rolled up at the waist and a striped T-shirt. Jamilo takes this in, opens her mouth and closes it, says nothing. She and Aaliyah are both particular about Aaliyah's appearance; her clothes fit perfectly, color-matched, socks just so. Dirt on the knees of leggings? Change them. Jamilo can't imagine what happened to her daughter's lavender dress.

Rested, Aaliyah goes back out to the kitchen and her cousins. They dig into a flat of strawberries still dripping with rinse water. Gone in one minute.

Jamilo locates Aaliyah's dress in a bedroom, slips it into a bag. "Mahad sanid," she says on her way out with the kids. *Thanks for the babysitting, thanks for the meal.* Her aunt nods. Aaliyah plucks their shoes from the overflowing rack by the door.

On the twenty-sixth day of Ramadan, an imam at the Portland mosque finds a handwritten note in the mail: "Muslim, I will enjoy the sight of the blood of you and your fellow vermin running into the streets. It will be a great experience come August. Life will never be the same again."

Police call it a hate crime and open an investigation. The note came from outside the US; detectives won't say where. The imam and the mosque president downplay the incident—the sender likely saw too many anti-Islam messages on TV. They're comfortable in Maine, they say, with good relations. Most of the mosque's five hundred members agree. With their backing, the imam continues to leave the doors open through the final days of Ramadan, so people can come anytime and pray.

Three days after the Portland incident, worshippers stream into the Lisbon Street mosque. After the service people will murmur on the sidewalk about the hate-crime investigation, but now it's about tarawiy. Could tonight be al-Qadr, the Night of Power? Excitement always builds as Ramadan nears an end. The last ten evenings are special, more so the odd-numbered ones and al-Qadr most of all. Muslims believe Allah blesses the Night of Power more than any other. The veil between heaven and earth thins, and prayers count more than those of a thousand months.

No one knows when al-Qadr will occur—even after it's come and gone. People say Allah offers hints: an unusually azure sky, an unseasonable storm, a strange tranquility. Describing this, a man smiles. "You have to say it's a good way of getting people to go to the masjid."

This particular evening, the twenty-ninth of Ramadan, could well be it. Inside a mosque bathroom, women use a footbath. A big mop stands ready in case of splashes. The room smells of soap and smoky-sweet oud perfume.

Long nights at the mosque during Ramadan draw the city's most observant Muslims. Everyone celebrates Eid—much as nearly everyone of Christian background celebrates Christmas—but throughout the year far fewer abide by each Islamic custom or routinely go to mosque. Still, even the less overtly religious seem to hold their faith close. Jamilo, who's home tonight with the kids, often mentions Allah in conversation. Her most deeply held belief is personal: without Allah, she wouldn't have survived to make it to America. She sees herself as an imperfect Muslim who keeps trying: *If others judge me, that's their problem. Only Allah sees all.*

Masjid A-Nur is a humble row house that fronts on Lisbon and backs onto Canal Street. Women pray in the finished basement, men on the first floor and sometimes the second. (Women typically attend mosque less often.) Kids have dugsi classes on the third. Right now, men spending the final days of Ramadan here have taken over the third floor, stacking prayer rugs as beds.

Apart from the chance that tonight is al-Qadr, it's special too because the final thirtieth of the Quran will be read aloud, marking the end of Ramadan. A leader lines up women shoulder to shoulder. Every inch counts—the room will be packed.

The imam's voice over the PA system intones the first prayer cycle. "Allah Akbar . . ." Everyone bows at the waist, hands to knees, straightens. Then they drop to their knees with a collective sigh, rest foreheads on the carpet. The women's backs—diracs, hijabs, shaashes—merge into a mosaic.

The basement door opens and closes, opens. Women keep coming. I recognize a few as moms, probably late from finishing iftar and putting kids to bed. Better some prayer than none. They shuck off flip-flops and sneakers, go to the footbath or directly join the others.

Half an hour later, after many cycles—a break. Everyone relaxes cross-legged or stretches out their legs. A few sit in chairs alongside older women who've done salah seated. The imam begins to read the last section of the Quran, in Arabic. In the rear of the room, three girls play tic-tac-toe in a notebook and whisper. One doodles a face that might be her own. Two others get up and return with water. It's warm in the basement and getting warmer.

Occasionally the kids' voices rise or there's too much activity. An adult turns, and the kids quiet. The older woman who's been living all month at the mosque, Habo, doesn't turn. She's absorbed, eyes closed but scanning behind her lids as if she's reading along.

Two hours later, after more prayer and the final verses, Habo moves through the crowded room handing out dates and tea. Women laugh and chat and hug one another. They embrace Habo, too. *Congratulations!*—her long nights at the masjid are nearly over.

Was this the Night of Power? Were the gates to Paradise open? No one will ever know. Women sent up their most closely held prayers, in case.

Sunday brings Eid at last. Jamilo and the kids are up before 5:00 a.m. By 5:15, she's posted a photo of Aaliyah in a black abaya and Hamzah in kameez. This year Lewiston has two Eid services—the one at the Armory and another in the Ramada Inn ballroom. Jamilo opts for the latter, as do many other Somali Bantus. She promises Aaliyah and Hamzah she'll take them someplace fun afterward if they're good.

They're good. They sit, atypically quiet, beside Jamilo on the carpet. The ballroom fills. Kids climb around them in the crowded space to reach pitchers of ice water along a wall. Then they're back for more ice water. Soon parents are stepping around Jamilo and Aaliyah and Hamzah to take their kids to the bathroom. Abdikadir and Ikran are here with all four children, plus his parents and the rest of the family—close to forty people. Abdikadir wears white shoes and a suit jacket over his kameez. Carries Jaseem tucked against his hip.

Salah resembles tarawiy at the mosque, but fewer prayer cycles, different readings, and far more people—all dressed up. The sense of relief that Eid has arrived is palpable. No more struggling at dinnertime while hunger gnaws at you, and the kids fight, and it's still three hours until sunset. No more long nights at the masjid. The near-constant pressure to be preternaturally kind? Mashallah, today that lessens too.

After salah, worshippers filter into the summer-perfect day until all that remains in the ballroom are the scent of incense and a left-behind pair of socks. Kids unwrap candies handed to them from uncles who filled their pockets before leaving home. A boy does handstands in the grass. Hugs and kisses all around, hundreds of cell photos. Hotel guests passing through the parking lot smile at the celebrants. A few guests look the other way.

No matter. Jamilo and the kids gather with their group of friends, figuring out where they'll go. The water slide in Old Orchard? A picnic at Sabattus Lake? It's a perfect June morning in Maine. *Eid Mubarak!*

The day after Eid, the Supreme Court upholds parts of Trump's travel ban. It goes into effect for anyone lacking a "bona fide relationship with any person or entity in the United States." Students accepted to US universities, people with job offers, and relatives of citizens remain exempt. The Court will hear arguments in the case next fall.

In Lewiston, new immigrants react to this news with little more than a collective shrug. More Trump, more politics. Anyone resettled in Lewiston as a refugee would likely be doing so to join a relative, in any case. A lawyer Jamilo recently spoke with told her she should go ahead with DNA testing to verify her mother and father are in fact her parents. She added that to the list of things to save for.

Aaliyah did get her backpack for pre-K. Brand-new, adorned with characters from *Frozen*. It's wrapped in tissue paper and stored in the trunk of Jamilo's Versa with other things she wants to keep safe until she and the kids are in their own place. Her close friend Fatima's brother Mohamed bought it. Like Jamilo he's known for kind gestures, stepping up for people in need.

Jamilo gives the backpack to Aaliyah the night before summer pre-K starts. The next day Aaliyah wakes up first, checks her pack to make sure the snacks she and her mom loaded into it are still there. Chips, apple juice, Oreos. All good. She puts on her favorite outfit: the star-spangled red, white, and blue skirt they bought at Walmart before the Fourth of July, adds shirt and leggings.

Good-byes at the doors of Longley Elementary—tears from Jamilo, Aaliyah stoic. Jamilo's morning drags. She goes home and mops Fatummah's floor, tidies the apartment. She doles out drinks to the other kids and walks them to the park. Her work training isn't until later in the day. All morning she wonders what Aaliyah is doing.

When pickup time arrives, Jamilo's twenty minutes early at the bus stop. Later she'll reflect that this day meant so much because she never had anything like pre-K. There were few books in Dagahaley, teachers sometimes hit kids, no one learned that much. The first day of school in America: a milestone in a childhood so different from Jamilo's. It makes her happy and excited for her daughter—and a little sad for her girl-child self.

At the bus stop, Jamilo is so antsy she can hardly stand it. Finally the bus pulls up. Aaliyah descends the steps with a cousin, both of them grinning. Jamilo beams, waves. The girls cross the street.

"How was it?" Jamilo asks.

Aaliyah nods, gives a thumbs-up.

"So what did you do?"

Silence, thumb still up.

Jamilo turns to the cousin. "How did it go?"

The cousin: "Good."

Jamilo rotates her hand toward her, like *What else?*

The girls seat themselves on the stoop of the cousin's apartment building. They've been at school all morning; they're big kids now—a mom's questions can wait. Aaliyah unzips her backpack, removes the Oreos and hands them around to the cousin, herself, and a couple of other kids who materialized when the cookies came out.

Finally Aaliyah addresses Jamilo. "You don't bring snacks to school."

"What?"

"No snacks. The teacher said."

"Oh, okay. No problem. What did they have for lunch?"

"Carrots and an apple. Cheese."

"What else did you do?"

Aaliyah nibbles on her Oreo. No answer. As the afternoon goes on, she parcels out information. They sang a song. She played with dolls. She wants to go back tomorrow.

Pre-K comes at the right time. It's high summer, still cool in the foothills but sun-baked in the Lewiston flats. A good time to spend the heat of the day indoors. And Aaliyah wants to learn—whenever the ABCs or counting come on kids' TV, she moves in closer.

Things are tough at Fatummah's. She's on the verge of overwhelmed, taking care of her four plus Aaliyah and Hamzah sometimes while Jamilo's at her training. Fatummah nurses her newborn girl, warming bottles for her toddler daughter because the eighteen-month-old is jealous. Hamzah is jealous, too—but he's considered too big for bottles. He still tugs the baby's curls sometimes, still wants whatever lap he can find. One day while Jamilo's out and Hamzah acts up, Aaliyah threatens him with a time-out. She goes into their room, wheels out the stroller where Jamilo makes him sit. "Nooooooooo!" Hamzah wails. "No time-out, Aali."

"Then be a good boy."

He grabs her toy cell phone. She takes it back. He grabs it. She yanks it away. He wanders over to the TV and rubs his hands across the monitor, drawing a reprimand from Fatummah on the couch with the baby. Hamzah's eyes darken. Tears roll down, drip onto his belly. He howls. Fatummah looks at him. "Hamzah," she says quietly, not unkindly. Fatummah speaks barely any English. She puts the baby to her breast.

After a while, Aaliyah suggests to Hamzah that they go rinse his face. Sobbing, he agrees then sits on the living room rug, hiccupping upset. *Sesame Street* comes on. Aaliyah hums along to the ABCs. This morning her mom told her their new apartment will be ready really soon. She turns and reminds Hamzah of this. Big Bird looms over them both.

July drags on. Hot windless days with no AC, nights when the air still doesn't stir and the trash smells of diapers. It's time for Jamilo and the kids to be in their own place. Jamilo knows it. Fatummah knows it. Everybody waits it out.

At last the day comes. There isn't much to move. Jamilo pulls the kids' toys out of storage, arranges trucks and dolls and a drum in a corner of the new living room. In the other, she sets up an inflatable bed as a couch. Aaliyah's princess bed goes into one bedroom. The other will stay empty until Jamilo has money to furnish it. For now she'll sleep with Hamzah in the living room.

On the drive over with the kids, she tells them they're going to their new apartment. "Our nice new home," she says.

They cross the Androscoggin, slow and low in its summer bed. Two miles on they pull into the complex, drive past the small pond and up along the driveway. It's a place apart from downtown Lewiston's triple-deckers and brick mill buildings. Red maples dot a stretched-out lawn. Cars park in front of the low-slung buildings.

They climb the stairs to their unit, take off their shoes. The apartment has beige carpet and light gray walls. Smells of fresh paint.

Aaliyah pokes her head into one room after another, sees her bed and grins. She imagines her *Frozen* rug right here, on the edge of the bed so she steps onto it in the morning. They'll unpack her clothes and her stuffies. They can leave toys out overnight, and nothing will get lost!

Hamzah strides through the living room, past the sliders to the deck, through the kitchen and the hall. He throws his arms in the air. "Home," he says.

"What did you say?" Jamilo asks.

"Home!"

"Yes," Jamilo says. "Home."

"Home!" Hamzah runs to the toy corner. When friends come over later, he designates himself the greeter. "Door down there," he says, gesturing from the deck to the building's entrance. And, after they're inside: "Need bathroom? Here!" He leads the way down the hall.

"My little family is settling in," Jamilo says.

In this new home, it's peaceful at dinnertime when they sit down to eat. No honking horns, no crying infants. Sparrows fidget in the trees behind the complex, and Aaliyah and Hamzah have met kids at the play space. Sometimes Jamilo wakes up before dawn, pulls on leggings and a long shirt. Outside on the dew-damp grass, she stretches and jogs in place, happy to be there as the sun rises. Inshallah, good things will continue.

They do. Aaliyah likes pre-K a lot; she makes two best friends, and the teacher says she's a good listener. One of Jamilo's favorite uncles arrives in the US from Dagahaley. He and his wife aren't much older than Jamilo, and both love kids. Soon they're babysitting Hamzah and Aaliyah during Jamilo's shifts—a quantum improvement from the patchwork of babysitters she had before.

One day in the apartment parking lot Jamilo buckles Hamzah into his car seat and closes the door. She pulls on the driver's door. It won't open. Pulls again. Nothing. *Subhanallah, she's locked him in.* It's 85 degrees. She yanks on the door a third time, tries the others. From inside the Versa, Hamzah watches her. Jamilo can almost feel the temperature inside the car rising. Panic wells in her chest. She pulls out her phone, calls a mechanic friend to come pop the lock. People gather. Smash a window, someone suggests. Jamilo is crying. Inside the car Hamzah is not, although his forehead glistens with sweat.

Faces peer in at him. Why are all those people standing there? They shout, pointing at his car seat. "Unbuckle yourself!" But he's not supposed to do that—Hooyo tells him not to. They keep gesturing. "Unbuckle it!" And so he does. Jamilo raps the driver's side window. "Go push the buttons!" He's not supposed to touch any of the controls, either. But she keeps pointing. "Push them." *Too hot in here.* Hamzah wants out. He climbs into the front, steps into the driver's seat. He's never sat here. Touches the steering wheel, the blinkers. Presses buttons. The flashers go on. *Fun, but still too hot.* More people watching now. *Why is Hooyo crying?* Hamzah keeps pushing. The door lock pops. Hooyo jerks the door open, grabs him. People cheer. Alhamdulillah!

These days, problems have a way of righting themselves, Jamilo says later. She was set to break that window. Who'd have thought Hamzah would unlock the door?

Around this time, Jamilo shaves her head. She says she wanted to treat her dry scalp, but also that she wanted a change. Something to signify new beginnings. Inside the apartment, without hijab and without hair, she is startlingly young. As if sprung in reverse from her children, she looks like a cross between them: Hamzah's eyes, Aaliyah's smile, Hamzah's forehead, Aaliyah's lashes.

Not that things don't sometimes tug her backward. One morning Jamilo finds a rose and a Milky Way bar on the windshield of her Versa. She's pretty sure who left them—confirmed soon after by a text from Mustafa with those same symbols. He knows Milky Way is her favorite. He knows everything about her. Her heart lurches, but resettles sooner than it would have last spring.

Mustafa—one day I bump into him downtown. He's giving away Qurans in front of a store. Islam represents the one true diin (pathway to God) he tells those who stop. People don't convert to Islam; they revert to a monotheism that encompasses both Christianity and Judaism. Allah is the God of all, Mustafa says.

Three months after Providence, he still seems free of rancor. He loves Jamilo, Mustafa says—he would take her back. He left the rose and the candy bar to suggest that. But she'd have to want him. Mustafa says he realizes this: Jamilo is the woman he's loved most in his life. He thinks often of their time in Providence. They were happy, but so briefly.

Jamilo said she left because of Aaliyah, and that's partly true, Mustafa says. But his overall take hasn't changed: he was ready, she was not. He knows how much she's been through, he says, the scars she carries. Sometimes she feels compelled to just keep moving. And she needs a lot of affirmation. Mustafa says he also sees her pure-heartedness. He's glad she went back to Lewiston rather than someplace bigger—her family notwithstanding: "She'd get chewed up and spit out in a big city."

Like the Somali community's willingness to take Jamilo back after Providence, Mustafa's loyalty to Jamilo belies Western stereotypes of Muslims as strict and unyielding. Are the stereotypes way off? Is Islam mutable in the US, evolving?

On a late-August afternoon, Jamilo takes Aaliyah to Five Below. It's payday. Jamilo lets Aaliyah load her kid-size cart: a few discount toys and clothes, couple of items for the kitchen. Aaliyah picks out a ball for Hamzah, tosses that in. They're on a mom-daughter outing but can't forget him. Hamzah is having a hard time again. His honeymoon in the new apartment didn't last. The tantrums are back, and naughtiness. He smears the fridge with Nutella, cracked the window in Aaliyah's room. Jamilo gives him time-out, and he rages.

One day Jamilo goes to pick up the kids. Her uncle, the one just in from Kenya, watched them alone while his wife was out. He opens the door. He looks exhausted. "I cannot believe Hamzah," he says. The uncle, who has a background in mental health care, chased after him all day long. Something isn't right, the uncle tells her. Hamzah is smart and full of life. But he can't sit still. He's too easily frustrated. The uncle thinks Hamzah may have ADHD.

Jamilo calls Early Intervention, schedules an evaluation. She's fortunate, she knows, to be able to do this—reach out and get help. Still, it's one more thing. She forces herself to remember how good everything felt just a couple of weeks ago. Inshallah, it will all work out.

13

Bulshada Aayar Ar (Making Community)

Summer 2017

Carrys, Jamilo, Abdikadir

I STOP HEARING FROM OR SEEING JARED. TENTATIVE PLANS TO meet fall through; the frequent emails cease. Eventually he contacts me, though his tone is cool. It's possible his wife and sons, less political than he and wary, convinced him to pull back. More likely he's decided that if he can't convince me of Islam's threat, then I'm not worth his time. He's told me he's "a black and white kind of guy." My shades of gray must gall him.

He's come at me hard at times, in episodic bouts of disgust. Accusations and characterizations pile up in my inbox—"You're asleep." "Your side of our society is going to be entirely responsible for destroying America." "You must shake off the daydream of unicorns." He prods: How am I going to use the platform of this book? Will I cross over and portray Islam for the risk it poses, or will I write liberal blather?

This hard-edged Jared is at odds with the easygoing guy I meet at Dunkin' Donuts—a man I've watched absorb others' feelings, like Fatuma's when she testified about her FGM. This Jared seems embittered. Is it that he cares deeply about the anti-Islamist movement and he's upset I don't fall in line? This Jared is the same person who posts vitriolic comments online and in letters to editors. Does frustration make him mean?

Frank views me similarly. "I don't know how [much] clearer I can present this threat before you open your eyes," he writes one day, arguing that the goals of the Muslim Brotherhood and violent jihadists are the same. His displeasure culminates in an email telling me he's "done." I'm a "lost cause," he says. And I don't adequately respond to the questions he poses. He writes, "I will do everything in my power to defeat the 'Unholy Alliance,'" by which he means an association between leftists and sharia-adherent Muslims against American democracy. His parting line: "Have a nice life as a seditious, unpatriotic sympathizer to your Muslim 'friends.'"

His dismissal stings but isn't unexpected. I write back that our transaction, as I understood it, was he'd share his perspective, and I would render it on the page. I've responded to questions as best I can, and can't pretend to agree if I don't. After that, apart from emails broadcast to his contacts list, I hear little from him again.

But Jared and Frank are wrong if they believe I absorbed nothing they and other anti-Islamists said or that my thinking didn't shift, however incrementally. The refugee vetting process, for instance—I think it warrants examination. In war-torn nations, where civil and legal systems have been gutted—sometimes for many years—systematic record-keeping of births, marriages, international travel, arrests all but disappears. The vast majority of potential immigrants pose no security threat, of course, but mechanisms for identifying the few who do can be compromised when records are sparse. (This is poignantly apparent in Lewiston on New Year's Day, when many refugees observe the January 1 birthdays assigned them.)

Other realities compound the record-keeping issue. Catherine Besteman and others say refugees sometimes are told to reconfigure their personal histories to conform to resettlement requirements. "[Refugees] crafted a narrative of suffering that matched UNHCR's desire for victimization," Besteman writes in her book, referencing the United Nations High Commissioner for Refugees. Scholars describe widespread atrocities—murder, rape, pillaging, torture—converted into accounts of individual trauma. Anthropologist Cindy Horst talks about mukhalis (brokers) who, for a fee, coach refugees on what to say. Beyond the substantial matter of fairness, the recasting of personal narrative obviously means people could try to obscure their pasts.

I've come to believe, too, that questions of how long refugees take to become self-supporting, and where money comes from in the meantime, are valid—and necessary, to challenge the view that they benefit from big-government backing at the expense of other Americans. Finding answers is difficult. In Lewiston, City Hall has some figures on General Assistance, for instance, and Catholic Charities offers a general understanding of federal monies refugees receive when first resettled. The state keeps records on TANF, SNAP, and MaineCare—but not closely parsed by demographic.

And the answers, when they do come, are inconsistent. Analyses ranking Maine's welfare benefits relative to other states, for instance, yield wildly differing results. They range from middle-of-the-pack to third in the nation—depending, unsurprisingly, on the lens of the measurer. I also think journalists, including me, sometimes don't push for answers lest they appear insensitive or out of fear they'll provide ammunition to haters. But not asking and not knowing provides fertile ground for rumors to flourish. It's also patronizing; Lewiston's newcomers can withstand the scrutiny.

I take in what Jared and Frank say, yet often they lose me through overstatement. Sometimes I hear a kernel of truth, but it's embedded in extremity: all Muslim refugees pose a risk; none can be trusted; Islam is an imminent threat to life in the United States. I find it more convincing, for instance, when Jared acknowledges that sharia is not really yet a problem in US courtrooms—but that the growing number of Muslim tribunals in England makes him worry it could become one.

I come away from considerations of the anti-Islamist stance sure of one thing. With so much at stake and such complexity, an Us vs. Them, Good vs. Bad reduction—whether conservative or progressive—does disservice to us all.

~

THE STATE LAW ending General Assistance to asylum seekers after two years goes into effect. Anyone who started receiving GA on or before July 1, 2015 is no longer eligible.

In Lewiston, no one loses benefits—yet—and statewide only a handful of people do. This is partly because asylees often get work permits as soon as the six-month moratorium ends. Many find jobs soon after, partly because officials steer people slated to lose assistance toward employment-training programs well before the deadline. The new law, enacted after the governor refused to reimburse cities for GA to asylees, continues assistance but also imposes the cutoff. Some cities, including Portland, are looking into how to provide support beyond two years without the 70 percent state reimbursement that keeps most GA budgets afloat.

Carrys doesn't know anyone directly impacted by the new law. He's been in the US long enough that almost all his asylum-seeker friends and acquaintances have full-time jobs, or part-time if they're students.

He's away from Maine this summer in any case, interning with a Boston engineering firm in its mechanics and infrastructure group. He lined up the job months ago: sent an inquiry, word-processed his résumé, gathered references—including one from a USM math professor who described Carrys as among his most talented students. After the firm offered him the position in April, Carrys located a room with shared kitchen and bath, a twenty-minute bike ride from the office.

The sublet is small and barebones. Carrys spends his first weekend in Boston "making it pretty," he says. The firm where he works, on the other hand, is fancy. Paintings hang on the walls, and employees get free lunches at midday lectures. Carrys has his own cubicle, small but outfitted with a nice workstation and high walls for privacy.

He helps with several projects. The first is an investigation of water damage resulting from the failure of a fire sprinkler system in a Florida high-rise condo. Using Bluebeam on PDF drawings, Carrys identifies leak locations and enters data about each. For another investigation, he documents corroded samples of steel plumbing pipe. He makes a field trip to nearby Cambridge to oversee the removal of pipe specimens.

Much of the firm's work involves the forensics of engineering failures. "I find it very interesting," Carrys says. "Actually, I am learning a lot." His supervisor calls him "adept and quick." And well liked. The openness that drew co-workers and customers last summer at Argo results now in invitations to barbecues and birthday parties. In the long summer evenings he sometimes plays tennis with a housemate, a Chinese graduate student at Brandeis University who's becoming a close friend.

Carrys enjoys Boston. His supervisor talks with him about transferring schools, suggests Tufts, Northeastern, MIT, or Worcester Polytechnic Institute. Carrys isn't sure. For the coming year, at least, he'll stay in Maine at USM.

Still no word on a date for his asylum hearing. Still widespread instability in Congo and no presidential election. More and more, Carrys imagines himself living in the US after he graduates—if his asylum comes through. He misses his family, but the fighting there seems endless. No sooner do things settle down than violence breaks out again. Prospects for young people look dim. As Carrys puts it, "I am having trouble seeing myself in that life."

He moves forward on faith and instinct, every day a little deeper into his life here. This fall when he returns to Portland, he'll take a dispatch job at AAA routing tow trucks to stranded motorists, to help pay school and household costs. His English flows easily, French-accented but fluent.

Now, in June, he saves most of his earnings, cooking in the communal kitchen almost every night. One evening he splurges on ingredients and makes chicken paprika, smothered in onions and peppers and served with plantains. The smell wafts through the house and out the open windows.

JAMILO WAITS IN line with friends at a clothing store. Behind them, a woman mutters something into her phone then, loudly: "It's those people we don't like." The woman narrows her eyes, sneers. A manager asks her to leave. She drops the clothes she's holding and storms out.

Has Trump's presidency emboldened people? Jamilo can't say. Lewiston police don't report a rise in anti-Muslim incidents. And things like this happened before the election—that day Jamilo was with other moms, their babies in strollers, and a white teen yelled, "Go back to Africa, n—ers"; the time a woman was caught making up stories to get her Somali neighbors in trouble.

Jamilo recounts incidents like these matter-of-factly, not unlike the way Fatuma talks about waking up one morning a few years ago to an epithet scribbled on her front door. The family didn't call the police. Instead they repainted the door themselves. There's weariness in the telling. "Look, the US can be a racist place," Fatuma says. As part of her work at the IRC she teaches tolerance—but its opposite does not surprise her.

One day Aaliyah and I go to a nail salon I'd tried before and liked. She wears her favorite hijab. "What do you want?" a man asks when we step inside. He waves toward the polish, hurries us to sit. I ask for a test color on one nail. He glares. "Do it yourself," he says.

The woman who paints Aaliyah's nails speaks to her sharply. "I told you to sit still!" I think of leaving, but don't want to upset Aaliyah. The man cuts me with his nippers. "Go to the dryer now," the woman commands Aaliyah. Both of us have polish slopped onto our cuticles. The salon feels completely different from last time. I talk to the manager in code: ". . . unwelcoming, aggressive . . ." The manager's face says, *I don't care.*

Jamilo goes through every day knowing some don't want her here. She's mindful of how others see her. One afternoon she's talking with friends about cheap places to buy groceries, then the topic shifts to upcoming Eid al-Adha. The date has been uncertain because Muslim holidays are determined real-time, based on new moon sightings. "I'm so glad it won't be on September eleventh," Jamilo says. "People might misunderstand when they see us hugging and, you know, happy." The other women nod. "I mean, I feel terrible about that day," Jamilo says, her face grave. I think of reminding her that she was seven years old on 9/11, still living in Kenya, but of course she knows.

Then there are the scary incidents, like the time a few years ago that Jamilo went late at night with friends to McDonald's and, on the way home, a man tried to run them off the road. She'd been the one to dial 911. The man, who turned out to be a former LHS classmate, was charged with two felonies.

Many things stay below the radar, talked about but not reported. At the café where she works, Sadio Aden is asked by a male customer for a hug. When she hesitates he says, "In my culture we hug everyone" and pulls her close. The embrace shocks Sadio, who's never been hugged by a male stranger. Anger flushes her cheeks, prickles the back of her neck. *How dare he?* Later, she talks it over with friends. Was he sexist? Anti-Muslim? Maybe just plain ignorant?

Jamilo often looks for reasons to explain things away. The woman in the clothing store might have been high. That kid who yelled the n-word seemed drunk. Still. She decides not to take the kids to Fourth of July fireworks. The guy calling her out for her hijab happened months ago, but it seems pretty recent. And the Fourth "feels like a time when something bad could happen," Jamilo says. She doesn't like the white-hot flashes overhead, the pops like gunshot. She and the kids stay home and watch a movie instead.

What helps: all the normal interactions, the weeks that go by without incident, the times when Jamilo and Sadio and Fatuma feel more like other Lewistonians than *Muslim woman in headscarf*. When others see them just as fellow residents.

Work is one place where that happens. Sadio applied for her job at the café knowing few Somalis go there; she could have worked at one of the African-owned shops nearby. But she loved the café's smells of baking bread and fresh-ground coffee. She learned the job quickly. Soon managers were giving her all the hours she wanted and asking her to help train new hires. She made friends with co-workers—with them she figured out what she'd say if a man ever approached her like that again.

Him: "In my culture we hug everyone."

Sadio: "In my culture, we don't."

At nonprofit Trinity Jubilee, the mix of people on a typical day reflects that of the tree streets neighborhood: white, African American, mixed race, Somali and other Africans. It's a busy place. Aba Abu, the single mom and caseworker, hustles from one task to the next. She speaks English with a Lewiston-Mainer twang, same as her white coworker; unless you're in the room, you can't tell them apart. People flow in and out of her office all day long. "Where's Aba?" an older white guy asks one afternoon. He's filling out a form. "She's the one I want to help me."

New immigrants work throughout L-A—in both of the hospitals, Argo, Bates College, the cities' banks and hotels, manufacturing plants, Walmart, supermarkets, and as childcare providers, shopkeepers, farmers, caseworkers, home health aides. Anti-Islamists claim that refugees and asylum seekers take jobs that should go to native-born citizens. But Maine needs workers. It still has the highest median age of any state—and labor shortages in several sectors, including agriculture, hospitality, and retail. For years Maine's innkeepers and restaurant owners have imported workers on H-2B visas to fill summer jobs.

According to Phil Nadeau, by late 2002 close to half of Lewiston's adult Somalis had found jobs. As more refugees arrived, that percentage remained steady for years before rising at the end of the decade. Early news stories reported employers reluctant to hire Somalis because of concerns about Muslim culture. But by 2007, when I wrote a magazine piece about Lewiston, things were changing. I profiled Mohamed Maalin, who worked on the manufacturing floor at Dingley Press. If he needed to pray during a shift, a crewmate covered for him. "It's worked out," a manager said. "He's a great employee." Last summer, driving west on Route 196 into Lewiston, I noticed Dingley had a recruiting table set up outdoors. It was there for days. One afternoon I saw a van pull up. Two black men got out, walked toward the table. The company's workforce is now 20 percent Somali and other African newcomers.

The availability of workers in the L-A area has drawn employers. L.L.Bean opened a new boot-making plant in Lewiston in June 2017. "Demographics are definitely part of it," says Bean shift manager Rick Valentine. "We wanted to feel confident we could fill the jobs." In some cases, Bean also receives tax credits for hiring refugees.

When machines at the new plant and in nearby Brunswick are fully running, 450 boot-making employees will beat back a near-constant backlog. Twenty-seven-year-old Abdiweli Said is one of them. He grew up in Dadaab and came to the US with older siblings. At LHS he played varsity soccer. After that he went on to community college and then to USM, where he studied international relations until the costs and the commute got to him.

In the four years he's worked at Bean, Abdiweli has absorbed the lore. How back in 1912, L.L. got tired of wet feet while hunting and designed himself some boots. Founded a company, mailed one hundred pairs of boots to customers—satisfaction guaranteed—and got ninety back. Nearly went out of business, but figured out just in time why the bottoms were tearing from the uppers. Last year the company produced 600,000 pairs of its iconic boot. Abdiweli owns a pair. Actually, he owns two, but a friend appropriated the other pair last winter.

One summer afternoon, Abdiweli works second shift. He and his crewmates surround a device that forms polymer soles and bottoms. Leather uppers get sewn on later. On the manufacturing floor: a mechanical roar but surprisingly little smell. People fit socks onto sized lasts, which disappear via conveyor into a molding machine. Inside, polymer flows around the last. The resulting piece—picture a rubber moccasin with no sole—is heat-fused with its matching bottom into a waterproof half-boot. An aperture opens and, in a maneuver that conjures a sportsman being ejected feetfirst, the boots emerge soles-up on metal legs.

Robotic arms pluck the boots off the feet. Abdiweli trims excess fabric. Someone applies the Bean label. Two others pack. Boom, a dozen pairs of half-boots—done. Next stop, Brunswick.

Valentine calls a break. Workers gather for a photo for an upcoming grand-opening celebration. The mayor has been invited, and the governor. Bean executives will be here, too, to watch the crew run the newest million-dollar molder. After the photo comes stretching: backs, shoulders, arms, even fingers. Abdiweli leads a soccer stretch—crosses legs, reaches hands toward feet, 1-2-3-4.

Two-thirds of Abdiweli's crewmates come from Somalia or other parts of Africa. The rest are white. "It's a premier company," he says. "We work hard, but they take really good care of us"—by which he means the breaks and the stretching, plus state-of-the-art workspace, good pay, high-end health plan, employee fitness room, and a designated space where he goes for salah.

The prayer space, and the fact that Bean gives Muslims paid holidays on Eid-al-Fitr and Eid-al-Adha, means a lot. Abdiweli's co-worker Safiya Khalid remembers a different experience at Kmart where a supervisor admonished her for speaking Somali during a break. "There was no understanding," she says.

"Expect diversity," people are told when they apply to Bean. Valentine says he sees people and personalities, not ethnicity. "When you work with someone day after day—skin color, head coverings, all that sort of disappears." Everyone is known for something particular to their person—Abdiweli's quick hands and droll sense of humor; Safiya's ability to multitask two stations at once.

As immigrants in Lewiston have gained traction and established lives, some have expanded their social networks to include longtime residents who seem in need. Aba Abu, the Trinity Jubilee caseworker, also drives a bus that picks up kids with special needs. One of her passengers is a white boy who lives with his father. The father, overwhelmed, often sends his son to school wearing the same clothes as the day before. "It was sad to see him like that in the morning," Aba said. So she started buying shirts to send home with the boy.

Acculturation has turned out to work both ways. Newcomers adapt but also influence the broader community. At CMCC an instructor reports that Somali eagerness for education is contagious. "When [other students] see refugees taking their educational opportunities seriously, it establishes a certain climate," he says. Last winter, on an afternoon when Nasafari was in class, about a third of the students in the CMCC cafeteria were new immigrants.

Sports have been a big unifier. Jamilo and Abdikadir have played pickup soccer with white players, and Sadio ran varsity girls cross-country at LHS. Carrys made many of his American friends playing tennis and soccer. And everyone still talks about the city's 2015 championship soccer team and its diversity of players. The way that season played out—the comeback from the previous season, the hundreds of Lewistonians who became new soccer fans—well, it's the stuff of Abdikadir's dreams. Integration—one team, one Lewiston: more than anything, this is what he wants.

To Abdikadir and others, that team showed the possibilities when differences are set aside. As Catherine Besteman put it in a *Maine Sunday Telegram* op-ed, the Blue Devils exposed "the lie in the anti-immigrant argument that immigration weakens our national fabric and challenges our cultural integrity."

The team didn't take the 2016 championship. But it has a chance in 2017—players look good on the field this summer, and Coach McGraw is optimistic. In the meantime, L-A youth soccer thrives like never before. Black kids and white kids want to be Maulid Abdow, scoring the winning goal that makes teammates weep with joy. They imagine themselves doing flip throw-ins like his, so the ball rockets toward the goal.

Yet—that championship team that brought the city together? At a home game the next fall, a member of the opposing team uses a racial slur. Apart from a few Facebook posts, nothing seems to have been done about it. And one night a white teen named Avery Gagne is eating dinner with his parents at IHOP when he overhears a waitperson tell a table of Somali teens they have to pay upfront. It's a "new-generation thing," she says. When Gagne posts about the incident, it goes viral. "That's crazy," Jamilo responds in an online comment. "I usually go to that IHOP with my family."

Most upsetting to him, Gagne says, is that when he and his mom went over to the teens' table, one said, *It's okay.* Writes Gagne, "No . . . This is NOT okay."

At the institutional level, advocates say racial equality is closer than it was a decade ago—but not achieved. "Look, we've made progress in Lewiston, but we're not there yet," says Fowsia Musse, director of Maine Community Integration. Musse and others cite improvements: organizations in which services are provided horizontally rather than vertically—that is, new immigrants helping each other rather than being "helped" by white administrators; newcomers employed in city institutions as other than interpreters and cultural brokers; a school system that while imperfect still graduates most of its new-immigrant kids—and sends many on to college.

Sometimes it seems even the well-intentioned view newcomers as less than full-fledged equals. In 2016, I moderated a New Mainer panel discussion. The venue was filled with people eager to hear immigrants' stories. Audience members listened avidly as Abdikadir and Jihan Omar talked and took questions. Then an audience member asked whether refugees had considered relocating to this midcoast part of Maine. "We have an aging population here," he said. "We're going to need a lot of home health aides as we get older." So there would be many jobs. Others chimed in—"Yes, there will be jobs!"

Abdikadir smiled, nodded. So did Jihan. Did they feel uncomfortable or affronted? They didn't say so later. But Jihan is completing a master's degree, and Abdikadir already co-leads a large nonprofit.

Unwitting condescension will abate as more newcomers enter the same professions as those in the audience that night. But then there are Mainers who remain convinced Somalis and other Muslims pose an irremediable threat. Most who believe this are less visible than Jared and Frank. One summer day, I meet a guy named Ed at Dunkin' Donuts. I'm there with my laptop; he asks what I'm doing, and I tell him. Lewiston may be sitting on a "time bomb," Ed casually tells me. "All it will take is a couple of Muslim men combined with the wrong Islamic leader, here or online."

He says harm might not come to Lewiston itself but that "harm will definitely come." What sort of harm? Ed reminds me of "that guy in Freeport." He's talking about Adnan Fazeli, the same self-radicalized man LePage mentioned in his 2016 letter to Obama. Fazeli left his wife and children and went to Turkey, purportedly to visit his father. Instead he became an ISIS fighter. He was killed in Lebanon in 2015.

Being held accountable for beliefs and actions they reject, in nations they left, frustrates Muslims in Maine. As Jamilo puts it: "These are people we hate, too. They want the opposite of what we want." Her cousin was accosted by al-Shabaab in Kismayo and pressured to join. "He ran away," she says. "He was scared to death."

I mention to Ed that Fazeli was one man two years ago, one refugee out of thousands in Maine. That his family informed the FBI of his radical ties. That Fazeli didn't do anything in America. Ed still doesn't like the odds: "Where there's one, there could be others."

Among some, the less extreme but ingrained belief persists that new immigrants are entitled and don't conform to American cultural norms. A waitperson at an Auburn restaurant put it this way: "A lot of them don't have manners, at least not American manners. They come in and demand a lot of things, and then don't leave a tip. . . . It doesn't seem like they're thinking of the other person." Later I ask the manager of another restaurant whether new immigrants tip his staff. More and more, they do, he says, especially as some take service jobs themselves.

Shared experience, day by day by week by year—through work or school or just through circumstance—builds understanding and empathy. Professional relationships deepen. A white health aide describes a Somali case manager she works with as "one of my besties." They met two years ago, realized they were both in their early twenties, both married, both with two kids. Same city, similar jobs. "We always have a lot to talk about," she says.

A sense of humor helps bridge gaps. When the aide wears khakis, her friend jokes about "man pants." The friend, in turn, gets ribbed about the layers of clothes she comes to work in, even on the hottest days.

One day I tell Abdikadir I like his shirt. He looks down ruefully at the madras fabric. "Me too," he says. "But now that you've said that, in my culture I'm supposed to take it off and give it to you." We laugh. He keeps his shirt. But for me, it's a gentle lesson in toning down compliments, especially to Muslim men.

For some in Lewiston, the kinship they feel with Muslim neighbors and colleagues started out as wariness. The south end of Lisbon Street holds most of the Somali-owned shops. Banks, law offices, and restaurants occupy the northern blocks. Dube's Flower Shop sits in between. Inside, it could be 1980 or 2020. Deb and Skip Girouard intend it that way. Deb's been making a version of that daisy-dotted get-well arrangement for a quarter of a century. The air smells good, of plant respiration and flowers. A wedding, a birth, a funeral, wedding, birth, funeral, weddingbirthfuneral. The Girouards will keep helping to mark occasions until they decide to stop.

Eighteen years ago, when the first Somalis showed up, Deb and Skip didn't know what to think. They were not overjoyed. The city had been through so much already. Dube's was doing okay, but Deb and Skip were far from rich.

A Somali store opened next door—the now-familiar assortment of fabrics and foodstuffs. Men in macawis started congregating outside on the sidewalk. They weren't unfriendly, but they weren't that warm. Deb felt intimidated, coming and going from her shop. She told Skip. Skip avoids confrontation. He thought a long while about what to do. Weeks passed. Deb still felt unhappy. Both worried their customers might stop coming.

Finally Skip went over to talk with the men and the storeowner.

"What happened next," Deb says, "what happened next was they listened to Skip."

Skip: "They were respectful and polite."

The men stopped gathering on the sidewalk. "A big relief," Deb says. Over time, the Girouards became friendly with the storeowner. A few Somalis came into the flower shop to buy things. Then a few more. A woman ordered floral arrangements for her daughter's wedding.

A year passed. Skip started carrying slips of paper in his wallet, useful phrases in Somali. He still has them, dog-eared now. Good Morning—*Subax wanaagsan.* How are you?—*Iska waren*...

"Skip was interested in their culture," Deb says. She's reserved. He's more outgoing. Over time, Skip got close with two young Somali guys. They stop in with friends sometimes to chat and ask for advice about, say, buying a car or renting a tux.

"Things are pretty good," Skip says of his and Deb's relations with the newcomers now, and of the city's overall. "It did take a while to adjust," he says, the same way it did with earlier immigrants. Skip is French Canadian—he grew up hearing stories about families like his coming down from Quebec. The resistance they encountered, the discrimination.

There's one noticeable difference though, Skip says. "Work."

Deb rolls her eyes. He's conservative, she not so much. "Skip," she says.

"No, listen. The French Canadians would move in one day and start work the next. That was just what they did."

"Things were different then, Skip. Lots of jobs, for one thing. And don't forget, they weren't refugees," Deb says.

"These young Somali guys come in, I tell them listen, my grandfather came from Canada, and right away he got a job," Skip says. "Back then, it was 'If you can walk, you can work.' Every able-bodied person should work. I could take someone down right now and get them a job at Burger King."

Deb: "Burger King doesn't pay a living wage. Most of the mill jobs did."

Skip pauses. "That's true," he says. He has other opinions. He wishes, for instance, that women would remove their hijabs when not in the mosque so they wouldn't stand out so much.

Deb reminds him most women choose to cover their head. It's their right, she says.

Skip nods, smiles wryly. He and Deb differ on some things, but they let it go. He thinks it should be that way with the newcomers and longtime residents. Everyone's neighbors now, so they need to get along.

Deb and Skip have changed. A Somali café owner who's since moved used to come in a lot and buy flowers. He and Deb would chat. One day at a meeting of local business owners, he said, *I go into the flower lady's shop, but she's never come to my restaurant.*

"He was right. I never had," Deb says. She went in a few days later and ordered food.

"Delicious," she says. "I don't know why I didn't do it sooner."

"You weren't ready," Skip says.

Deb nods. "You have to be ready."

For Skip and Deb, community formed over time. But it can happen in an instant. One night six months from now, Jamilo will be driving to work a health-aide shift at a new location. She'll get lost and, turning around, slide off an icy country road and get stuck. It's near zero outside. Jamilo isn't dressed for it. She calls her supervisor, who tells her to find a street sign so she can come and pick her up. Jamilo gets out, starts walking in the dark to the end of the road. Ice crackles underfoot. Wind blows through her hijab. Her ears start to go numb. After a while she sees headlights—a car. It pulls up, stops. Mashallah, she's not alone.

A man unrolls his window, smiles. "Hey, are you okay?"

"My car is in a ditch," Jamilo tells him. She explains someone's coming to help but needs to know the street name.

He tells her the name and says she can sit in his car while she waits. She thanks him, asks him instead to drive her back to her car. He offers to stay but Jamilo says thanks, she's okay now. Tells him she's really grateful. Her supervisor shows up twenty minutes later. They agree—the incident likely wasn't life threatening, but because of the cold and because Jamilo had no idea where she was, it was pretty scary.

Later on Twitter, the man—Mike Jones—describes coming across "this lady shivering and walking in the middle of nowhere." She was sweet but "scared and couldn't catch her breath." He was glad he could help, he says.

Jamilo's supervisor sees the tweet and recognizes Jones's name—they're friends. She sends it to Jamilo, who reposts it on Facebook. "This guy saved me last night," she writes and adds, Jamilo style, five exclamation points.

~

AT BARAKA, A few days after a man rams his car into a group of counterprotesters at a white supremacist rally in Charlottesville, North Carolina, Mohamed and two nieces talk about racial conflict. Mohamed thinks people are making too much fuss over statues of Confederate generals. "I understand that it's painful for some people, but they need to move on," he says.

His nieces, both college students, eat Indian takeout at one of Baraka's tables. They see it differently. In their view, the statues should come down. They represent slavery. They belong in a museum.

The generals died over a hundred years ago, Mohamed says. People should focus on going forward, not focus on the past. And, he says, white people in the South consider someone like Robert E. Lee part of their background. "They feel like you're taking away their history," he says of the statues' removal.

The nieces hold firm. The statues should come down. They cause too many people pain.

Mohamed doesn't give in, but agrees that racism is a plague. "Humans have a darkness in the heart," he says. "Think about it—we live in a world of technology miracles, where we can explore the moon and other planets. But we still think the color of a person's skin matters. How can this be?"

14

Fall 2017

Nasafari, Jamilo, Abdikadir

LATE AUGUST—I'VE NEVER SEEN WALMART SO BUSY AT NINE p.m. Shoppers lift clothes from the racks, choose notebooks and pens, load up on cartons of Capri Sun. About half of the families are black, half are white. And all over the store—kids. Toddlers kick from the seats of shopping carts or trot alongside. Kids push carts until parents protest. Girls burst from the fitting rooms in new outfits. Boys sit in the aisle to try on sneakers. Kids way outnumber adults.

Back-to-school time—next week Aaliyah continues pre-K at Longley Elementary. In the state that still ranks as the nation's second-whitest, two out of three students at Longley are black or mixed race. The majority of students come from new-immigrant families.

For Aaliyah, her classroom at Longley is as comfortable as home. It's a place where she eats breakfast and lunch, listens to stories and practices the alphabet, rests when things get hectic. Her teacher and thirteen classmates don't mind if once in a while when her mom works a back-to-back and there's no time to bring Aaliyah home from her uncle's to change, she comes to school in the same clothes two days in a row. Jamilo worries about it, but then she picks her up and the teacher says everything went fine. Aaliyah being Aaliyah, her outfit stayed clean anyway.

Two months ago the city broke ground on its new school, which will replace Longley and another older elementary. Capacity will exceed nine hundred students—among the largest K–5s in the state. As with many new schools, the state is paying most of the construction costs.

Soon after Aaliyah goes back to school, the Supreme Court blocks a ruling that granted an exemption from the travel ban to refugees with contractual confirmations from US agencies. The lower court ruled that ties to a volag like Lewiston's Catholic Charities constituted a "bona fide relationship." The Supreme Court decides otherwise. The lives of twenty-four thousand people green-lighted for resettlement go back on hold. Those with close relatives in the US remain exempt. Still, the news makes Jamilo wonder whether her parents will ever make it to America, even if she pushes as hard as she can from this end. "Everything keeps changing," she says.

Then, at month's end: the third version of the ban, issued as a presidential proclamation, indefinitely bars citizens of Iran, Libya, Syria, Yemen, Somalia, Chad, and North Korea. The proportion of new Muslim refugees already has decreased. In Obama's final year, equal numbers of Muslim and Christian refugees entered the United States. In June 2017, according to Pew Research Center data, Muslims accounted for 31 percent and dropping.

~

THE FRIDAY BEFORE college starts, Nasafari rear-ends another car—an awful thud, the seatbelt yanking her shoulders and chest. *Have I hurt someone? Please God, no.*

A man gets out of the car she hit. He's okay, neither car much damaged. Even so, Nasafari is in trouble. She drove unaccompanied on her learner's permit, and police are on their way to investigate the accident. She sits in her car, shaking with anxiety. *What was I thinking? Why didn't I wait for Nabega or Dad to come with me?*

She's a US citizen, so she's not worried about issues with ICE. But Nasafari can't stand disappointing people. For so long she's been the good girl, the one who studied hard and toed the family line. Her dad tells people that Nasafari learned from her sisters' mistakes. But actually, she carved her identity from turf Antoinette and Nabega didn't claim.

After Antoinette left for Arizona, after Nabega moved in with Tyler, adolescent Nasafari became the daughter who did things differently—obeyed curfew, went uncomplainingly to church. Her sisters had pushed back. She tried not to—even while she struggled with her father's strictness. Her sisters weren't traveling to Rwanda with their father for their uncle's wedding? Nasafari would. And she didn't regret it. She came home holding her new Rwandan family close, especially her grandfather. *What will he think when he hears about the accident?*

She loses her permit for six months, has to pay for the other car's repair. She gets fined. Altogether it costs more than $1,000. Nasafari is stoic, but still, it stings. Norbert and Kamakazi are not helicopter parents. They leave her to figure out how to make things right. So, consequences. Paying the fine and repairing the cars means Nasafari has to work as many extra hours as she can at TJ Maxx and Lever's Daycare. She drops two of her five classes at CMCC. Not what she imagined a year ago when St. John's hung in front of her like an apple she could reach out and pick.

Patient Journey—Nasafari's name sometimes inspires her, sometimes seems ironic. Her goals haven't changed. Major in paralegal studies, enroll in law school, specialize in child advocacy. But getting there, accommodating the unanticipated, comes harder than she'd thought.

For now: she'll go to work, to CMCC, to church. She'll spend time with her family and baby Azaleah, whom she tries to see every day. She does love watching her niece grow—learning to roll over, sit up, crawl. "THE BIG GIRL" Nasafari calls her on Facebook. Now Nasafari gets what her dad means when he says time goes by too fast. And Azaleah isn't even her baby; what will it be like to have a child of her own? Thinking about that—the future, a husband, a home, children: too much. For now, she steers clear of the boys who let her know almost every day, wherever she goes, that they're interested.

More and more, Nasafari believes she'll settle down here in Lewiston when the time comes. But her heart's still set on transferring to St. John's after her associate's at CMCC. One night at home, she brings this up again. Norbert rolls fufu between his fingers—the little orbs always accompany his plate of whatever Kamakazi fixes. There's no fuss over Nasafari's pronouncement. No arguments from him. Nasafari will be ready, Norbert told me earlier, to go to New York in two years if that's what she wants. In spite of the accident—maybe in part because of it—she is learning to be responsible, he said.

Norbert turns to Christina. "How was kindergarten today? Are you still making new friends?" Yes, Christina says, she is. And school was good, yes. "Are you listening to your teacher? You must listen to her." I listen, she tells him.

Nasafari looks on, absorbing the exchange. Now her dad is focusing that fierce love of his on the younger kids. She beams at her sister. "I'm sure you're doing great."

Nasafari bites into the cheeseburger and fries she buys after work on Thursdays. Once a week she splurges. She hands fries to Moses and Christina to go along with their muamba. Norbert says nothing; more and more he picks his battles, and Nasafari's fast food at the dinner table is not one he's willing to fight.

Kamakazi cooked the meal on her new flat-top stove. It gleams, except for a dull spot from a bit of burned-on food that Norbert can't seem to remove. The spot has been bugging him since he noticed it a couple of days ago. He wants that stove mint, like his Avalon. But really, this is a minor problem. He acknowledges that. Things overall are good: Nasafari liking college and paying the costs of her accident; the younger kids doing well in school; Antoinette coming home around Christmastime for a visit. And Nabega—here again tonight with Azaleah, who just turned eight months old.

Kamakazi sits with the baby in her lap, feeds her bits of fufu dipped in muamba. Azaleah: plump, pink-cheeked. The little pouf she wears on top of her head has more heft than it did a month ago. She smacks her lips, *More*.

Kamakazi laughs, speaks in Kinyamulenge—"Look at this child who enjoys her African food!"

Watching her mother feed her baby, Nabega's face is awash with love. So is Norbert's, watching his daughter watch her mom.

~

JAMILO KEEPS REMINDING herself she's strong. For so long she felt otherwise. She shares a Facebook post. "Make sure you don't start seeing yourself through the eyes of those who don't value you. Know your worth even if they don't." She comments, "I got options!"

On an October afternoon that hints of cold to come, she's home with the kids—she worked last night, will work again tonight. Meanwhile, it's toddler marathon with Hamzah. Jamilo puts a diaper on him. Hamzah peels it off. He considers himself toilet-trained, which intermittently he is. While he's at it, he pulls off his shirt, pants, and socks. Dashes naked for the deck, tipping over Jamilo's shaax along the way. She grabs him, locks the slider.

He's still tantrum-prone. The Early Intervention evaluation hasn't happened yet. Instead of punishment, Jamilo is trying distraction and, okay, bribery to encourage good behavior.

Would Hamzah like pizza when it arrives? "Yes!"

Then he needs to stop climbing onto the counters. And give her that bag of chips.

Slowly, the apartment is filling up. Leatherette sofa, rug, clock with a molded Quran, quilt for Aaliyah's bed. The kids watch YouTube—*Barney* and *Sesame Street* and a Muslim kids' show that teaches Arabic—on a flat-screen propped against the wall. Jamilo sprawls on the sofa. At work she can sometimes doze between midnight and five a.m. while her clients sleep. She never feels completely rested. Arriving home after a shift, the first thing she does is brew shaax.

But she likes her life right now, she says. Outside later, the kids play in the sandbox. Jamilo sits on the grass. "You hear about the American Dream. The big house, the SUV, the career. Those things don't mean that much to some people. I mean, I feel I'm living my version of the American Dream. I have a nice apartment... We have a car, food, education." She sweeps an arm around the complex. "Look at this, Mashallah." She has her friends, too. Aspen and Binto have been there for her day by day during these hard months. And she counts on the twins, Fatima and Mohamed, to help keep her centered—Fatima a good listener, Mohamed funny and warmhearted.

Money is still tight. With overtime, Jamilo is earning $950 every two weeks. After rent, food, utilities and biil—her sister in Africa needs more eye surgery—she usually runs short. There's still some child support, but not enough to cover what it really costs to raise two kids, she says.

The sun drops below the horizon. Aaliyah puts on her jacket. Jamilo rewraps her headscarf, calls out, "Hamzah, are you cold? You might need a sweater."

He plucks at his T-shirt. "Have sweater right here."

"That's a T-shirt."

"Have T-shirt!"

After an adventure involving salad and juice mixed in the pizza box lid while Jamilo wasn't watching, she carries Hamzah to the bathtub.

He howls. She washes him. He settles down with Aaliyah in the shallow water. Jamilo lights incense, rinses dishes a few feet away in the kitchen. Hamzah shows up again. He trots in and out of the bathroom, carrying handfuls of little plastic foods from Aaliyah's room. Finally gets back into the tub. Jamilo shakes her head. "At least he never runs out of ideas."

It's a good day overall, comfortingly ordinary.

The next one brings tragedy. That morning, Jamilo learns Yussuf's brother has died in a Mogadishu bombing. Two truck bombs detonated, destroying buildings and setting dozens of cars on fire. Over the coming weeks, the death toll will climb to four hundred.

Yussuf's brother and his family had moved to Mogadishu from Dadaab a year earlier. They'd hoped to come to the US but left the camp because the resettlement process was so slow. People in Lewiston learned what had happened after the brother's thirteen-year-old son texted, "My father is dead." Jamilo didn't know her ex-brother-in-law well, but she and her mom had shared a meal with his family when Jamilo visited Dadaab.

All day and night people flow into Yussuf's mother's apartment. Jamilo and the kids go that afternoon. Together in the same room, she and Yussuf are polite with each other, careful, trying not to let the strain between them show. Not here, not today. Details come via text: the brother's wife is pregnant; he'd gone out to pick up his paycheck at the hotel where he worked; officials blame the blast on al-Shabaab; many of the bodies are unidentifiable.

The scale of the devastation stuns even those who lived in Somalia for years during the civil war. Where, Jamilo wonders, is #IamMoga dishu on Instagram and Twitter?

The following Friday, Lewistonians gather at Shukri's Hall for a remembrance of the victims. Jamilo has to work. More than a hundred others come to the afternoon service. People know Yussuf's brother and two other men who died: a music teacher and an older man from Minnesota who'd gone to Mogadishu to see family.

Inside, the room is draped in blue, the color of the Somali flag. On the walls, someone has taped photographs of dismembered bodies amid the rubble. People walk the perimeter, taking in the images. A man stands in front of a photo of an ashen figure no longer distinguishable as female or male. He shakes his head. "We must look, and we must remember," he says. Others dab their eyes. One woman leaves, weeping.

Along with grief is outrage toward whoever set off the blast. During the service, speaker after speaker steps to the microphone and denounces what happened. "They who did this are evil-hearted," says the Somali man who organized the memorial. The attacks happen so frequently, take so many lives. They inhibit progress, he says. "We stand united in the fight against terrorism." People nod—almost everyone in the room came to the US at least in part to escape terrorism.

Imam Roble cites an oft-quoted verse from the Quran—killing one innocent person is the most egregious of sins, akin to killing all of humankind.

The terrorists have no religion and they have no names, another speaker says.

Mama Shukri's husband hands around an image of two boys carrying a cardboard box with their mother's remains. "I share this tremendous pain," he tells the mourners.

The most emotional testimony comes from a woman in blue warm-ups—a former athlete and teacher in Somalia. "I wanted to be there. I wanted to help," she says. She chokes up. "I am very sorry."

Listening to her, the man beside me sobs. Earlier he told me his mother lives in Mogadishu. He visited her in July, had to pass through checkpoints guarded by armed soldiers. Three car bombs went off while he was there. *This is no way to live*, he said.

Other Lewistonians offer condolences—a city councilor, school superintendent Webster, a mayoral candidate. State representative Jared Golden, who will soon announce his candidacy for US Congress, takes the microphone. The bombing is a reminder of the necessity of advocacy, he says. "We need compassionate foreign policy. [We must be] mindful of the need to have our arms open to refugees."

After the service, Golden tells me he spent three years in the Middle East, first deployed as a marine in Afghanistan and Iraq and later as a teacher. He came away with heightened empathy. "People there live with terrorism as a daily reality," Golden says. "This is not something Americans can really understand, what it's like to go through every day with that open threat."

And what if, in reaching out to refugees, the US winds up bringing in an extremist? Golden's eyes travel to the photos on the wall. He clears his throat. "The courageous thing to do, the humane thing, is to take that risk."

~

AT FIRST, BRIAN Ingalls wanted to bring the city's Muslims to Jesus. When he started his Lewiston ministry in 2013, he reached out. He combed downtown and the park for newcomers, talking with whoever would listen. Few would, but one afternoon a Somali man stopped for a while then invited Ingalls and his copastor to visit Masjid-A-Nur. Ingalls was excited. He'd grown up in Lisbon, watched as Muslims moved by the hundreds to Lewiston. Who better than he to approach the new neighbors with the word of Christ? Ingalls felt ready. He'd studied the Quran extensively, spoke some Arabic. At twenty-five, he woke every morning lit with conviction.

A few days later at the mosque, the imam and men who'd come for salah were waiting. Ingalls and the other pastor hunkered down on the rug and faced the congregation. A man got right to it: "So you think Jesus Christ is the son of God?"

Ingalls did. He quoted from the Bible and the Quran, mentioned a declaration in the Hadith that Jesus was sinless. The men listened skeptically, counterpointed Ingalls's assertions with their own. The Bible contains factual errors, someone said. Jesus was a prophet, but not divine. Intense energy filled the room. Souls were at stake: a whole roomful from the pastors' perspectives; theirs from the point of view of the Muslims. Not to mention being "right" in the here and now on Earth. "It was intimidating but exhilarating," Ingalls says.

But for all his efforts, that day and many others, Ingalls converted only a single Muslim—a young man who abandoned his nascent Christianity after his father took his Bible away. The man got another, a miniature one he hid under his mattress, but went back to Islam soon after.

Ingalls has since stopped proselytizing the city's Muslims. He describes them as "closed to Christianity." He's thought a lot about why. There's cultural opposition, he says, and the dishonor that conversion would bring to the family.

But Ingalls believes something else is at work, too. "We've lost our testimony, our credibility. The biggest reason Muslim refugees don't give Christianity a thought is that too much of the emphasis in modern Christianity and American culture is on personal prosperity and possessions," he says. "When it comes down to it, most individual Christians don't do that well helping people in need. In many ways, we've relegated the task of caring for the poor and needy to the government." Ingalls believes newcomers see this. And even though that same government helps them, too, they view skeptically an ideology that doesn't hinge on direct, individual responsibility for others.

Some of what Ingalls says comports with what I've noticed. Many Muslim immigrants hold traits that seem at odds with each other, at least by left/right measures: traditional social views; belief in broad government support of education and healthcare; emphasis on the primacy of faith; communitarianism. My sense is that they're not so much closed to Christianity as contented in Islam and in African values of resource sharing and nonpermissive childrearing.

Among parents, especially, there's mistrust of American pop culture, which many see as condoning substance abuse and promiscuity. But people seem neither threatened by nor reactive against Christianity. In fact, Somali parents who send their kids to private school sometimes choose Christian-run ones. Fatuma's oldest daughters both attended Catholic high school.

Many of the city's new immigrants, even teens, do hold conservative social views. Reposting a piece about Parkland school shooter Nikolas Cruz that referred to him as a "broken child," Sadio Aden wrote, "19 years old and they call him a child?" Nasafari responded with a rolled-eyes emoji. Earlier Sadio had posted that she refused to blame the shooting on Cruz's mental illness. And informally polling newcomers one day, I found not one who wasn't pro-life.

Yet you'll see pro-life Muslims alongside Planned Parenthood supporters in protest of Medicaid cuts—because of a belief that health care is fundamental. Among new immigrants, you'll hear support for enhanced ELL programs *and* for standardized graduation requirements. Job-training programs *and* tax reform. To many, these are simply practical, first-order concerns.

The city's newcomers have a rising interest in politics. In November, three Somalis run for School Committee. None wins, but Rita Dube, founder of the Gendron Franco Center, likens their expanding presence in civic affairs to an earlier Franco one. It's "history repeating itself," Dube tells the *Sun Journal*. It's also the city's newcomers heeding urgings, post-Trump, to run for office or at least to vote. Many of L-A's 2,500 new-immigrant voters went through the MIRS citizenship program Abdikadir helped develop.

Even Abdikadir has politics that don't cleave neatly left or right. He's pro-business and entrepreneurial yet socially progressive. And flexible. When Governor LePage shows up in town to celebrate the mayoral victory of Republican Shane Bouchard, Abdikadir will appear with them in photos. He didn't support Bouchard—will in fact be disappointed by progressive Ben Chin's loss. But—*democracy*. Bouchard got the most votes. He must have his chance.

Brian Ingalls is right that most of the city's Muslim newcomers are clear about their beliefs. Most aren't searching for alternatives—religious or otherwise. Ingalls has shifted the direction of his outreach; now he co-runs Cell 53, a storefront church on Lisbon Street. The focus is on the city's very poor and homeless—and substance abuse, family dysfunction, isolation. The loneliness: the way Ingalls sees it, in addition to the comfort of Christ, Cell 53 offers companionship. And a sense of community—which too many in Lewiston lack.

BY SEPTEMBER, MY sister and I agree Mom shouldn't live on her own much longer. She insists otherwise. She's fine, everything's good in Florida—this despite a banker calling me worried she's not on top of her finances, and a nurse concerned she missed an appointment. When I mention these, my mom gets angry. People should mind their business, she says.

She's decided, at least, that eventually she'll come to Maine—but at a time and to a location of her choosing. Without telling her, my sister and I look for more assisted-living places in Maine where she'd have her own apartment. Somewhere between us, somewhere that offers things she likes: exercise classes and bridge, a lot of indoor light. We find a good one, but there's a waitlist. We ask them to add her to it.

My mother has never asked whether she could live with my family. But I feel conflicted that I haven't asked *her*. Mohamed is part of it. He doesn't mean to cause upset. Or maybe he does, a bit—challenging the Western way of doing things, questioning American values. Questioning mine, for not insisting she move in. In any case, he works on me.

"The mother," he says one day. It's Friday jumuah, quiet until people surge later into Baraka from the mosque, hungry. "I've been thinking about the mother."

"How so?"

"The mother is the most important person in the eyes of Allah. Always, she should be respected."

He doesn't know my relationship with my mom isn't always easy. At least, I haven't told him outright.

No matter what kind of mother she is, Mohamed says, the Quran holds her in esteem. "She gave you life." He goes on: Allah has ninety-nine names—"Ar-Rahman, Ar-Rahim, Al-Malik, Al-Quddus, As-Salam. . . . People ask, why only ninety-nine? Some Muslims believe there is not a hundredth name. But the hundredth is womb, *rahem*."

The hundredth name for Allah is "mother's womb." He's right, I think, about respecting her no matter what, being thankful she gave me life.

I go home and call her. "I'm fine," Mom says. On the way out the door to lunch with friends. Then she brings up the car I just bought. Am I sure it didn't cost too much?

We say good-bye. Ahhh, the mother's womb.

Still—Mohamed's mother died of illness in Somalia a few years ago. I should be grateful my mom's with us.

A week later, I'm outside in the yard. Leaves coast from the trees. Canada geese fly overhead. My cell rings—my mom's third call today. A friend drove her to the doctor for a follow-up appointment. She must be home now. I pick up.

"They tell me I have Alzheimer's," she says.

~

AALIYAH'S FIFTH BIRTHDAY—SAME orchard as last year, another nice October day. Fatima couldn't come from Massachusetts, but her twin,

Mohamed, did. He's gotten close with the family; Aaliyah and Hamzah have started calling him "Best Friend." Jamilo's friend Ishaa makes lasagna, like last year. Many of the same guests attend.

But this birthday goes differently from Aaliyah's fourth. This year, Jamilo orchestrates everything beforehand. She puts money aside, calls to reserve party tables, gets tickets for the corn maze, orders donuts and cider. This year she does it up. Does it like someone who knows how.

She's almost completely off public assistance—no TANF or SNAP, no housing voucher or subsidized childcare. Aaliyah and Hamzah still get MaineCare, but Jamilo's income is high enough that she no longer qualifies. "I want to make it on my own," she says. "It makes me feel good."

Kids find their way through the maze, play on the tractors. A few head off with adults to pick apples. Jamilo tends to a couple dozen guests in the outdoor party enclosure, urges everyone to eat the donuts while they're hot. Her face is lit with happiness.

Mohamed hangs out with Hamzah. At UMass Boston, Mohamed is majoring in communications, but he loves kids and wants to work with them. It shows. He knows how to manage Hamzah when he locks up, soft-spoken in redirecting him. "Let's go back to the table, Hamzah."

Hamzah [refusing to budge from the driver's seat of a tractor]: "Not now!"

Best Friend: "Come on down, I'll race you to the swings."

Later, Hamzah sits across from Aaliyah at a picnic table, eating the lasagna Ishaa packed with extra cheese and hard-boiled eggs.

Aaliyah asks, "How's your lasagna, Hamzah?"

"Is good. I like egg!"

"I know, I like it too."

Hamzah eyes the pile of opened birthday presents, including a huge stuffed pony all the kids love. "Is your birthday, Aali."

"Yes."

"Is your cake."

"Yes."

Aaliyah is over what Hamzah did earlier. No one saw what happened, but judging from the look of his dress shirt, he must have embraced the cake. Damage to the cake—marble, *Frozen*-themed—was limited, but he was a mess of blue and white frosting. When he was discovered, Hamzah's eyes glittered with tears—he knew he'd screwed up. Mohamed did what he could with napkins and water to wipe him clean.

But it was a kid-size mishap, nothing like last year's confrontation between Jamilo's friend and the employee who virtually accused her of stealing apples. Last year's party worked out in spite of everything. This one is a straight-up success.

Cake time—everyone sings "Happy Birthday." Aaliyah blows out her candles. It's still warm in the afternoon sun.

Hamzah heads for the gate, Mohamed brings him back. "Thank you," Jamilo mouths. The look that passes between them is indulgent.

Fall weather arrives a few days later, in time for Halloween. It's a holiday in flux for the city's Muslims. Some let their children dress up, many don't. Some think it's okay for little kids, but not for older ones who've gone through dugsi. Behind the counter at Baraka, Mohamed weighs in. Halloween is a pagan holiday; on the other hand, there's really no harm in letting kids dress up and go door to door with their parents. He doesn't officially have trick-or-treat candy at the store, but when costumed children come by, he lets them choose from his slim pickings of chocolate and other sweets.

At Ikran and Abdikadir's, Ikran frets as the two older kids get ready to go trick-or-treating in Heidi's neighborhood. Jamal wears a bee costume, Samia a ladybug. She loves the red sateen, keeps smoothing it. "Really, I'm not sure we should be going," Ikran tells Jamal, although any discussion is moot. The kids are dressed and excited. Pumpkin buckets wait by the door. Nor does Ikran want to disappoint Heidi, who's been a friend of hers and Jamilo's for years.

But one of Ikran's Somali neighbors criticized her for getting the kids costumes. Ikran rarely backs down and didn't this time either. Still, the judgment stung. And, technically, nine-year-old Jamal is grounded for not cooperating in brushing his teeth after Ikran leaves for work in the morning and Abdikadir supervises.

They go. At Heidi's house, her mom and husband exclaim over the kids' costumes. A lover of tradition, Heidi stands at the counter packaging candies and a hand-made message. "Always remember you matter and are someone's reason to smile. Happy Halloween! You make Lewiston rock."

Jamilo is here too. She avoids the Fourth of July, but Halloween is okay. She had money enough for one costume—Minnie Mouse, for Aaliyah. Hamzah wears his Spider-Man jacket and Aaliyah's fuchsia pom-pom hat. Jamilo and Ikran joke that their costumes will be themselves: head-scarfed Somali women.

The treat packets are ready. There are many photos, and last-minute costume adjustments to accommodate sweaters and coats made necessary by the dip in temperature.

Everyone troops outdoors. *Happy Halloween!* Tonight is an American night.

Among educators and community leaders, the premise in Lewiston is that new-immigrant kids who do best remain close with their ethnicity even as they're steeped in American culture in school and sports, with friends, through social media and TV. The emphasis is on acculturation rather than wholesale assimilation. The right balance of old ways and new differs for each person. Some young-adult Muslims rarely set foot in a mosque. Others go often. A woman who'd been an LHS honors student took my writing workshop. She'd downloaded a salah app—when it alerted, she stopped whatever she was doing to pray, sometimes at her desk.

And so it goes: the richness of having two cultures from which to forge your identity, the challenges. Jamilo and Ikran deal with them every day. People chide Ikran for letting her kids trick-or-treat, Jamilo for posting photos that bare her arms or neck. Ikran, in fact, has mentioned this to Jamilo—Ikran is more traditional. Jamilo prays to Allah and quietly ignores much of what Ikran says.

Outside Heidi's house, ghouls and vampires pass by. "They're only make-believe," Aaliyah reassures the littler kids and maybe herself. A teen dressed as Scream lifts his mask and grins. "Hello!" Then lowers it. In that moment, Hamzah's eyes grow fractionally more knowing.

Heidi leads the way. "Say 'trick or treat' and 'thank you,'" she reminds everyone.

The younger kids soon realize they're visiting families' homes. "This you door? This you house?" Hamzah asks a woman. Yes, she says, and yes. A few more places, and then a man comes to the door wearing a lion mask. It's realistic. The kids stand transfixed as he hands out candy with a paw. A few moments of silence, then Hamzah: "Take off you face?" The adults crack up.

The moon comes out. The wind comes up. Samia swings her bucket, and Jamal counts his loot. When the host at one house invites Jamilo and Ikran to come collect treats for themselves, they giggle and rush forward. They seem so far along in life—marriages, children, multiple jobs—sometimes I forget how young they really are.

At one house, with the decorated look that suggests it welcomes trick-or-treaters, nobody comes to the door. A woman is visible through the window, though. She stares out, unsmiling. Jamal rings the bell again. Nothing. The adults exchange glances.

Heidi shakes her head. "Let's move on." One sour apple—who knows why. No one says the words *racist* or *anti-Muslim*, but the possibility hangs there.

Onward. Everyplace else, people have been friendly. A dozen houses in, Hamzah ramps up his doorside questioning. "This you dog? This you car?"

Laughing, Heidi steps in. "Hamzah, this is not an interview!"

Like Kim Wettlaufer, Heidi is a go-to for new immigrants, especially young Somalis. They come to her for advice about work, housing, health issues. Her son is an LHS senior, so Heidi also knows the schools. People look to her, too, to interpret American culture. Jamilo and Ikran likely would have been angry alongside Heidi if she'd expressed upset over the woman who didn't open her door. And, had the kids not been here, Heidi might have. She's a straight-shooter—empathic yet frank. Sometimes her directness causes conflict.

A month from now on Facebook, a man will question why he got a parking ticket during Thanksgiving break, with city offices closed. Heidi will say meters have to be paid, regardless. She adds that enforcement is inconsistent, cites parking violations on Lisbon Street. She mentions two restaurants, her mother's apartment building, and the mosque as near where she means. The poster asks what the mosque has to do with his question. He's upset, perhaps thinking she's accusing Muslims of illegal parking. Heidi protests—she referred to the mosque as a locator.

Things escalate. The poster says Heidi went from his question to an unnecessary statement about rules. He charges her with failing to acknowledge inequality. She bristles: What inequality? She laments "how everything is political, how no one wants to hear what another person is saying." Another poster accuses Heidi of being among "the haters and the status quo lovers." The exchange is rife with misunderstanding—contextual, cultural, linguistic.

On Halloween night, all is well. Heidi has known Jamilo and Ikran for years, and they have a lot of ballast. If ever they get off course, affection rights them. House follows house follows house. The kids' buckets fill. Aaliyah yawns and rubs her eyes. Her face has the blank expression it gets when she's tired. She asks to be carried, falls asleep. Jamilo's tired too. She worked last night, got home this morning at eight thirty, then headed off to her community college class. She has another shift tonight.

Abdikadir missed the outing altogether. He's still at MIRS. The agency just moved into a bigger place on Bartlett Street. It's been a big transition. Later Abdikadir will wistfully say he wishes he could have been there to trick-or-treat with the kids. It's true that Ikran does more childcare, he says, more driving and cooking and clothes-washing but—at least when it comes to the kids—it seems she also has more fun.

~

IN NEW YORK City on Halloween night, an Islamic terrorist rams his car into a crowd and kills eight. ACT president Brigitte Gabriel appears on TV. She decries the lack of security in the US, describes how she recently traveled unchallenged to Boston, Miami, and Virginia on an expired driver's license.

Her message is a much-abbreviated version of the one I watched her deliver a few days earlier in Boston, where she received an award for anti-terrorism work from Christians & Jews United for Israel. There, Gabriel argued ISIS is mushrooming and increased vigilance is essential.

In Boston, Gabriel described being one of the "forgotten people" during the Lebanese civil war. For seven years when she was a child, she and her parents lived in an eight-by-ten-foot underground bomb shelter, she said. Islamic militants had destroyed the family's home during an assault on a nearby military base. Her anti-Islamist views solidified later, when she reported on terror attacks around the world as a TV news anchor. Gabriel told the audience, "We have never been faced with an enemy that is so direct... tells us exactly why they hate us, how they hate us, what they want to do us, how they want to kill us."

After the ceremony, people lined up for a heavily guarded meet-and-greet with her. Reaching the front, I described the Mogadishu remembrance a week earlier in Lewiston, the outrage and the repeated denouncement of terrorism by Somali Muslims. "Then let's go after the terrorists," Gabriel said. "That's why ACT exists." So, I asked, she doesn't think Islam itself or the Quran pose a danger?

Her response was quick and unrehearsed, less cautious than her carefully worded ACT emails. "The Quran does pose a danger. The Quran is the danger." But, Gabriel told me, many Muslims don't read the Quran, or live by it. Consider the Nation of Islam, she said. Most black Americans don't speak or read Arabic—Islam's appeal is its structure and routine.

My attempts at follow-ups—Wouldn't American Muslims read English translations of the Quran, even if they don't know Arabic? And, how can someone really be Muslim without a relationship with its holy book?—went unanswered. Gabriel and her handlers hurried me along. What I wish I'd asked: If Muslim extremists are so powerful, why can't they maintain dominance in places where they already have political and military hold?

Over the years I've been writing about Lewiston I've listened to dozens of women and men talk about what Islam means to them and why they're followers. That night in Boston, I left the ceremony with an understanding of how Gabriel came to her beliefs. But the Islam she described was so profoundly different from the one I see practiced every day in Lewiston that I hardly recognized it.

15

December 2017–March 2018

Fatuma, Nasafari, Jamilo

On December 30, a shocker: Mohamed asks Jamilo to marry him. She had no idea it was coming. His mom said they had a "present" for her, but Jamilo didn't know what. Looking back, she'll see hints. Mohamed asked how she felt about his family, how she felt about their friendship. *It's wonderful*, she told him. *I think so, too*, he said.

During a trip to western Massachusetts, Mohamed's extended family is together. Mohamed asks Jamilo to come with him into a bedroom, closes the door. They sit facing each other on a bed. Then: "Do you want to spend the rest of your life with me?" For a second, Jamilo wonders whether he's playing around. He has a good sense of humor, often jokes with her. But no, his eyes are serious.

Her heart pumps harder; she feels it at her throat. *Can she do this?* Since Mustafa, she has questioned herself. *Why did she go ahead with someone that much older, someone she wasn't absolutely sure about? Why didn't she more carefully consider how she felt about staying home full-time and raising his boys?* And then there's Yussuf. Will this inflame him all over again?

But she realized she loves Mohamed around the time of Aaliyah's birthday in October. And he loves her, too. They're equals, Jamilo says. When they do things together, he feels like the partner she's never had. She and the kids still call him "Best Friend." And Mohamed's family is the kind Jamilo always imagined having—supportive and close. His parents have been married for thirty years. They have nine children. Fatima, whom she's known since they were teenagers, is the one who brought her twin brother and Jamilo together one afternoon when they all went roller skating.

Mohamed is watching, waiting. A calmness comes over her. A quiet voice inside—it feels like Allah—tells her to go forward.

"Yes," she says. Her eyes fill. Mohamed reaches for her hands.

They do a nikah with elders but no imam. Jamilo's family in Lewiston wants in on the negotiations—Jamilo thinks it's more for their financial gain than her benefit. Mohamed's mother, Isha, wonders about getting their approval. No, Jamilo says, if you're going to talk with anyone, call my parents in Kenya. She tells Isha she'd rather her African family receive any nikah money to buy food for themselves and others. During the call, Jamilo's father gives his blessing, tells her he feels she's doing a good thing. Her mother says, *We are happy for you, hooyo.* Mohamed's father tells Jamilo's parents he's proud that she's joining the family.

Jamilo's heart is full—this is how it should be. Instead of a relationship imposed on her, her and Mohamed's love ripples outward to include those they care about. Her choice to leave her Lewiston relatives out of the nikah will have repercussions. She knows that. "They probably won't come to the aroos," she says. She's right. In March, when Mohamed's parents' house fills with relatives and friends—including many of Jamilo's—no one from her Lewiston family will be there.

Others in Lewiston react to news of the relationship with a mix of happiness and trepidation. Ikran puts it out there: "Jamilo will always be my friend, no matter what. But sometimes I worry about how people see her." Ikran is at home in Tall Pines as she tells me this, sitting on the sofa, the two youngest kids climbing her like a tree. "I asked her, 'Is Mohamed really the one?' She said she thinks so. I told her, 'You have to *know*. You have to make it happen. You have to think about the example you're setting for your kids.'" Ikran sighs, peels Siham from her shoulders. "I do like Mohamed a lot."

Jamilo feels sure. She and Fatima are like sisters, and have been for a long time. Jamilo has gotten to know the family well. And for months, she and Mohamed have been growing closer and closer. "This is it," she messages me.

LEWISTON WEARS WINTER well. The artifacts of nature—snow and ice, sharp light and shadow—show off the detail in the nineteenth-century buildings. Close your eyes, and newly arrived Franco women shepherd children past busy brick mills. Open them, and two moms in hijabs watch their kids toss snowballs at each other in Kennedy Park.

On a late January afternoon it's very cold, though not as bitter as two weeks ago when the temperature clung to zero for days and tree limbs moaned and cracked. Dark pushes in at five o'clock. By seven thirty downtown is zipped up—no one wants to be out later than they have to be.

Across the river in Auburn, Fatuma bundles baby Mohamed and Sanaa and Amina into her Ford Bronco. She pulls onto the highway from their snow-locked condo complex and heads south to pick up Isaaq and Ilyas from their school in Portland. Isaaq had indoor soccer practice; Ilyas had to wait there with him.

It's a tough trip. On the way, Mohamed overheats inside his snowsuit and throws up. Coming home, Ilyas gets tearful over having to stay at school so long without the math book he needed for homework. Everyone is tired. By eleven o'clock they're all asleep. Muktar is on the road, partway to Philadelphia with a loaded rig, so Fatuma and the baby go it alone in the big bed.

Short night—Fatuma's up again at four thirty. When I get there at five, she's already started a load of laundry, hand washed Mohamed's soiled clothes from last night, and dusted the well-used dining set. She goes up the stairs and down the stairs, up and down and up—checks the sleeping baby, lays an extra blanket on Amina and collects stray socks. With each trip, her knee hurts a little more. The surgeon recently removed the pins and plate from last winter's break, but her knee won't be the same again. Chores are harder now.

Still, Fatuma loves this time of day—the quiet, the thinning dark, the hour that belongs to her alone. She brews shaax, decaf so the kids can drink it too when they wake up, drops a couple of cardamom pods and a cinnamon stick into her cup. For a minute or two she sits at the counter nursing it, watches the snow go from slate gray to silver.

Muktar will be calling soon to check in from the road. By now he should be in Philadelphia. He recently changed brokers—more money, tougher trips. She wants to hear how this one's going. Almost daylight now. She switches off the kitchen light. Upstairs she opens the door of the bedroom Ilyas shares with Idris. Ilyas needs to finish that math. Fatuma goes to his bed, speaks gently. "Ilyas, it's almost time to get up. Don't you have homework to do?" He groans.

Fatuma presses. "Ilyas, do you have schoolwork?"

Ilyas mumbles that he'll bring his textbook and do the assignment during his extra period. Don't worry, he set his alarm for five thirty. He slides deeper under the covers. A last few precious minutes of sleep.

Downstairs Fatuma starts breakfast. Often it's oatmeal. Today she makes malawax, similar to crepes, with milk and egg and flour—

gluten-free for Amina. While the first batch cooks, Fatuma packs snacks for Amina: popcorn plus special crackers and pretzels. Anything to get a few extra calories into her and still adhere to the restrictive celiac diet. In the laundry room, wet clothes go into the dryer and another load gets started. Necessity has honed Fatuma's skills at multitasking.

She's particular. That often-used cookware that over time can get a little grungy? At Fatuma's, the bottoms and the handles gleam. She insists. And so later while she's cooking dinner, when she lets Mohamed open cabinets at her feet, pull the pots out and play with them—smudge them—this is an act of love. The lime-green smears on the living room sofa signal love, too. Against her better judgment, Fatuma let Amina and a friend make slime one afternoon; Sanaa got into it and imprinted the silky fabric with her fingers.

The warm smell of malawax fills the kitchen. Idris pads down the stairs with Mohamed on his hip. More than ever, the baby looks like Muktar. Same easy smile. Same calm eyes. Mohamed reaches out for Fatuma. She settles him against her.

"How did you sleep?" she asks Idris. He nods. "Good."

She serves him malawax with shaax poured on top. He eats. She hands a similar bowl to me. Soft and creamy—comfort food.

Ilyas comes rushing downstairs to the first-floor shower. Then Amina shows up sprite-like at Fatuma's side, leans in for a hug. Already the house feels full, but Isaaq is still asleep in his bedroom in the basement. Sanaa is there too, sharing a bed with Nafisa who's home for a few days.

Amina barely touches her malawax, even though she usually likes it, even though Fatuma coaxes. "Come on, let's see you eat a little more."

Most mornings the babysitter would arrive soon, but Fatuma plans to work at home today finishing some reports. It's easier here than at the office, where it's always hectic. Nafisa will watch the younger kids, so Fatuma can settle at the dining table. Already her cell is ringing—she was scheduled to lead a training today; now the team will go without her. They have questions. Fatuma talks for a bit, hangs up. Amina chatters on. Idris says something. "Sorry, sorry," Fatuma says. "I'm a little preoccupied."

A flash of yellow out the kitchen window—the school bus on East Hardscrabble Road, turning into the condo complex. Time for Isaaq and Ilyas to go. "The bus is almost here," Fatuma calls. "Don't forget to put on lotion!" The boys shrug into backpacks, sit beneath the Nerf hoop in the foyer and pull on shoes. Fatuma follows them to the door and watches them board the bus. Asks me, "Did it look like it was going too fast when it came around the corner?" She sighs. She worries. She pushes those boys. It will be twelve hours before she picks them up. "They do work hard," she says.

So does Fatuma, seventy hours a week. And that's just at the office. But her long hours are of her own volition. She admits—her kids are under a lot of pressure. She wants them to earn A's. Wants them to get into top colleges. To reflect well on the Somali community. And to be happy, of course. *In America, you can be whatever you want to be*: she tells them this a lot. But to get there, they have to study and do right. Whenever the topic of drugs comes up, Fatuma tells them she will kill them—she uses this word—if they ever get into that kind of trouble. She's exaggerating. But: "I'd rather go to jail than see them having all this privilege and screw it up."

For Fatuma, Utanga refugee camp and all that preceded it—separation from her parents, the death of her sister, those hard years in Atlanta—backgrounds everything. Her kids will have what she did not, and they will play their part in getting there.

Meaning: it's not easy being the child of a refugee parent. Qamar Bashir, who arrived in Maine around the time Fatuma did and is similarly driven, says, "The kids are burdened. We want them to achieve, to have a better foundation than we did. We want them to grow up to support their families, here and in Somalia." Then there are the social challenges, says Qamar. "They are black, they are Muslim, and they are Somali in Lewiston."

Fatuma sees all this. The kids carry heavy loads of parental expectation. And Islamophobia persists. So does racism—even at her boys' exclusive high school, they've heard other students use the n-word. Fatuma believes the bar is both higher and lower for black students there. A faculty advisor, also a person of color, is demanding and exacting but then tells Fatuma that the college Isaaq likes most is too much of a reach. Fatuma does not want to hear that.

Sometimes the kids in turn exert pressure on their parents. When Qamar's son, now a college junior, was going through the application process he applied to many schools. For nearly two decades, as he grew from baby to kindergartner to young man, Qamar had hung on to the idea that her family might someday return to Somalia. Might someday go home. She wanted her son to attend college but resisted the scope and the intensity of his process. "Really, why are you doing all this?" she asked. "Why so many schools?" She didn't say, *when we might not stay here*, but it was implied.

Her son told her, "Mom, we aren't ever going back. Until you accept that, you can't move forward." Qamar thought about this for weeks. By the time his acceptance letters started coming, she felt herself changed. "We are not leaving. It took me twenty years to realize that."

The same realization has come to Fatuma. It's partly why she's bringing her mother and father to stay with her this spring. Boxed-up furniture waits in the garage; she and Muktar will redo a ground-floor living space for the extended visit. Inshallah, her parents will come. If their health holds up. If Trump doesn't keep them out.

Trump. How can Fatuma say this? So much energy expended in reaction to his policies and positions. Does she really still have to justify the Somali presence in Lewiston or, more broadly, new immigrants in

Maine? Already there's barely enough time for her work at the IRC. As it is, things get compromised at home. She should have introduced more solid food to Mohamed by now. And Sanaa seems a little slow to talk, Fatuma says, maybe because she's spent so much time with babysitters.

At the counter, Amina still picks at her malawax. A look passes between her and Fatuma. This is an old battle, Amina's eating. A compromise—Fatuma hands her a drinkable yogurt. "Finish this and I'll bring you pizza at school for lunch."

"Yes!" Amina guzzles the yogurt. Fatuma packs carrots to go with the pizza.

Upstairs, Amina dresses quickly. The sooner she gets to school, the sooner Hooyo and the pizza will arrive. Today she chooses a blue hijab—sometimes she wears one, sometimes not. Her closet looks just like Fatuma's, arranged by color and by type: skirts with blouses, dresses with sweaters, a section for small-size abayas.

Out the door and into the Bronco, everyone buckled in. Five-minute drive to school, good-byes. Amina hops out, starts toward the entrance. Fatuma watches her, then puts the truck in park and gets out to walk her all the way in.

That night, President Trump gives his first State of the Union address. He touts as achievements tax reform, rising wages, low unemployment. "This, in fact, is our new American moment," Trump says. "So to every citizen [no matter] where you've come from, this is your time. If you work hard, if you believe in yourself, if you believe in America, then you can dream anything, you can be anything, and together, we can achieve absolutely anything." Among his concerns, Trump cites the visa lottery, chain migration, and terrorism.

Does he include Lewiston's newest citizens in the portions of his remarks he intends as inspirational? Most share the dreams he describes. And most arrived here as Muslim refugees or through the chain migration he aims to eliminate.

Campaigning in Portland in summer 2016, Trump suggested Somali refugees were a security threat. As far as I know, he's never been in Lewiston apart from passing through the day of his rally. If he had attended the service in Shukri's Hall for the Mogadishu truck-bomb victims, he'd have seen the pain and the outrage—and maybe would have realized how badly Somali refugees want ISIS eradicated. And if Trump had spent time in Lewiston in the 1980s and '90s, he would have felt how moribund the city was: ever-smaller classes graduating from LHS, many of those graduates moving away.

Things needed to change. Things did.

~

ON A JANUARY morning, Nasafari supervises snack in the three-year-olds' room at Lever's Daycare. The kids at small tables eat their orange slices and Cheerios, or they don't. They spoon cereal into their mouth and giggle and occasionally poke one another. Some gaze through the windows at the snowy outdoors. A boy named Jacob begins to cry. "I miss my mimi," he wails.

"Ohhh Jacob, it's okay," Nasafari tells him. "You'll see her soon." Jacob sniffles, goes back to his cereal. He lives with his grandmother—his mimi—and his grandfather, has a hard time parting from them in the morning.

Feelings run high here in the three-year-old room, Nasafari says. Happy to sad to silly to sleepy. It helps to read the kids' faces to anticipate what's coming. What she likes about this job, what she loves, is how unique each child is. They're so young, she says, yet already whole people.

The classrooms at Lever's don't fully reflect Lewiston's new demographics, but they come close. The kids are white, mixed race, and black. Lever's families speak a half-dozen languages. Here at school, everyone uses English.

It's circle time—a penguin story, counting, some songs. Nasafari is called Fari in the three-year-old room. Fari sings and recites the ABCs. She reaches around the boy who's plopped in her lap and claps. His jeaned legs dangle over her raspberry Roxy ones.

The kids sing about the days of the week. What's today, the head teacher asks when it's done. "Monday!" Yes. What is the weather? A girl peers outside. Sleet stings the pane. "Cold?" she asks. Yes, cold. And what do you wear when it's cold? Another girl comes alive. Every day on cue she jumps into the middle of the circle. "Coat! Boots and mittens and a hat!"

At 10:45 a.m., after her three hours, Fari will board the Lever minibus. She'll get dropped off at CMCC for her first class of the new semester—public speaking, which she's good at, which she's loved ever since her time at the State House. That class will be easy. So, she hopes, will ethics. Statistics will be challenging, but Nasafari did well on the math placement exam so maybe it'll be fine. Psychology starts later in the semester.

For now she's here, twenty hours a week in pretty much her favorite place. One constant in her life is her love of kids—their well-being remains her incentive for becoming a lawyer and a child advocate. Her sister Nabega is also here, running the after-school program and working mornings in a classroom. Every so often, Nabega or Nasafari goes into the baby room to visit Azaleah. Nabega likes working at Lever's, too. Tyler picked up a job on a fishing boat during the paving off-season—this place makes her loneliness manageable while he's out to sea.

On Christmas day at his parents' house, everyone around the tree, Tyler got down on his knee and asked Nabega to marry him. *Oh yes*, she told him. What a year. Nabega has said this before: She can't imagine her life other than as it is right now. All winter she's clomped around in the boots as big as bear paws that Tyler convinced her to wear, the two of them taking Azaleah sledding, going for walks with her on Tyler's shoulders. Nabega used to think of the Maine woods as colorless during winter. But no—there are red-berried bushes, green pines, sky like Tyler's eyes.

Azaleah is thriving. So are Nabega and Tyler. Every day, Nasafari sees the evidence of this. It's becoming clearer to her that happiness comes in many forms, and that it's impossible to completely engineer the future. It doesn't make her want St. John's or law school any less; it does take the edge off the longing. "I still want it all," Nasafari says. But in the past year, her concept of "all" has broadened, as has the urgency around it. Not getting into St. John's disappointed her, yet here's the funny thing: she's actually happier now than she was twelve months ago.

God factors into this somewhere. His plan for her. Nasafari will keep working, keep trying for A's, and what's right will happen, she says. Maybe she'll meet a guy in a couple of years and take time off after her paralegal degree to get married and have kids. Or maybe she'll go straight through law school. She still believes she'll wind up practicing law back here in Lewiston. Maybe one day Azaleah will drop by after school to visit her auntie at the office on Lisbon Street.

After circle time at Lever's comes free play in the gym. The kids careen around in little cars. They manage to avoid Fari, or they don't. Jacob runs to her and raises his arms. *Pick me up.* So Nasafari does.

~

FGM IS BACK on the calendar in Augusta. On February 6, Heather Sirocki hosts a press conference at the State House to unveil the latest measure. Submitted this time as a governor's bill, the measure closely resembles the one Jared reached out to Heather to sponsor last year.

After the bill failed by one vote last summer, the governor's involvement this year seemed all but inevitable. Growing up under his hard-drinking father sensitized LePage to abuse. Fierce advocacy on behalf of children and victims of domestic violence stands out from his otherwise conventionally conservative politics. Heather approached him knowing he'd likely come down hard on FGM.

LePage is here today. So are CBS and ABC affiliates along with other media outlets. Almost every chair is filled. People stand along the sides. "FGM is finally getting heard," Heather says. Jared sits in the front row with his wife.

Heather scheduled the measure's unveiling to coincide with the United Nations' International Day of Zero Tolerance for Female Genital Mutilation. After her press conference was announced, Democrats called for one a day earlier to unveil an FGM bill which—Republicans quickly point out—looks much like the one that failed in the Democrat-controlled House last year. They grumble that both of this year's measures have the same core—making FGM a class A felony for the cutter, punishable by up to thirty years in prison and a $50,000 fine. The Democrats' measure calls for the funding of additional education and doesn't hold parents criminally responsible.

Last year's bill was amended and reamended to address objections, Heather says, yet Democrats wouldn't pass it. Now here they are with their own. In a radio interview she calls out partisanship. "We need to be debating bills on the merits of the bill, not who can put a feather in their cap. . . . The Democrat Party wants credit [for anti-FGM legislation]. . . . They also have egg on their face because we have roll calls to show that so many Democrats voted against this."

Partisanship likely played a role in the bill's failure. But so did its association with ACT. The measure's opponents, including Fatuma, view any ACT-supported initiative as biased. They see ACT as espousing not just anti-extremist but anti-Muslim rhetoric. Fatuma and other Somalis gathered here yesterday to back the Democrats' version.

Fatuma sees it as essential that the Somali community helps craft any FGM legislation; the fact that Democrats asked for her input shows her they get that. And Fatuma opposes criminalizing parents.

"These individuals are not wrong, but rather misguided," she'll later tell the criminal justice committee. "If we want to eradicate [this], let's do it in the right way. But let's not attack immigrant women who have never stepped in a classroom, who have never advocated for themselves, who have never had any right over their body. . . . I plead with you, let's pass something, but it has to be all of us working together."

At the press conference, Heather steps to the microphone. Two dozen Republican legislators stand behind her. Most wear pink—shirts, jackets, ties, sweaters—to signify support of the bill. Heather says much of what she said last year, emphasizing FGM is a human rights violation that results in psychological damage and health complications. She holds up a US map with twenty-six states pinked in, signifying passage of anti-FGM legislation. Maine must become the twenty-seventh.

The governor follows Heather at the podium. He calls FGM a "horrific form of child abuse" that needs to be aggressively prosecutable. "People ask, 'Is this happening in Maine?' The answer is simply 'yes.'" He cites the MaineCare numbers—more than $300,000 billed under FGM-related codes in 2016 and 2017 (though those numbers remain disputed because it's not clear when or where the FGM occurred).

Next comes a woman introduced as F. A. Cole. She grew up in Sierra Leone, she says. She was eleven the day her stepmother brought her to a place where she was stripped, tied down, and blindfolded. Several women pressed in and held her immobilized. Then one of them excised her clitoris and part of her labia, probably with a preused razor blade.

People sit as stunned and still as they were when last year Fatuma stepped to the podium. Cole continues. She was left scarred "physically, mentally, emotionally," she says. "I'm pleading with the legislature in Maine, please protect these girls."

After Cole finishes, people hesitate—how to respond? While Cole talked, Heather cried, tears sliding down her face. Jared's cheeks are reddened. A woman stands. Another. More people, until almost everyone is on their feet.

During the Q&A, someone asks Cole whether she believes parents should be held criminally responsible if they choose to have their daughters cut. "Most definitely," she says—this is part of why she travels around the US, telling her story.

After the press conference Heather brings up, again, that the Senate repeatedly passed the measure last year. She seems incredulous over the necessity of a do-over. A nurse she spoke with a week ago said she'd treated three young women and girls for complications from FGM—"one of them recent." How recent? Heather won't say.

My perspective has changed. I still think education is most crucial in protecting Maine girls from FGM. But if there's a chance a state law will save someone from undergoing the procedure—here or sent to Africa for it—then I believe it should be on the books as a felony for the cutter and for accomplices. A law also helps ensure mandated reporters report FGM if they ever see it. (This will seem more pressing after a Michigan district judge finds the federal FGM law unconstitutional in November 2018. He'll claim Congress overstepped in enacting the ban and criminal law generally should be left to states.)

Something a Somali woman who works as a case manager said factored into my shift. Talking about domestic violence among the state's new immigrants, and the necessity of ongoing funding to educate women about their rights, she used the phrase *culturally ingrained*. "It's not something you easily eliminate," she said. My mind flashed to FGM. What if girls *were* being sent to Africa? Even one. How could anybody be certain?

After the press conference, I look for Jared but he's gone. He seemed unhappy with me today. Earlier, when I sat beside his wife, Jared leaned over and glared. "Do you have any connection with the

SPLC?" The Southern Poverty Law Center—No, I don't. The next day he emails. "I wish to apologize for being so abrupt. . . . My chapter has been compromised by the SPLC." He says someone infiltrated the group and shared his emails, along with his screen name, chapter location, and first name.

On the SPLC website, I find three of Jared's emails and an article headlined "Maine State Rep. Sirocki seeks support from anti-Muslim hate group for FGM bill." The article says, "In her attempts to promote the bill, Sirocki has recruited the help of a local chapter of ACT for America, the largest anti-Muslim hate group in the United States." Jared is angry—he feels they've misrepresented Heather's actions. He's upset too that self-appointed "thought police" have labeled ACT a hate group, yet not groups on the left that promote violence. He doesn't hate Muslims, he says, though he does hate Islamists.

Jared is also displeased with ACT National. It won't stand up to the SPLC, he says, instead reprimanding him for outspokenness and for using "Infidel" in his e-signature. He's complained about ACT's leadership before, but now it's personal—he doesn't feel it's backing him.

A few days later, he resigns as chapter head. "We've done a lot of good educating the public," Jared writes in a final email to members. "Maine is WAY more cognizant about jihad and the implications thereof much because of all of your efforts. I'll stay in the fight and hope you do as well."

Within weeks, he and Frank will align themselves with a new conservative news site, MaineFirst Media. They and their aliases begin showing up there when immigration stories run. Their comments strike me the way they often do, as fact-dotted yet narrow, a careful marshaling of only that which supports their argument—and thereby misleading. The tone is often derisive, the same one they've sometimes used in emails to me, the one that makes it hard to absorb the substance of what they're saying.

And so the anti-Islamist movement morphs and redirects. The same night as Heather's press conference, a man named James Mosher addresses the Lewiston City Council in opposition to another piece of state legislation—LD 1492, "An Act to Attract, Educate and Retain New Mainers to Strengthen the Workforce." Mayor Macdonald also opposes the bill, which would appropriate $1.5 million over two years. The money would fund English language and work training programs, as well as support state welcome centers, including one in Lewiston. Most of the councilors are for the bill. New immigrants are among residents who've come to the meeting to speak in favor of it.

Mosher is adamant. "I disagree with the premise that Maine's economic problems come from being too old or too white. I do not believe that mass immigration is the remedy," he says. "[New immigrants have] run Maine's economy into the ground.... Assimilation, it's not happening." He talks about Muslim "no-go zones" and says that in speaking with police, he's heard "it's getting that way here, too."

Mosher continues. "We're facing an existential threat. The economic impact pales in comparison to the ideological, sociological, and cultural shift if the progressive elites get their way." At the end of his remarks, he circles back to economics. "The welfare state doesn't mix well with open borders.... The productive will end up paying dearly for all of this."

Maine Community Integration director Fowsia Musse listens to Mosher's remarks. She considers herself among "the productive." She moved to Lewiston fifteen years ago, has raised three children here and worked during much of that time.

At the podium, Musse addresses Mosher directly. She doesn't mention that last year her family paid thousands of dollars in state and federal taxes. She doesn't say that in Lewiston she's also known as someone who presses fellow Somalis to avoid leaning long-term on interpretation services—to learn English and find work.

Instead, she tells Mosher he can't blame everything that's wrong with America on refugees. "I am not your issue," Musse says. "I am not your enemy."

In April, the state legislature will fail to agree on either FGM bill. The House passes the Democrats' version but not the Senate. Then the Republican-controlled Senate passes Heather's—but in a tense, late-night session, House Democrats kill it. My take: If a group other than ACT had reached out for support of the measure, it might have passed. But rather than prompting straightforward consideration of whether the state needed an anti-FGM law, the bill came to represent intolerance. Many House members voted as much against ACT as against the measure itself.

Through the lens of Jared and Frank and James Mosher, the state's Muslims are a threat, an entity to be legislated against. But seventeen years in, many newcomers view themselves as full-fledged American citizens. Fowsia has lived in Lewiston since 2003; she's at least as convinced of her right to speak up as Mosher is of his to argue that she shouldn't be here.

THE DOCTOR IN Florida tells us my mom's memory impairment is still mild. Another physician suggests her cognitive issues may stem from not taking medication as prescribed. A family friend who's a health aide begins helping with my mother's meds. We decide to confirm the Alzheimer's diagnosis in Boston when she comes north.

If she comes north.

She bristles when I urge her. Her friends are in Sarasota, and so is warm weather. She loves her home and garden. She hates the cold. *Do you know how much I hate the cold?* (I do.) But, she concedes, my sister and I do live up north. So do her grandkids. And, Mom says, Maine is ultimately where she needs to be. It's where her husband is buried.

Maine is home. She's even willing to consider the assisted-living place we finally told her about, the one we think she'd like.

Then the doctor says my mother must stop driving. A sad, huge loss. This is it, my sister and I tell each other. Now she'll be ready. But no, Mom pays the aide to drive her: to the grocery store, the hair salon, to visit friends. Her tenacity surprises us, though it really shouldn't. One afternoon the aide messages about an outing that includes stops at a dozen nail salons until my mother finds one that suits her.

My sister and I listen as Mom goes over options, but we don't pressure her. A spot hasn't yet opened on the assisted-living waitlist. And we're worried about the real possibility she won't like it when she gets here. Then what?

I don't talk much about this with Mohamed. When he asks, "How's Mom?" I tell him she's okay. She signed up for tai chi. She's spending time with her friends and enjoying the Florida weather. Mohamed knows about her diagnosis but not the extent of our uncertainty.

My heart moves in one direction, my head in another. In a way, I envy the Somali assumption that an aging parent will of course live with an adult child. That the family, the community, heaves a little, shifts and resettles, and life goes on. I wish it were so straightforward for us. It's strange to stand among my new-immigrant friends, people who have endured so much yet mostly managed to right themselves, and feel a lack of ballast.

The family on my father's side lived generation to generation in the same Maine foothills. They were farmers, teachers, homemakers, business owners, and one Olympic athlete. Photographs of the extended family show seated adults thronged by many children. They were religious and close-knit. Hardly anyone moved elsewhere. In my family, achievement and independence came to outweigh community. People fell away from faith.

Last summer the woman who owns the house where I grew up messaged me on Facebook. She was putting the place up for sale. Was

I interested? For a day or two I imagined it: move back, start a kayaking business on the newly clean Androscoggin. Open the old house to my children and stepchildren. Invite my mom. I didn't think, *reclaim and right the past*, but that was part of it.

"What?" my husband said when I told him. "You don't really want to live there."

The fantasy evaporated. He was right. There's little to go back to. The village is run down. The church closed years ago. Most of my relatives have moved away, and the mill operates fewer and fewer machines.

When my parents separated, my father assumed the role of single dad with grace. He was the parent we relied on—the tuned-in one who asked, "How are you, pup?" and listened fully present as we answered. He was a force of kindness. But, hooyo—my mom read to me every night when I was young. She modeled snowplow turns down the ski slope. She brought my sister and me to her office at the university. And she introduced us to a world beyond western Maine.

Now, there's that part of her that more and more, when her own needs aren't pressing in, allows her to simply *be* with us. And even with her cognitive issues, there's a new, sly sense of humor. Of the name of a Lewiston law firm, Fales & Fales, she tells me, "They might want to consider changing that."

And indomitability: During a fall visit to Sarasota, my sister and I find her forgetful, yet very much herself. She chooses where we eat and mostly how we spend our time. One night, my mom and sister in their rooms, I slip out for a walk. When I get back, Mom is standing at the door, arms crossed. "Where were you? You should be in bed." Later, I remember being fifteen and hospitalized overnight with a concussion after a car accident. My mother no longer lived with us, but when I woke she was in the room. My first thought: "She is here." Is it like Mohamed says, that everything stems from mother?

In late March, I get a call from the assisted-living place. After five months, my mom has reached the top of the waitlist. An opening will be coming soon. If she's interested, she can share a suite with another woman; each will have a bedroom and a bath. Does my mother want it?

Yes, Mom says. She says she's ready now, for sure, to come north. It's the easiest, quickest phone call my sister and I have had with her in months. She's happy, we're happy. My sister and I hang up relieved. I begin imagining her there—walking around the pond every morning, playing bridge, watching *American Idol* with us and her suitemate in their living room.

Mom is coming home to Maine. Now we know this much.

~

MARCH 3, 2018—JAMILO marries Mohamed.

At his parents' home outside Boston, guests crowd a living room decked out with black and white streamers and balloons. Kids play on the layering of Oriental rugs in the otherwise emptied room where people later will dance past midnight. The doorbell chimes—another group of six or seven—and a few minutes later chimes again. Friends from Lewiston, from Boston, from western Massachusetts are showing up for the aroos. Flowers and gift bags pile up. Mashallah, this day comes after a big nor'easter earlier in the week. Another will follow a few days from now. Today is windy, but at least there's no snow or rain.

In an upstairs bedroom, Mariama does Jamilo's makeup while other friends get the bride's gowns and shoes and shaashes ready. By now Mariama has made up Jamilo's face so many times, for so many occasions, that she knows it well. The right foundation and brow color. The perfect lip-liner. Tonight Mariama chooses cobalt for the lids—to accent the jewel-toned sarong Jamilo is wearing first.

While Mariama works, Jamilo drinks shaax to power up for the hours to come. She holds out her forearms, studies the henna tattoos that twine up from her hands. Mariama did them, too. "These are amazing," Jamilo says. She looks at her work-in-progress face reflected in the mirror, smiles at it.

Earlier she was pensive. On this more than any other day, she misses her mother. Last night on Facebook she posted a single cry: "HOOYO!"

The reasons her Lewiston family didn't come are varied and, ultimately, disappointing. Whatever each person's excuse, the fact that no blood relatives other than Aaliyah will witness her marriage hurts. But Jamilo's battalion of longtime friends—more than a dozen in and out of the room with her right now—consoles her: *We're here. We love you. You wouldn't even want guests who weren't excited to come.*

A tap at the door. Isha enters. She carries a cloth packet that she sets on the dresser. From its folds, she pulls gold bracelets and a necklace she fastens around Jamilo's neck, looking into her eyes in the mirror. Jamilo holds the gaze. "They're so beautiful, thank you," she says. Isha holds Jamilo's shoulders—*Of course.* To her it couldn't be more straightforward. "Mohamed is my son," she told me earlier. "And now Jamilo is my daughter."

Isha exudes warmth and stability. She and Mohamed's father saved for many years to buy this house with six bedrooms where eleven people live. For now, the newlyweds and Aaliyah and Hamzah will be back and forth between here and Lewiston. Mohamed has his UMass classes and food-service job in Boston; Jamilo and the kids have their lives in Lewiston. They'll decide where to live permanently in a few months.

Already Jamilo and Mohamed have furnished their Boston bedroom with a four-piece Italianate king-bedroom set, rugs and throw pillows, and a constellation of framed signs. "You are loved." "You make me happy." "Every love story is beautiful, but ours is my favorite."

From her spot by the door, Aaliyah watches the progress. The helpers drape a gold belt around Jamilo's hips, add a medallion headpiece.

"Mohamed is going to be so happy when he sees you, Mama," Aaliyah says. Hamzah stayed in Lewiston—Jamilo decided tonight was too late and too much for him.

"The dancing is going to be fun," says Aaliyah. "But no twerking for kids, right?"

"That's right," Jamilo tells her. "When you're a grown-up, you can twerk if you want. But only in your own house."

Mariama adjusts the shaash atop Jamilo's braids, gives her makeup one last check. Jamilo straps on her three-inch heels and stands.

It's time. She's never been surer of anything. She didn't feel like this, certain in her heart, with Yussuf or with Mustafa. Alhamdullilah—she's going downstairs to begin the rest of her life with Mohamed, the man she loves, the husband she knew she'd find. The doubters and the skeptics, they no longer matter.

People fill the living room three deep against the walls. They clap and ululate as the wedding party enters and circles the bridal chair. Somali music plays. The room bursts with color: the women's dresses, the drapes and carpets. It's winter outside, spring and summer here. Still circling, Jamilo dances with one woman after another, until finally she sits. She holds a Somali milk jug; a tray filled with perfumes and incense lies at her feet. All symbolize abundance.

Isha steps in, passes scarves over Jamilo's head—the shaash ceremony. Mohamed looks on, pride and joy all over his face. *Jamilo, his wife*. Earlier he told me, "I know I will always love her."

Mohamed doesn't really like to dance, but now he dances anyway. He takes Jamilo's hands. She smiles encouragement. They move together, and everyone applauds. People join in. Soon the floor shakes with dancing. The Quranic wall hangings vibrate, and Aaliyah squeezes in with Jamilo and Mohamed.

Tomorrow the sun will rise on the same problems: custody of Hamzah, Jamilo's Lewiston family's antagonism, Trump's policies, the need to get her parents out of Dadaab. But now—dancing with

Mohamed, with her friends and his family surrounding them—Jamilo has a moment of seeing things from outside herself. *Praise Allah, here she is—she and Best Friend, her husband, together in this packed room, moving forward. Alhamdullilah, these are the people who love her, who have stood by her.*

Early in the new year, Jamilo and Mohamed come to a decision. They're going to live in Lewiston. Jamilo feels Boston is a good place but "there's something about Maine." She cites the safety, the openness and the quiet, the fact that she and the kids know so many people and they in turn know her and Aaliyah and Hamzah. And she's finally making good money—got a recent raise and works a lot of overtime. Her two-week paycheck tops $1,600.

"I just really like it there," Jamilo says of L-A and the apartment through which Hamzah danced room to room. So does Mohamed. He brings the kids to Kennedy Park, to IHOP, to visit friends in the tree streets. He's going to take part-time work as a homecare assistant and commute to UMass. In her heart, Jamilo says, she is a Somali Mainer—and soon Mohamed will be, too.

So they load up the Italian bedroom set and the "Every love story is beautiful" wall hangings and move them north.

Guriga waah Lewiston.

16

Summer 2018–January 2019

On June 12, thirty-eight-year-old Donny Giusti is badly beaten during a brawl at the edge of Kennedy Park. Three days later, he dies in the ICU at Central Maine Medical Center.

How Donny wound up with a fatal head injury on the same block where Jamilo lived with Fatummah is complicated and tragic. Different factions tell different stories about what led to the fight.

This much seems clear: At about 10 p.m. several teens drove by in a car on Bates Street and shot pellet or BB guns into a group of people in the park. A man from the park group later told me Donny and others had gathered to "settle" a dispute with some new immigrants. The car continued on Bates, turned right onto Spruce and started down toward Lisbon Street. At least three people from the park, including Donny, ran after it. Reaching Spruce, the men were confronted by more than a dozen teens armed with rocks and bricks. Donny was struck and fell to the pavement. The assailants fled.

Tensions rise further after Donny dies on Friday, June 15. Social media erupts in rumor: the teens involved are Somali and Congolese;

they lured Donny to their neighborhood; Donny's friends plan retaliation; police did little about a park skirmish that occurred in May.

There's nastiness—Heidi Sawyer bans posters from bashing new immigrants on a Facebook page she moderates. A man responds by calling her a "race traitor." Anti-Muslim comments pile up at the ends of news stories. There are calls for deportation and claims the newcomers will never coexist peacefully in Lewiston.

The weekend passes. At a packed city council meeting on June 19, the police chief sets forth facts. Interviews of witnesses and possible suspects are proceeding slowly because many are juveniles. Police are working with the new-immigrant community to begin identifying those involved, he says. Three months of rising tensions in the park preceded Donny's death, the city's first homicide in four years.

Cell phone video of the earlier May skirmish showed several African teens brandishing sticks and striking out at two men as onlookers egged them on. A police officer told me that incident resulted from conflict between new-immigrant youths and other downtown residents over turf. No one filed charges. The cell phone video wound up on Facebook. Someone commented, "Teens/preteens beating on a man in Kennedy park . . . here we are again."

Youths involved in recent conflicts do sometimes go unsupervised, the police chief says at the city council meeting. During the meeting's public comments period, residents point fingers in various directions: new-immigrant parents in the downtown neighborhood need to keep closer watch on their kids; bystanders must speak up quicker; police should maintain a stronger presence in the park; people must not take matters into their own hands or retaliate—and adults should never escalate conflicts with teens.

To many, it feels like a disheartening echo of the 2008 episode of group muggings and kids clashing with park-goers before parents and community leaders got together and turned things around.

This time, someone is dead. Donny Giusti was a hard worker and a church volunteer who deeply loved his children, one of his uncles tells me. He was also "trying to get his life straightened out" after a history as a brawler, a friend tells a news reporter.

At a press conference new-immigrant leaders hold after Donny's death, Fatuma offers condolences on behalf of the community. "Violence has no place in Lewiston," she says. "We condemn what happened in the strongest terms." Abdikadir is also there, as is Fowsia Musse. All three look deeply weary in the photo a *Sun Journal* reporter takes, as if they carry the burden of accountability for a whole community.

Fatuma talks more about the attack with the host of a morning radio show. It's a time of "mourning and reflection" for Lewiston, she tells him. There are challenges: Some first-generation newcomers are not integrating quickly enough, not acculturating the way they should. Their children struggle, Fatuma says. Also—residents across the city need to reach out and talk with one another more, neighbor to neighbor. It's time for everyone to "dig deeper and understand their biases" around race and religion.

Lewiston will find its way through this tragedy, Fatuma says. Overall, the city is stronger and more resilient than in the early 2000s. More united, even if there's a distance left to go. "We have a good foundation to work from," she tells the host.

There's evidence she's right. Heidi says people posting racist and anti-Muslim comments are a "vocal minority" emboldened by online anonymity. The man who called her a traitor? Other posters bashed him. And new immigrants who work downtown, including Fatuma, see an increase in friendliness from white people in the weeks after Donny's death, as if to acknowledge the unfairness of blaming many for the actions of a few.

At the city council meeting, a white landlord says residents can't let what happened be reduced to an Us vs. Them racial issue. Instead, he says, it's about two factions that lack direction, lack jobs or families or dreams, because "you don't hang out at night in a park if you have [any of] those." Other speakers call for unity. One of Donny's friends asks for Somali language workshops so residents can better understand their neighbors.

During the meeting, most of those who step to the microphone defend the new immigrants. Sitting there, I again note that the most vocal anti-Muslim voices around the state seem to belong to those who neither live among nor know newcomers.

On Thursday, Donny's family and friends hold a barbecue in Kennedy Park. Word goes out that all are welcome. A few new-immigrant boys hang back until a white woman urges them to join the line for hamburgers and pasta salad. Near the end, with twilight coloring the park, Abdikadir and other new-immigrant leaders show up with a check to contribute to Donny's funeral expenses. Distress tugs at the corners of Abdikadir's mouth as he tells one of Donny's friends how sad he is about what happened.

Two days later, a peace rally in the park draws a diverse crowd. Organizers talk about community empowerment and bystander intervention. Fowsia Musse tells the crowd her five kids include "three Mainers who were born here." She came to America for one primary reason, she says: peace. Describing being drawn by music coming from a church while she was still new to the US and struggling with trauma-related depression, she breaks down. "So I find myself in the church [and a woman begins to sing]...I remember crying nonstop, I had goose bumps—I couldn't figure out why, because I'm Muslim."

Fowsia says she'll sing what she heard that day. She begins: "Amazing grace, how sweet..." then stops. "I was lost that day, but I feel I was found afterward...[In Lewiston] I feel whole, belongingness, and a sense of connectedness."

On the same day that Donny Giusti was beaten, a thirteen-year-old named Rayan Issa drowned during a school trip to a nearby pond. The next day close to three hundred people from across the city gathered at the middle school. They wore red, Rayan's favorite color—T-shirts, shorts, hijabs, skirts—and remembered him as a funny, kind-hearted kid.

The turnout didn't surprise Fatuma. It's the base she talks about that's been broadening for years, the one the city will rely on as people join forces to find Donny's killers and to heal from his death and Rayan's drowning. To move the city forward. "This is our home, for all of us," she says.

It's the same thing Jamilo says, and Abdikadir, and Nasafari. The same thing Donny's uncle, Jim Thompson, says. He was at that press conference with others from Donny's family when new-immigrant leaders expressed condolences. Afterward, Thompson thanked them. Fowsia asked whether everyone wanted to join hands for a moment of silence. A circle formed. People cried. Still holding hands with Fowsia and another Somali leader, Thompson called for an end to the conflict. "This is our community, our city, our people," he said. "We're all one... We're all a country of immigrants."

Seventeen years in, Fatuma is right that Lewiston has become a different city. It's more diverse, more vital—yet still vulnerable. Parts of downtown remain among the poorest neighborhoods in New England. Poverty, abuse, and anomie determine too many lives—both black and white. That dream the landlord at the city council meeting mentioned is hard to keep hold of when you're hungry, or sick, or strung out. Hard if you're struggling to pay rent or suffering the effects of PTSD.

Speakers at the city council meeting kept saying what happened that night in the park wasn't about race or religion. I think they're right. It's about what occurs when two traumatized factions intersect.

In Lewiston, those factions represent fragments of the city's population, but until both groups have the resources to move forward, the city will struggle episodically.

Depending on who holds power, national leaders by turns welcome refugees or spurn them, failing to provide consistent support. For some, the eight months of federal assistance is enough to propel them to independence. For others, it's not. About continuing support until refugees are self-sufficient, Phil Nadeau says, "Don't rescue me and give me a life I can't maintain." And, apart from refugee policy: partisanship at all levels has stymied our nation's ability to address mental illness, addiction, and generational poverty.

Since the first Somalis moved to town, Lewiston and its people have risen to the occasion despite the challenges. Kids keep heading off to college in ever-rising numbers. The wan service economy of the 1990s continues slowly to expand. And, as the mayor pointed out again after Donny's death, the city's violent crime rate remains among the lowest in Maine. (A spate of nonfatal drug-related shootings not tied to new immigrants will inflate this year's numbers.) What Lewiston needs now is what Fatuma and Phil Nadeau and the school superintendent have pointed out: for good kids to settle down here and keep building lives.

It will take time to fully understand what happened in the park that night. Jared sees Donny's killing as more evidence that Islam is a negative force in America and that hijrah is coming. But in my view, Donny's death isn't about hijrah, much less Muslim hatred of kafirs. It's about a handful of inadequately parented young people who made grievously wrong decisions.

Don't sugarcoat the challenges, Fatuma told the radio host. Talk about the hard stuff. Ask her anything. Even ask her whether she's a terrorist, Fatuma said—and come see how she lives. Jared complains often about what he sees as the abridgement of free speech in America, the gag of political correctness. He should talk openly with Fatuma—she'd talk openly with him. If only they'd met up last spring after they spoke at the State House and Fatuma suggested he come to Lewiston and visit her.

Inevitably, their paths will cross again. So maybe he still will.

~

LATE JULY. ON a 90-degree day Jamilo, Mohamed and Aspen sit in the shade outside the apartment. Jamilo just got home from her shift. Mohamed leaves soon for his. Now they drink ice water and play a ruthless game of UNO while a neighborhood teen watches the kids. Jamilo slaps down a Draw Four, laughs. Mohamed groans and picks up. Jamilo wins; she's taken almost every hand. Mohamed is quick, she's quicker. "I'm done for now," Aspen says. A few more rounds and Jamilo glances at her phone: time for Mohamed to get ready. "You'd better go shower," she tells him. He nods, stands.

It's been an uneasy summer in Lewiston. A *Sun Journal* story that runs in August bears the headline "Lewiston police say 'a perfect storm' of violence overshadows low crime rate." The story reports that rapes, robberies, motor vehicle thefts, and arson have fallen to a twenty-four-year low. But, it says, those numbers don't reflect drug-related arrests—up 50 percent, attributed by police to outsiders coming in with illegal substances—or tensions over the lack of an arrest in Donny Giusti's death.

Kennedy Park seems quiet to me—fewer kids, fewer moms with babies, fewer families out for walks in the evenings. Part of that is the result of a new ten p.m. park curfew. Jamilo isn't avoiding going there—she still takes the kids to the pool—but she's not seeking it out, either. Her take on Donny's killing: although she thinks it's likely new-immigrant youths were involved, police have to go forward carefully to make sure they don't arrest the wrong people.

The drug arrests, plus Donny's killing and another in which a white man stabs a woman to death: all of it makes for lingering anxiety. A police officer quoted in the *Sun Journal* piece says Lewiston has "big-city problems, but we don't have big-city funding or resources."

The midterm election cycle heats up around these issues and others—Medicaid expansion, jobs, education. LePage is term-limited out. Maine attorney general Janet Mills—who spoke against anti-sharia legislation at the ALAC hearing—runs on a progressive platform. Her opponent is Republican Shawn Moody, who espouses a toned-down version of LePage's politics. Democrat Jared Golden, the state rep and ex-marine who attended last year's remembrance for the Mogadishu bombing victims, is vying for the US congressional seat of Bruce Poliquin.

Fall arrives, with dropping temperatures and busyness. Nasafari starts her third semester at CMCC. She's in steady-state, still working at Lever's, liking school—except for math—still hoping to transfer to St. John's after she gets her associate's.

Her sister Nabega is pregnant for the second time—a boy she and Tyler plan to name Ashtyn. Nasafari wonders: can she possibly love a new baby nephew as much as she does Azaleah? Two months ago the family moved into a new house—a large two-family in a neighborhood near Bates, a few blocks from where my Aunt Nell used to live. Norbert rented out the first floor to a pastor friend and plans to turn the third floor into another apartment. In the meantime, Nasafari sleeps up there in an aerie-like room with Christina.

Carrys enters his sophomore year at USM. Anxiety over whether he'll ever get an asylum hearing—much less asylum itself—wears on him. Some of his friends have been denied. He also worries, as ever, about Congo and his family's safety. Rebel groups have made much of the eastern part of the country unlivable; desperate civilians are fleeing to Uganda by the thousands. Amid the peril, medical workers struggle to contain the nation's worst-ever Ebola outbreak. And the long-promised presidential election has been postponed again, and again, and again. Carrys finds himself distracted, focuses in on his schoolwork then drifts and focuses again. "I have thoughts that trouble me," he says.

Finally, in December, general elections will take place in Congo—two years after Joseph Kabila's term officially ended. But afterward, allegations of electoral fraud and manipulation will surface immediately. A peaceful transition of power seems unlikely. By then, Carrys's own position will be precarious. Work permit expired, he has to leave his dispatch job at AAA and can't pay his upcoming USM tuition. As he has before, he rights and reorients himself. He barebones his spending, applies for another permit and enrolls in some noncredit classes at Southern Maine Community College. He will get through this.

Jamilo is carrying worries, too. One of her stepbrothers in Dadaab was badly injured after a motorbike struck him. He lay semiconscious at home until the family got enough money together to take him to the hospital, where they learned his leg was severely broken. "I feel so helpless," Jamilo says of her inability to be there in Africa for her family. She still sends bill, and she'd like to take Mohamed and Aaliyah and Hamzah there to visit. But how, with the kids in school and she and Mohamed working full-time-plus? Amid political uncertainties and safety concerns?

When Jamilo closes her eyes, she can feel the Dagahaley breeze, the African sun on her face and red sand beneath her toes. But in a few months, three years will have passed since she was there.

By October, campaign signs for the US midterm election are posted all over Lewiston. On stormy days they cartwheel down streets before they're reanchored and then, in the next squall, uprooted again.

As it did in the 2016 presidential election, Maine carries disproportionate heft this time around. A win by Golden could be the one that gives the US House to Democrats—and Poliquin is the sole Republican representative from New England. At the state level, a Mills administration would look profoundly different from the current one. If her campaign isn't explicitly anti-LePage, it's implicitly so, with references to broken government and promises to bring the state to higher ground.

Tightening, the congressional race turns personal. Poliquin refers to Golden as "a young radical with a socialist agenda." Golden takes his own shots. Aboard a lobster boat in a TV ad, he drops traps into the water. It's time to show Washington what needs to go, he tells viewers—including partisanship, special interests, and "career politicians like Bruce Poliquin."

During the home stretch, commentators call Maine a national bellwether. Outside money has poured in, close to $10 million for the congressional race. Ads fill the airwaves—over two hundred TV spots on one day alone. In Lewiston, home and cell phones ring with call upon call, and texts stream in. Downtown at Forage Market and in the aisles of Hannaford, residents commiserate over the repeated rounds of door knocking.

The high pitch fires up some. Ever since he became a citizen, Abdikadir has loved elections—to him they epitomize democracy. He avidly supports Golden and Mills. His Facebook page fills with posts—Samia waving a handful of small American flags, Abdikadir's own urgings to vote, a group photo that includes Mills and him with others at MIRS. He posts a shot of himself standing on a rocky beach backdropped by the Atlantic. His home state of Maine is beautiful, he writes.

Abdikadir has yet to announce if or when he'll run for office himself, but more and more he sounds and feels like a candidate, still attending every civic event and forging alliances with other progressive leaders around the state. His life is packed full, in any case. MIRS recently celebrated its tenth anniversary. And, on a spring day seven months ago, Ikran convinced him they should try for another baby. She's now pregnant with their fifth.

Halloween comes, with the annual Muslim debate over trick-or-treating. Mohamed prefers Aaliyah and Hamzah not go. Jamilo isn't sure—the kids liked it last year, but this fall Heidi has a new baby and will stay home and hand out candy. Plus, it's a workday and a school night. Jamilo comes up with an alternative: she buys the kids costumes they can wear to Aaliyah's upcoming Chuck E. Cheese birthday party. Then, on Halloween night, she'll take them to Walmart and let them pick out candy.

She doesn't anticipate Hamzah. On the afternoon of October 31 he asks, "When are we trick-or-treating?" Jamilo talks him into a nap, thinking he might wake with something else on his mind. He doesn't. He presses. Aaliyah sees their chance, jumps in. *Hamzah doesn't want candy from Walmart. Hamzah wants to go to people's houses and knock on their doors like last year. He wants to dress up.* It's clear the Walmart thing isn't going to work, no matter how many Kit Kats and Sour Patch Kids Jamilo bribes them with.

She capitulates: They'll go visit Heidi's baby girl and trick-or-treat around her block. The kids race to put on Elsa and Spider-Man.

Mohamed doesn't mind. He and Jamilo see some things differently—that's normal, he says. When Hamzah and Aaliyah get home with their hauls, Mohamed shares a couple of their candies and says nothing about his earlier reservations.

Jamilo and Mohamed—whenever I see them, they seem stronger than the time before. As their relationship deepens, they remind me more and more of Mohamed's parents—solid, clearly partnered. One night Jamilo describes how it is: Mohamed is different from anyone she's ever been with. He's her husband, but also her friend. She tells him everything. They laugh a lot, have fun. He's really good with the kids. And—he lets her be her. Other men have wanted to mold her.

Not that there aren't challenges. At Aaliyah's Chuck E. Cheese party (she's six), Jamilo and Mohamed uneasily await the appearance of Aaliyah's father, who asked Jamilo if he could come. He doesn't show up, but the next day he calls her. He gets right to it: would Jamilo want to be with him again? She can't believe what she's hearing. He knows she's married now. And this is someone who left her when she was most vulnerable. She tells him that. The answer is *of course not*, she says. If she once imagined being back with him, she hasn't for a long time. She tells him that, too: "I've really moved on."

"I was desperate," she says later of that time—a new mom with an infant, heartbroken, little family support. Those months in the shelter were awful. "He had power over me. Now it's me who has power," she says. "Now it's me who's happy."

The next time he calls, she doesn't pick up. Instead she plans a weekend in Vermont with Mohamed to celebrate one year of being together. She books a motel that gets great reviews, signs them both up for massages, figures out which restaurants they'll try.

November 6 finally comes, and Janet Mills wins big. "It is time...for hope once again. We will lead Maine in a new, better direction," she says in her acceptance speech. Neither Poliquin nor Golden gets a 50 percent majority. The state's new ranked choice kicks in, which means the second-place picks of those who voted for other candidates count instead. The process takes days. Abdikadir posts on Facebook that he's feeling optimistic. On a Democrat-blue background he writes, "Fingers crossed 4 my Golden." On November 15, Golden is declared the winner.

Jared, when I ask how he feels about Mills, writes "I do not like [her] one bit." Of the turnover in political power he says, "We'll now see what the dems will really do—unfortunately, I fear." Poliquin, meanwhile, announces he's going forward with a lawsuit to challenge the constitutionality of ranked-choice voting. And Paul LePage, who previously said he was retiring to Florida, now says he'll keep his Maine residency and consider a 2022 run against Mills.

But in the here-and-now of 2018, the people of Maine have spoken. The state went Democrat. There was no referendum on refugees on the ballot (and attitudes toward immigrants don't fall neatly along party lines, in any case), yet in voting blue many people took a stand.

Refugees and asylees are a visible change in Maine. Integrating them has been hard work—for them and for the cities where they settled. It's taken time and money and concerted effort. It still does. One message of the 2018 midterm seems to be that Mainers feel the effort is worth it, that they believe they're collectively becoming something greater than they used to be.

Fatuma talks a lot about the generosity of Americans, and Mainers: "I see it. I live in it... [It's] because of the generosity of the people of Maine that [new immigrants here] are thriving," she says. But the newcomers haven't been passive recipients. They've helped themselves—become business owners and healthcare providers, Walmart stockers and team members at L.L.Bean. They've become Lewistonians and Mainers—while also remaining Somali Muslim, or Congolese, or Sudanese.

Two decades ago, Lewiston was a beautiful old ghost of a city. It needed to stake a claim in the twenty-first century. It has. The new elementary school has a name now—Connors, after a well-loved former superintendent who died a few years ago. Many of the hundred rooms are nearing completion, including six classrooms for each grade. It will open in fall 2019 with 750 kids. Capacity is one thousand. Planners intentionally left room to grow.

In Lewiston, "Peace in the Park"—the volunteer foot patrol Fatuma cofounded after Donny Giusti's death—winds down as winter approaches. For months, pairs of trained volunteers wearing yellow T-shirts walked the paths in Kennedy Park each afternoon. They struck up conversations with people along the way and kept an eye out for trouble. Fatuma had help: Lewiston police advised on how to keep the fifty volunteers safe. Bates College and a social services agency provided space so the volunteers could be trained in how to de-escalate conflict. The Chamber of Commerce donated the shirts.

The volunteer effort was "ensuring that we do what we need to do," Fatuma told a news reporter who showed up to write about it.

Residents were already telling her they felt safer, she said, and—at least as important—more connected to one another.

The volunteers—black, white, young, old, female, male—included Donny Giusti's father and his Uncle Jim. All together it was proof to Fatuma that over time, progress only moves in one direction.

The governor-elect apparently agrees. In her January 2019 inaugural address, Janet Mills says the state will find unity "from the tree streets of Lewiston to the rolling fields of [Aroostook] County." She tells the capacity crowd at the Augusta Civic Center that "when a family, a community, a state believe in [and] help each other . . . great things can happen."

Fatuma and Abdikadir are there to hear her say it.

Afterword

SHORTLY AFTER DAWN on April 11, 2019, a team of Lewiston and Maine State police pulls up in front of an apartment on Ash Street. A second team arrives at an apartment near the corner of Knox and Birch.

Within minutes, the police make two arrests in connection with the beating death of Donny Giusti: 23-year-old Pierre Mousafiri and a 13-year-old boy whose name is not released. Both are charged with misdemeanor assault.

A third person, 17-year-old Emmanuel Nkurunziza, is arrested at a jobs training program in Limestone and charged with manslaughter, which is punishable in adult court by up to 30 years in prison. During the police investigation Nkurunziza admitted throwing a rock into a group that included Giusti, but in Lewiston's 8th District Court he denies the manslaughter charge.

A medical examiner found that blunt-force trauma to Giusti's head caused his death. He also suffered a broken clavicle, a rib fracture, and a shoulder injury.

The two teens are taken to the Long Creek youth detention center in South Portland. Mousafiri is released on bail with a June 2019 court date.

Author's Note

MY MOTHER DIED suddenly on April 19, 2018, of a cerebral hemorrhage, just after she moved north to Maine. We held services in Florida and in Maine, and laid her to rest beside my stepdad in Portland. She was eighty-seven.

As we often said in the family, she was small but mighty. We miss her terribly.

Acknowledgments

I AM INDEBTED to the Lewistonians who carry the main threads of this book and who opened their homes and hearts to me. My deepest gratitude goes to Fatuma Hussein, Jamilo Maalim, Nasafari Nahumure, Abdikadir Negeye, and Carrys Ngoy. I hope they find themselves and their loved ones accurately reflected in these pages.

Many others generously shared their stories and their perspectives on life in Lewiston: Shukri Abasheikh, Aba Abu, Farah Adan, Sadio Aden, Best Ali, Qamar Bashir, Mary Bedard, Jared J. Bristol, Mohamed Dekow, Frank, Deb Girouard, Skip Girouard, Mohamed Heban, Mohamed Hussein, Brian Ingalls, Isaac Kabuika, R. K., Safiya Khalid, Ikran-Sahra Khalif, Moe Landry, Jeannie Martin, Binto Matan, Mike McGraw, Aliya Mohamed, Zamzam Mohamud, Muna, Fowsia Musse, Phil Nadeau, Nabega Nankema, Kamakazi Nyagichumbi, Jihan Omar, Ashley P., Paul Poliquin, Mustafa Ramos, Renee, Norbert Rwambaza, Shoboh Saban, Abdiweli Said, Heidi Sawyer, Heather Sirocki, Julia Sleeper-Whiting, Mary Theriault, Jim Thompson, Rick Valentine, Bill Webster, Kim Wettlaufer. Thank you, all.

This book originated decades ago. I fell in love with Lewiston as a kid sitting with my family on Aunt Nell's porch, riding the elevator at Peck's, walking to Great Falls lookout. Later my friend Lynn and I took dance lessons at Ellen Cooper's studio and explored the length of Lisbon Street. We spent hours with Lynn's mémère and her aunt, who lived nearby. I'm grateful for those times.

Several news and magazine editors supported my earlier writings about Lewiston's transformation. I owe thanks to Scott Armstrong at the *Christian Science Monitor*, Mel Allen at *Yankee* magazine, and the editorial teams at *Huffington Post*, *The Hill*, *Forbes*, and *World Policy Institute*. Paul Doiron published a feature on L-A's new immigrants in *Down East*; I'm grateful for that and for his insightful read of an early draft of this manuscript. Jane Friedman and Jessica DuLong also helped during the initial stages of the project and, before that, colleagues at Boston University led me to realize there was a book to write.

The work of many authors and writers provided valuable context—notably Ben Rawlence's *City of Thorns: Nine Lives in the World's Largest Refugee Camp*; Catherine Besteman's *Making Refuge: Somali Bantu Refugees and Lewiston, Maine*; Dave Eggers's *What Is the What*; Debi Goodwin's *Citizens of Nowhere*; Nuruddin Farah's trilogy *Maps*, *Gifts*, and *Secrets*; Cindy Horst's *Transnational Nomads: How Somalis Cope with Refugee Life in the Dadaab Camps of Kenya*; Abdi Nor Iftin's *Call Me American*; Jennifer Hyndman's *Managing Displacement: Refugees and the Politics of Humanitarianism*; Amy Bass's *One Goal: A Coach, a Team, and the Game That Brought a Divided Town Together*; and a collection of narratives titled *Somalis in Maine: Crossing Cultural Currents*. The sound reportage of the *Lewiston Sun Journal*, the *Bangor Daily News* and the *Portland Press Herald* enhanced my understanding of past and present events in Lewiston. Pieces about the city in the *New Yorker* and the *New York Times* offered additional perspectives.

A lot of hands helped out along the way. Loving thanks go to Andre Dubus II's Thursday Nighters—Lori Ambacher, Louie Cronin,

Judy McAmis, Dick Ravin, Adair Rowland, Bob Steinberg, Jep Streit, Frankie Wright—for twenty-plus years of friendship and chapter-by-chapter support; special shout-outs to Dick and Frankie, who provided wise commentary on the complete manuscript. Mark Kramer's kitchen workshop—Sarah Bates, Kathleen Burge, Michael Fitzgerald, Dan Grossman, Anna Kuchment, Nell Lake, Gabriela Soto Laveaga, Stacy Mattingly, Judy Rakowsky, Farah Stockman, and Chris Woodside—also offered astute feedback on work in progress. Big thanks to Mark for his close attention to these pages. For their careful reads and for their friendship, I'm grateful to Robin Schoenthaler, Amy Yelin, Sandra Miller, and Tracy Mayor, who combed the final galley.

My agent, Jennifer Carlson, expertly guided this project from proposal through final revision. I'm also indebted to my editor, Ben Adams, whose keen instincts and vision were crucial throughout the writing and revision process, and to the PublicAffairs editorial and publicity teams for helping the book find its readers. Special thanks to Eric Rayman, Brynn Warriner, Jocelyn Pedro, Linda Mark, Lindsay Fradkoff, and to Amy Toensing, for her beautiful photographs.

I owe much to my family: love and gratitude to my husband, Flip, who always said yes when I asked him to read a paragraph, a page, a chapter. He was there throughout, and this book bears his mark. My daughter Katherine offered many insights—and showed steadfast faith in the project from the beginning. Thanks, too, to Erik, McKane, Clint, Sam, Sarah, Kevin, Jake, Livi, and Luca for their loving support, and for helping me stay mindful of life's lightness.

Finally—to my sister Jill, with whom I shared the journey of our mother's last year: We learned much about family along the way, and I can't imagine a more caring companion. Jill, this book is for Mom—and it's for you, too.

SALLY PASLEY VARGAS

Cynthia Anderson is a cross-genre writer who grew up in western Maine. She graduated from Cornell University with a degree in mathematics and has worked as a computer programmer, pipefitter's helper, and journalist. Her collection of stories, *River Talk* (C&R Press), was a Kirkus Reviews' Best Books of 2014 and received the 2014 New England Book Festival award for Short Stories.

Other work has appeared in *Boston* magazine, the *Christian Science Monitor*, the *Miami Herald, Huffington Post, Redbook, Flash Fiction Forward* (W.W. Norton & Co.), the *Iowa Review*, and others.

Anderson lives with her family in Maine and Massachusetts. She teaches writing at Boston University, from which she holds an M.S. in Journalism.

PublicAffairs is a publishing house founded in 1997. It is a tribute to the standards, values, and flair of three persons who have served as mentors to countless reporters, writers, editors, and book people of all kinds, including me.

I. F. Stone, proprietor of *I. F. Stone's Weekly*, combined a commitment to the First Amendment with entrepreneurial zeal and reporting skill and became one of the great independent journalists in American history. At the age of eighty, Izzy published *The Trial of Socrates*, which was a national bestseller. He wrote the book after he taught himself ancient Greek.

Benjamin C. Bradlee was for nearly thirty years the charismatic editorial leader of *The Washington Post*. It was Ben who gave the *Post* the range and courage to pursue such historic issues as Watergate. He supported his reporters with a tenacity that made them fearless and it is no accident that so many became authors of influential, best-selling books.

Robert L. Bernstein, the chief executive of Random House for more than a quarter century, guided one of the nation's premier publishing houses. Bob was personally responsible for many books of political dissent and argument that challenged tyranny around the globe. He is also the founder and longtime chair of Human Rights Watch, one of the most respected human rights organizations in the world.

• • •

For fifty years, the banner of Public Affairs Press was carried by its owner Morris B. Schnapper, who published Gandhi, Nasser, Toynbee, Truman, and about 1,500 other authors. In 1983, Schnapper was described by *The Washington Post* as "a redoubtable gadfly." His legacy will endure in the books to come.

Peter Osnos, *Founder*